Sound and Sense

An Introduction to Poetry

SIXTH EDITION

Sound
and
Sense

An Introduction to Poetry

SIXTH EDITION

Laurence Perrine
With the assistance of
Thomas R. Arp

SOUTHERN METHODIST UNIVERSITY

HARCOURT BRACE JOVANOVICH, PUBLISHERS
SAN DIEGO   NEW YORK   CHICAGO   ATLANTA   WASHINGTON D.C.
LONDON   SYDNEY   TORONTO

ISBN: 0-15-582606-9

Library of Congress Catalog Card Number: 81-82425

Printed in the United States of America

COPYRIGHTS AND ACKNOWLEDGMENTS

LEONARD ADAME "Black and White" from *American Poetry Review*, Vol. 6, No. 3, May/June 1977, by permission of the author.

SAMUEL ALLEN "To Satch" from *American Negro Poetry* by Samuel Allen. Reprinted by permission of the author.

KINGSLEY AMIS "The Last War" from *A Case of Samples* by Kingsley Amis. Reprinted by permission of A.D. Peters & Co. Ltd.

MARGARET ATWOOD "Landcrab" from *Field #22*, Spring 1980, by permission of *Field* Magazine.

W. H. AUDEN "O where are you going?" copyright 1934 and renewed 1962 by W. H. Auden. "That night when joy began" and "O what is that sound" copyright 1937 and renewed 1965 by W. H. Auden. "Musée des Beaux Arts" and "The Unknown Citizen" copyright 1940 and renewed 1968 by W. H. Auden. Reprinted from *Collected Poems*, by W. H. Auden, edited by Edward Mendelson, by permission of Random House, Inc. and Faber and Faber Ltd.

DONALD W. BAKER "Formal Application" from *Saturday Review*, May 11, 1963, by permission of the author.

MATSUO BASHO/MORITAKE Two Japanese Haiku "Fallen petal rise" and "The lightning gleam" from *Introduction to Haiku* by Harold G. Henderson. Copyright © 1958 by Harold G. Henderson. Reprinted by permission of Doubleday Company, Inc. Basho, "The lightning flashes!" translated by Earl Miner, reprinted from *Encyclopedia of Poetry and Poetics* by A. Preminger, F. Warnke, & O. Hardison by permission of Princeton University Press. Moritake, "The falling flower." Reprinted from *Poetry Handbook; A Dictionary of Terms* by Babette Deutsch. By permission of the publishers, Funk & Wagnalls, New York.

ELIZABETH BISHOP "One Art" from *Geography III* by Elizabeth Bishop. Copyright © 1976 by Elizabeth Bishop. Reprinted by permission of Farrar, Straus and Giroux, Inc.

Copyrights and acknowledgments continue on pages 328–333

True ease in writing comes from art, not chance,
As those move easiest who have learned to dance.
'Tis not enough no harshness gives offense,
The sound must seem an echo to the sense.

Alexander Pope from *An Essay on Criticism*

preface

The sixth edition of *Sound and Sense*, like the earlier editions, is written for the college student who is beginning a serious study of poetry. It seeks to give that student a sufficient grasp of the nature and variety of poetry, some reasonable means for reading it with appreciative understanding, and a few primary ideas of how to evaluate it. The separate chapters gradually introduce the student to the elements of poetry, putting the emphasis always on *how* and *why*: *How* can the reader use these elements to get at the meaning of the poem, to interpret it correctly, and to respond to it adequately? *Why* does the poet use these elements? What values have they for the poet and reader?

In matters of theory, some issues are undoubtedly simplified, but, I hope, not overly so. The purpose of the simplification—as with the approach in general—is always to give the beginning student something to understand and use. The first assumptions of *Sound and Sense* are that poetry needs to be read carefully and thought about considerably and that, when so read, poetry gives its readers continuing rewards in experience and understanding.

Each chapter is divided into two parts: a discussion of the topic indicated by the chapter title, with illustrative poems, and a relevant selection of poems, with study questions, for further reading. The division between the two parts is visually indicated by a row of asterisks. The whole book is similarly divided into two parts: Part One consists of the sixteen discussion chapters; Part Two of poems, without study questions, for further reading.

The sixth edition differs from the fifth chiefly in the following respects. About twenty-eight percent of the poems are new, including some poems first published in the past five years. Canadian poets have been included. Chapter 12, Rhythm and Meter, has been rewritten using a different illustrative poem, and a supplemental note has been added.

A book of this kind inevitably owes something to all who have thought or written about poetry. It would be impossible to express all indebtedness, but for personal advice, criticism, and assistance I wish to thank my wife, Catherine Perrine; Professor Maynard Mack, Yale University; the late Charles S. Holmes, Pomona College; Donald Peet, Indiana University; James W. Byrd, East Texas State University; Calvin L. Skaggs, Drew University; Willis Glover, Mercer University; and Margaret Morton Blum, Southern Methodist University.

I would also like to thank the following instructors, who have sent me helpful reactions and suggestions for this sixth edition of *Sound and Sense:* Anne Agee, Anne Arundel Community College; Carolyn R. Allison, Essex Community College; Leroy Earl Ater, Los Angeles Pierce College; Joseph Barba, College of the Sequoias; Donna Bauerly, Loras College; Ronald E. Becht, Marquette University; Hazel M. Benn, Northern State College; Mark Bernheim, Miami University; Paul Borgman, Northwestern College; Phillip E. Bozek, Illinois Benedictine College; Stuart Burns, Drake University; Ronald W. Butler, Henderson Community College; John Canuteson, William Jewell College; Mary Casper, West Valley College; Helen G. Chapin, Hawaii Pacific College; M. G. Cheney, Weber State College; Penelope Choy, Los Angeles City College; Tony Clark, Paris Junior College; Lawrence Clayton, Hardin-Simmons University; Betty C. Clement, Paris Junior College; Burt Collins, Kankakee Community College; E. Wayne Cook, Mt. View College; Ethel F. Cornwell, Shepherd College; Lynn Cox, Lincoln Land Community College; Gordon Curzon, California Polytechnic State University; R. W. Danielson, Grossmont College; Pauline Douglas, Prairie State College; M. Duggar, Chicago State University; Janet E. Eber, County College of Morris; C. H. Edgren, North Park College; Robert A. Elderdice, Salisbury State College; Fiona I. Emde, West Valley College; Gene Fehler, Kishwaukee College; Virginia G. Fick, Davidson Community College; John W. Fields, Weatherford College; Frank M. Flack, Los Angeles Pierce College; Robert Foxworthy, Fullerton College; Gary Grassinger, Community College of Allegheny County; Jane Grissinger, Shepherd College; John K. Hanes, Duquesne University; Nikki Hansen, Weber State College; Marvin Harris, East Texas Baptist College; Carol T. Hayes, Holyoke Community College; Ann Hostetler, Golden West College; Thomas R. Howerton, Jr., Johnston Technical Institute; Betty Hughes, Beaufort County Community

College; Irene O. Jacobs, Frederick Community College; Sandra T. Jackson, County College of Morris; John Keeler, County College of Morris; Jeannette E. Kinyon, South Dakota School of Mines and Technology; Audrey S. Kirby, Forsyth Technical Institute; P. Kistel, Los Angeles Pierce College; Patricia C. Knight, Amarillo College; Allen J. Koppenhaver, Wittenberg University; Sister Mary Conrad Kraus, Viterbo College; Reverend Laurence Kriegshauser, OSB, St. Louis Priory School; Donald Kummings, University of Wisconsin, Parkside; William Landau, Los Angeles Pierce College; Lyle Larsen, Santa Monica College; Dixie LeHardy, Hagerstown Jr. College; Joanne H. McCarthy, Tacoma Community College; Jo Ray McCuen, Glendale College; T. Marshall, Robert Morris College; Joan Mathis, Paris Junior College; Don Meyer, Ventura College; Virginia R. Mollenkott, William Paterson College of New Jersey; George E. Montag, Longview Community College; Judith A. Oliver, Robert Morris College; Alice Omelia, Essex Community College; Roger J. Owens, Los Angeles City College; John Peters, Los Angeles Valley College; Gloria Dibble Pond, Mattatuck Community College; Kurt V. Rachwitz, Bellevue College; Noel Peter Robinson, County College of Morris; James C. Schaap, Dordt College; Gloria Schleimer, Compton College; Kent Seltman, Pacific Union College; Beth B. Shelton, Paris Junior College; Keith Slocum, Montclair State College; William F. Smith, Fullerton College; Mary S. Spangler, Los Angeles Valley College; Jacqueline Stark, Los Angeles Valley College; Maurine Stein, Prairie State College; Eric Steinbaugh, U.S. Naval Academy; J. M. Stiker, Lewis University; Harryette Stover, Eastfield College; Peter J. Ulisse, Housatonic Regional Community College; Charles L. Van Hof, Dordt College; Mike Vanden Bosch, Dordt College; Sandra C. Vekasy, Evangel College; Mary Waldrop, Tyler Junior College; Robert K. Wallace, Northern Kentucky University; Clifford Warren, Prince Georges Community College; John P. Weber, Cypress College; J. L. Wheeler, Southwestern Adventist College; Richard W. White, Edison Community College; J. Peter Williams, County College of Morris; Marianne Wilpiszewski, Prince Georges Community College; Robert W. Wylie, Amarillo College; Clemewell Young, Manchester Community College; Sander Zulauf, County College of Morris.

L.P.

contents

6. Figurative Language 2: Symbol, Allegory   75

7. Figurative Language 3: Paradox, Overstatement, Understatement, Irony 95

8. Allusion   115

9. Meaning and Idea 126

10. Tone 138

14. Pattern   203

*   *   *

15. Bad Poetry and Good   222

*   *   *

16. Good Poetry and Great   238

*   *   *

part two   Poems for Further Reading

part one

The Elements
of Poetry

1. What Is Poetry?

Poetry is as universal as language and almost as ancient. The most primitive peoples have used it, and the most civilized have cultivated it. In all ages, and in all countries, poetry has been written—and eagerly read or listened to—by all kinds and conditions of people, by soldiers, statesmen, lawyers, farmers, doctors, scientists, clergymen, philosophers, kings, and queens. In all ages it has been especially the concern of the educated, the intelligent, and the sensitive, and it has appealed, in its simpler forms, to the uneducated and to children. Why? First, because it has given pleasure. People have read it or listened to it or recited it because they liked it, because it gave them enjoyment. But this is not the whole answer. Poetry in all ages has been regarded as important, not simply as one of several alternative forms of amusement, as one person might choose bowling, another chess, and another poetry. Rather, it has been regarded as something central to existence, something having unique value to the fully realized life, something that we are better off for having and spiritually impoverished without. To understand the reasons for this, we need to have at least a provisional understanding of what poetry is—provisional, because people have always been more successful at appreciating poetry than at defining it.

Initially, poetry might be defined as a kind of language that says *more* and says it *more intensely* than does ordinary language. In order to understand this fully, we need to understand what it is that poetry "says." For language is employed on different occasions to say quite different kinds of things; in other words, language has different uses.

Perhaps the commonest use of language is to communicate *informa-tion*. We say that it is nine o'clock, that there is a good movie downtown, that George Washington was the first president of the United States, that bromine and iodine are members of the halogen group of chemical elements. This we might call the *practical* use of language; it helps us with the ordinary business of living.

But it is not primarily to communicate information that novels and short stories and plays and poems are written. These exist to bring us a sense and a perception of life, to widen and sharpen our contacts with existence. Their concern is with *experience*. We all have an inner need to live more deeply and fully and with greater awareness, to know the experience of others and to know better our own experience. Poets, from their own store of felt, observed, or imagined experiences, select, combine, and reorganize. They create significant new experiences for their readers—significant because focused and formed—in which readers can participate and which they may use to give themselves a greater awareness and understanding of their world. Literature, in other words, can be used as a gear for stepping up the intensity and increasing the range of our experience and as a glass for clarifying it. This is the *literary* use of language, for literature is not only an aid to living but a means of living.*

Suppose, for instance, that we are interested in eagles. If we want simply to acquire information about eagles, we may turn to an encyclopedia or a book of natural history. There we find that the family Falconidae, to which eagles belong, is characterized by imperforate nostrils, legs of medium length, a hooked bill, the hind toe inserted on a level with the three front ones, and the claws roundly curved and sharp; that land eagles are feathered to the toes and sea-fishing eagles halfway to the toes; that their length is about three feet, the extent of wing seven feet; that the nest is usually placed on some inaccessible cliff; that the eggs are spotted and do not exceed three; and perhaps that the eagle's "great power of vision, the vast height to which it soars in the sky, the wild grandeur of its abode, have . . . commended it to the poets of all nations."†

But unless we are interested in this information only for practical purposes, we are likely to feel a little disappointed, as though we had

---

*A third use of language is as an instrument of persuasion. This is the use we find in advertisements, propaganda bulletins, sermons, and political speeches. These three uses of language—the practical, the literary, and the hortatory—are not sharply divided. They may be thought of as three points of a triangle; most actual specimens of written language fall somewhere within the triangle. Most poetry conveys some information, and some poetry has a design on the reader. But language becomes *literature* when the desire to communicate experience predominates.

† *Encyclopedia Americana*, IX, 473–74.

grasped the feathers of the eagle but not its soul. True, we have learned many facts about the eagle, but we have missed somehow its lonely majesty, its power, and the "wild grandeur" of its surroundings that would make the eagle a living creature rather than a mere museum specimen. For the living eagle we must turn to literature.

THE EAGLE

He clasps the crag with crooked hands;
Close to the sun in lonely lands,
Ringed with the azure world, he stands. *soaring has the whole world*

The wrinkled sea beneath him crawls;
He watches from his mountain walls,
And like a thunderbolt he falls. *aged decline*

has great power —Alfred, Lord Tennyson (1809–1892)

QUESTIONS

1. What is peculiarly effective about the expressions "crooked hands," "close to the sun," "ringed with the azure world," "wrinkled," "crawls," and "like a thunderbolt"? *Descriptions.*
2. Notice the formal pattern of the poem, particularly the contrast of "he stands" in the first stanza and "he falls" in the second. Is there any other contrast between the two stanzas? *At top of world until someone shoots him down.*

When the preceding poem has been read well, readers will feel that they have enjoyed a significant experience and understand eagles better, though in a different way, than they did from the encyclopedia article alone. For if the article *analyzes* man's experience with eagles, the poem in some sense *synthesizes* such an experience. Indeed, the two approaches to experience—the scientific and the literary—may be said to complement each other. And it may be contended that the kind of understanding we get from the second is at least as valuable as the kind we get from the first.

Literature, then, exists to communicate significant experience—significant because concentrated and organized. Its function is not to tell us *about* experience but to allow us imaginatively to *participate* in it. It is a means of allowing us, through the imagination, to live more fully, more deeply, more richly, and with greater awareness. It can do this in two ways: by *broadening* our experience—that is, by making us acquainted with a range of experience with which, in the ordinary course of events, we might have no contact—or by *deepening* our experience—that is, by making us feel more poignantly and more understandingly the everyday experiences all of us have.

Two false approaches often taken to poetry can be avoided if we keep this conception of literature firmly in mind. The first approach always looks for a lesson or a bit of moral instruction. The second expects to find poetry always beautiful. Let us consider a song from Shakespeare:

WINTER

When icicles hang by the wall,
    And Dick the shepherd blows his nail,
And Tom bears logs into the hall,
    And milk comes frozen home in pail,
When blood is nipped and ways be foul,   5
Then nightly sings the staring owl,
      "Tu-whit, tu-who!"

A merry note,
While greasy Joan doth keel° the pot.   skim

When all aloud the wind doth blow,   10
    And coughing drowns the parson's saw,
And birds sit brooding in the snow,
    And Marian's nose looks red and raw,
When roasted crabs° hiss in the bowl,   crab apples
Then nightly sings the staring owl,   15
      "Tu-whit, tu-who!"

A merry note,
While greasy Joan doth keel the pot.

William Shakespeare (1564–1616)

QUESTIONS

1. What are the meanings of "nail" (2) and "saw" (11)?
2. Is the owl's cry really a "merry" note? How are this adjective and the verb "sings" employed?
3. In what way does the owl's cry contrast with the other details of the poem?

In the poem "Winter" Shakespeare is attempting to communicate the quality of winter life around a sixteenth-century English country house. But instead of telling us flatly that winter in such surroundings is cold and in many respects unpleasant, though with some pleasant features too (the adjectives *cold, unpleasant,* and *pleasant* are not even used in the poem), he gives us a series of concrete homely details that suggest these qualities and enable us, imaginatively, to experience this winter life ourselves. The shepherd lad blows on his fingernails to warm his hands; the milk freezes in the pail between the cowshed and the kitchen; the roads are muddy; the folk listening to the parson have colds; the birds "sit brooding in the snow"; and the servant girl's nose is raw from cold. But pleasant things are in prospect. Logs are being brought in for a fire, hot cider or ale is being prepared, and the kitchen maid is making a hot soup or stew. In contrast to all these homely, familiar details of country life comes in the mournful, haunting, and eerie note of the owl.

Obviously the poem contains no moral. Readers who always look in poetry for some lesson, message, or noble truth about life are bound to be disappointed. Moral-hunters see poetry as a kind of sugar-coated pill—a wholesome truth or lesson made palatable by being put into pretty words. What they are really after is a sermon—not a poem, but something inspirational. Yet "Winter," which has appealed to readers now for nearly four centuries, is not inspirational and contains no moral preachment.

Neither is the poem "Winter" beautiful. Though it is appealing in its way and contains elements of beauty, there is little that is really beautiful in red raw noses, coughing in chapel, nipped blood, foul roads, and greasy kitchen maids. Yet some readers think that poetry deals exclusively with beauty—with sunsets, flowers, butterflies, love, God—and that the one appropriate response to any poem is, after a moment of awed silence, "Isn't that beautiful!" For such readers poetry is a precious affair, the enjoyment only of delicate souls, removed from the heat and sweat of ordinary life. But theirs is too narrow an approach to poetry. The function of poetry is sometimes to be ugly rather than beautiful. And poetry may deal with common colds and greasy kitchen maids as legitimately as with sunsets and flowers. Consider another example:

DULCE ET DECORUM EST

Bent double, like old beggars under sacks,
Knock-kneed, coughing like hags, we cursed through sludge,
Till on the haunting flares we turned our backs,
And towards our distant rest began to trudge.
Men marched asleep. Many had lost their boots,   5
But limped on, blood-shod. All went lame, all blind;
Drunk with fatigue; deaf even to the hoots
Of gas-shells dropping softly behind.

Gas! GAS! Quick, boys!—An ecstasy of fumbling,
Fitting the clumsy helmets just in time,   10
But someone still was yelling out and stumbling
And flound'ring like a man in fire or lime.—
Dim through the misty panes and thick green light,
As under a green sea, I saw him drowning.

In all my dreams before my helpless sight   15
He plunges at me, guttering, choking, drowning.

If in some smothering dreams, you too could pace
Behind the wagon that we flung him in,
And watch the white eyes writhing in his face,
His hanging face, like a devil's sick of sin,   20
If you could hear, at every jolt, the blood
Come gargling from the froth-corrupted lungs
Bitter as the cud
Of vile, incurable sores on innocent tongues,—
My friend, you would not tell with such high zest   25
To children ardent for some desperate glory,
The old lie: *Dulce et decorum est*
Pro patria mori.

Wilfred Owen (1893–1918)

Not sweet
but cruel

QUESTIONS

1. The Latin quotation, from the Roman poet Horace, means "It is sweet and
   becoming to die for one's country." (Wilfred Owen died fighting for England
   in World War I, a week before the armistice.) What is the poem's comment on
   this statement?
2. List the elements of the poem that to you seem not beautiful and therefore
   unpoetic. Are there any elements of beauty in the poem?
3. How do the comparisons in lines 1, 14, 20, and 23-24 contribute to the
   effectiveness of the poem?

Poetry takes all life as its province. Its primary concern is not with
beauty, not with philosophical truth, not with persuasion, but with expe-
rience. Beauty and philosophical truth are aspects of experience, and the
poet is often engaged with them. But poetry as a whole is concerned with
all kinds of experience—beautiful or ugly, strange or common, noble or
ignoble, actual or imaginary. One of the paradoxes of human existence is
that all experience—even painful experience—when transmitted through
the medium of art is, for the good reader, enjoyable. In real life, death and
pain and suffering are not pleasurable, but in poetry they may be. In real

life, getting soaked in a rainstorm is not pleasurable, but in poetry it can be. In actual life, if we cry, usually we are unhappy; but if we cry in a movie, we are manifestly enjoying it. We do not ordinarily like to be terrified in real life, but we sometimes seek movies or books that will terrify us. We find some value in all intense living. To be intensely alive is the opposite of being dead. To be dull, to be bored, to be imperceptive is in one sense to be dead. Poetry comes to us bringing life and therefore pleasure. Moreover, art focuses and so organizes experience as to give us a better understanding of it. And to understand life is partly to be master of it.

Between poetry and other forms of imaginative literature there is no sharp distinction. You may have been taught to believe that poetry can be recognized by the arrangement of its lines on the page or by its use of rime and meter. Such superficial tests are almost worthless. The Book of Job in the Bible and Melville's *Moby Dick* are highly poetical, but the familiar verse that begins: "Thirty days hath September, / April, June, and November . . ." is not. The difference between poetry and other literature is one only of degree. Poetry is the most condensed and concentrated form of literature, saying most in the fewest number of words. It is language whose individual lines, either because of their own brilliance or because they focus so powerfully what has gone before, have a higher voltage than most language has. It is language that grows frequently incandescent, giving off both light and heat.

Ultimately, therefore, poetry can be recognized only by the response made to it by a good reader, someone who has acquired some sensitivity to poetry. But there is a catch here. We are not all good readers. To a poor reader, poetry will often seem dull and boring, a fancy way of writing something that could be said more simply. So might a colorblind man deny that there is such a thing as color.

The act of communication involved in reading poetry is like the act of communication involved in receiving a message by radio. Two factors are involved: a transmitting station and a receiving set. The completeness of the communication depends on both the power and clarity of the transmitter and the sensitivity and tuning of the receiver. When a person reads a poem and no experience is transmitted, either the poem is not a good poem or the reader is a poor reader or not properly tuned. With new poetry, we cannot always be sure which is at fault. With older poetry, if it has acquired critical acceptance—has been enjoyed by generations of good readers—we may assume that the receiving set is at fault. Fortunately, the fault is not irremediable. Though we cannot all become expert readers, we can become good enough to find both pleasure and value in much good poetry, or we can increase the amount of pleasure we already find in poetry and the number of kinds of poetry we find it in. To help you increase your sensitivity and range as a receiving set is the purpose of this book.

Poetry, finally, is a kind of multidimensional language. Ordinary language—the kind that we use to communicate information—is one-dimensional. It is directed at only part of the listener, his understanding. Its one dimension is intellectual. Poetry, which is language used to communicate experience, has at least four dimensions. If it is to communicate experience, it must be directed at the *whole* person, not just at his understanding. It must involve not only his intelligence but also his senses, emotions, and imagination. Poetry, to the intellectual dimension, adds a sensuous dimension, an emotional dimension, and an imaginative dimension.

Poetry achieves its extra dimensions—its greater pressure per word and its greater tension per poem—by drawing more fully and more consistently than does ordinary language on a number of language resources, none of which is peculiar to poetry. These various resources form the subjects of a number of the following chapters. Among them are connotation, imagery, metaphor, symbol, paradox, irony, allusion, sound repetition, rhythm, and pattern. Using these resources and the materials of life, the poet shapes and makes his poem. Successful poetry is never effusive language. If it is to come alive it must be as cunningly put together and as efficiently organized as a tree. It must be an organism whose every part serves a useful purpose and cooperates with every other part to preserve and express the life that is within it.

*   *   *

SPRING

When daisies pied and violets blue,
   And lady-smocks all silver-white,
And cuckoo-buds of yellow hue
   Do paint the meadows with delight,
The cuckoo then, on every tree,   5
Mocks married men; for thus sings he,
          "Cuckoo!
Cuckoo, cuckoo!" O word of fear,
Unpleasing to a married ear!

When shepherds pipe on oaten straws,   10
   And merry larks are ploughmen's clocks,

When turtles tread, and rooks, and daws, *[handwritten: just how should winter isn't all bad - spring]*
And maidens bleach their summer smocks, *[handwritten: isn't all good]*
The cuckoo then, on every tree,
Mocks married men; for thus sings he,   15
                    "Cuckoo!
Cuckoo, cuckoo!" O word of fear,
Unpleasing to a married ear!

William Shakespeare (1564–1616)

QUESTIONS

1. Vocabulary: *pied* (1), *lady-smocks* (2), *oaten straws* (10), *turtles* (12), *tread* (12), *daws* (12).
2. This song is a companion piece to "Winter." In what respects are the two poems similar? How do they contrast? What details show that this poem, like "Winter," was written by a realist, not simply by a man carried away with the beauty of spring? *[handwritten: Reality of Spring]*
3. The word "cuckoo" is "unpleasing to a married ear" because it sounds like *cuckold*. Cuckolds were a frequent butt of humor in earlier English literature. If you do not know the meaning of the word, look it up.
4. Is the tone of this poem solemn or light and semihumorous?

[handwritten: sun is out & woman loose clothes loose life. Out.]

A BIRD CAME DOWN THE WALK*

A bird came down the walk.
He did not know I saw.
He bit an angle-worm in halves
And ate the fellow, raw.

And then he drank a dew   5
From a convenient grass,
And then hopped sideways to the wall
To let a beetle pass.

He glanced with rapid eyes
That hurried all around;   10
They looked like frightened beads, I thought.
He stirred his velvet head

Like one in danger; cautious,
I offered him a crumb,

*Whenever a title duplicates the first line of the poem or a substantial portion thereof, it is probable that the poet left the poem untitled and that the anthologist has substituted the first line or part of it as an editorial convenience. This is standard practice, and is true for this poem and for two of the three poems that follow in this chapter.

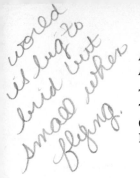

[handwritten margin notes: "world is big but bird but when small flying"]

And he unrolled his feathers *[handwritten: flew away afraid]*   15
And rowed him softer home

Than oars divide the ocean,   *[handwritten: bird—free]*
Too silver for a seam,   *[handwritten: when flying]*
Or butterflies, off banks of noon,
Leap, plashless, as they swim.   20

Emily Dickinson (1830–1886)

QUESTIONS

1. The poem is based on a pair of contrasts: that between the observer (the human world) and the bird (the natural world); and that between the bird on the ground (1–14) and the bird in flight (15–20). Discuss the first contrast. What is the relationship between observer and bird? How do their "worlds" contrast? *[handwritten: free → majestic   limitation]*
2. How does the bird in the air differ from the bird on the ground? How do the sounds of the words in lines 15–20 reflect that difference?
3. Discuss the appropriateness of the word "rowed" (16). What is referred to in line 18? What image is suggested in lines 19–20, and how is *it* lightly reflected in the sounds of the words used?

CONSTANTLY RISKING ABSURDITY

Constantly risking absurdity
                          and death
          whenever he performs
                    above the heads
                              of his audience   5
  the poet like an acrobat
                    climbs on rime
                          to a high wire of his own making
and balancing on eyebeams
                          above a sea of faces   10
          paces his way
                    to the other side of day
          performing entrechats
                    and sleight-of-foot tricks
and other high theatrics   15
                    and all without mistaking
          any thing
                    for what it may not be

      For he's the super realist
                          who must perforce perceive   20
          taut truth
                    before the taking of each stance or step

in his supposed advance
> toward that still higher perch
where Beauty stands and waits
> with gravity   25
> > to start her death-defying leap

And he
> a little charleychaplin man
> > who may or may not catch   30
> her fair eternal form
> > spreadeagled in the empty air
> of existence

Lawrence Ferlinghetti (b. 1919)

poets take risk wh writing, hope to capture beauty and essence in their work

QUESTIONS

why do they do it?

1. Vocabulary: *entrechats* (13). What meanings have "above the heads" (4), "sleight-of-foot tricks" (14), "high theatrics" (15), "with gravity" (26)?
2. The poet, it is said, "climbs on rime" (7). To what extent does this poem utilize rime and other sound correspondences? Point out examples.
3. What statement does the poem make about poetry, truth, and beauty?
4. What additional comments about poetry are implied by the figures of speech employed?
5. Does Ferlinghetti take poets and poetry seriously? Solemnly?

THE PASTURE

I'm going out to clean the pasture spring; *speaker is a nature lover*
I'll only stop to rake the leaves away
(And wait to watch the water clear, I may):
I shan't be gone long.—You come too. *- society*

I'm going out to fetch the little calf
That's standing by the mother. It's so young
It totters when she licks it with her tongue.
I shan't be gone long.—You come too.

Robert Frost (1874–1963)

QUESTIONS

1. Who and what kind of person is the speaker? Who is addressed?
2. Frost, as a poet, characteristically strove to capture the speech rhythms and language of the actual human voice in poems retaining a metrical form. In what lines is he particularly successful at this?

3. Originally the initial poem in Frost's second volume of verse, "The Pasture" was retained by Frost as the initial poem in collections of his verse. What additional meaning does the poem acquire from this position? Are poets usually concerned, would you guess, with the *arrangement* of poems in their books? Why or why not?

TERENCE, THIS IS STUPID STUFF

    "Terence, this is stupid stuff:
You eat your victuals fast enough;
There can't be much amiss, 'tis clear,
To see the rate you drink your beer.
But oh, good Lord, the verse you make,   5
It gives a chap the belly-ache.
The cow, the old cow, she is dead;
It sleeps well, the horned head:
We poor lads, 'tis our turn now
To hear such tunes as killed the cow.   10
Pretty friendship 'tis to rhyme
Your friends to death before their time
Moping melancholy mad:
Come, pipe a tune to dance to, lad."

    Why, if 'tis dancing you would be,   15
There's brisker pipes than poetry.
Say, for what were hop-yards meant,
Or why was Burton built on Trent?
Oh many a peer of England brews
Livelier liquor than the Muse,   20
And malt does more than Milton can
To justify God's ways to man.
Ale, man, ale's the stuff to drink
For fellows whom it hurts to think:
Look into the pewter pot   25
To see the world as the world's not.
And faith, 'tis pleasant till 'tis past:
The mischief is that 'twill not last.
Oh I have been to Ludlow fair
And left my necktie god knows where,   30
And carried half-way home, or near,
Pints and quarts of Ludlow beer:
Then the world seemed none so bad,
And I myself a sterling lad;
And down in lovely muck I've lain,   35

Happy till I woke again.
Then I saw the morning sky:
Heigho, the tale was all a lie;
The world, it was the old world yet,
I was I, my things were wet,   40
And nothing now remained to do
But begin the game anew.

    Therefore, since the world has still
Much good, but much less good than ill,
And while the sun and moon endure   45
Luck's a chance, but trouble's sure,
I'd face it as a wise man would,
And train for ill and not for good.
'Tis true, the stuff I bring for sale
Is not so brisk a brew as ale: 50
Out of a stem that scored the hand
I wrung it in a weary land.
But take it: if the smack is sour,
The better for the embittered hour;
It should do good to heart and head   55
When your soul is in my soul's stead;
And I will friend you, if I may,
In the dark and cloudy day.

    There was a king reigned in the East:
There, when kings will sit to feast,   60
They get their fill before they think
With poisoned meat and poisoned drink.
He gathered all that springs to birth
From the many-venomed earth;
First a little, thence to more,   65
He sampled all her killing store;
And easy, smiling, seasoned sound,
Sate the king when healths went round.
They put arsenic in his meat
And stared aghast to watch him eat;   70
They poured strychnine in his cup
And shook to see him drink it up:
They shook, they stared as white's their shirt:
Them it was their poison hurt.
—I tell the tale that I heard told.   75
Mithridates, he died old.

                         A. E. Housman (1859–1936)

1. "Terence" (1) is Housman's poetic name for himself. Housman's poetry is largely pessimistic or sad; and this poem, placed near the end of his volume *A Shropshire Lad,* is his defense of the kind of poetry he wrote. Who is the speaker in the first fourteen lines? Who is the speaker in the rest of the poem? What is "the stuff I bring for sale" (49)?
2. "Hops" (17) and "malt" (21) are principal ingredients of beer and ale. Burton-upon-Trent (18) is an English city famous for its breweries. Milton (21), in the invocation of his epic poem *Paradise Lost,* declares that his purpose is to "justify the ways of God to men." What, in Housman's eyes, is the efficacy of liquor in helping one live a difficult life?
3. What six lines of the poem most explicitly sum up the poet's philosophy? Most people like reading material that is cheerful and optimistic (on the argument that "there's enough suffering and unhappiness in the world already"). What for Housman is the value of pessimistic and tragic literature?
4. "Mithridates" (76) was a king of Pontus and contemporary of Julius Caesar; his "tale" is told in Pliny's *Natural History.* What is the connection of this last verse paragraph with the rest of the poem?

HAST THOU GIVEN THE HORSE STRENGTH

Hast thou given the horse strength?
Hast thou clothed his neck with thunder? powerful
Canst thou make him afraid as a grasshopper? meek
The glory of his nostrils is terrible.
He paweth in the valley, and rejoiceth in his strength: 5
He goeth on to meet the armed men.
He mocketh at fear, and is not affrighted;
Neither turneth he back from the sword.
The quiver rattleth against him,
The glittering spear and the shield.   10
He swalloweth the ground with fierceness and rage;
Neither believeth he that it is the sound of the trumpet.
He saith among the trumpets, Ha, ha;
And he smelleth the battle afar off,
The thunder of the captains, and the shouting.   15

From the Book of Job 39:19–25

These words are spoken to Job by the Lord, out of a whirlwind. In the Bible they are generally printed as prose. What justifies their being regarded as poetry?

2. Reading the Poem

The primary purpose of this book is to develop your ability to understand and appreciate poetry. Here are some preliminary suggestions:

1. Read a poem more than once. A good poem will no more yield its full meaning on a single reading than will a Beethoven symphony on a single hearing. Two readings may be necessary simply to let you get your bearings. And if the poem is a work of art, it will repay repeated and prolonged examination. One does not listen to a good piece of music once and forget it; one does not look at a good painting once and throw it away. A poem is not like a newspaper, to be hastily read and cast into the wastebasket. It is to be hung on the wall of one's mind.

2. Keep a dictionary by you and use it. It is futile to try to understand poetry without troubling to learn the meanings of the words of which it is composed. One might as well attempt to play tennis without a ball. One of your primary purposes while in college should be to build a good vocabulary, and the study of poetry gives you an excellent opportunity. A few other reference books will also be invaluable. Particularly desirable are a good book on mythology (your instructor can recommend one) and a Bible.

3. Read so as to hear the sounds of the words in your mind. Poetry is written to be heard: its meanings are conveyed through sound as well as through print. Every word is therefore important. The best way to read a poem is just the opposite of the best way to read a newspaper. One reads a newspaper as rapidly as possible; one should read a poem as slowly as possible. When you cannot read a poem aloud, lip-read it: form the words with your tongue and mouth though you do not utter them. With ordi-

nary reading material, lip reading is a bad habit; with poetry it is a good habit.

4. Always pay careful attention to what the poem is saying. Though you should be conscious of the sounds of the poem, you should never be so exclusively conscious of them that you pay no attention to what the poem means. For some readers, reading a poem is like getting on board a rhythmical roller coaster. The car starts, and off they go, up and down, paying no attention to the landscape flashing past them, arriving at the end of the poem breathless, with no idea of what it has been about.* This is the wrong way to read a poem. One should make the utmost effort to follow the thought continuously and to grasp the full implications and suggestions. Because a poem says so much, several readings may be necessary, but on the very first reading you should determine the subjects of the verbs and the antecedents of the pronouns.

5. Practice reading poems aloud. When you find one you especially like, make friends listen to it. Try to read it to them in such a way that they will like it too. (a) Read it affectionately, but not affectedly. The two extremes oral readers often fall into are equally deadly. One is to read as if one were reading a tax report or a railroad timetable, unexpressively, in a monotone. The other is to elocute, with artificial flourishes and vocal histrionics. It is not necessary to put emotion into reading a poem. The emotion is already there. It only wants a fair chance to get out. It will express *itself* if the poem is read naturally and sensitively. (b) Of the two extremes, reading too fast offers greater danger than reading too slow. Read slowly enough that each word is clear and distinct and that the meaning has time to sink in. Remember that your friends do not have the advantage, as you do, of having the text before them. Your ordinary rate of reading will probably be too fast. (c) Read the poem so that the rhythmical pattern is felt but not exaggerated. Remember that poetry is written in sentences, just as prose is, and that punctuation is a signal as to how it should be read. Give all grammatical pauses their full due. Do not distort the natural pronunciation of words or a normal accentuation of the sentence to fit into what you have decided is its metrical pattern. One of the worst ways to read a poem is to read it ta-*dum* ta-*dum* ta-*dum* with an exaggerated emphasis on every other syllable. On the other hand, it should not be read as if it were prose. An important test of your reading will be how you handle the end of a line when there is no punctuation there. A frequent mistake of the beginning reader is to treat each line as if it were a complete thought, whether grammatically complete or not,

---

*Some poems encourage this type of reading. When this is so, usually the poet has not made the best use of rhythm to support sense.

and to drop his voice at the end of it. A frequent mistake of the sophisticated reader is to take a running start upon approaching the end of a line and fly over it as if it were not there. The line is a rhythmical unit, and its end should be observed whether there is punctuation or not. If there is no punctuation, one observes it ordinarily by the slightest of pauses or by holding onto the last word in the line just a little longer than usual, without dropping one's voice. In line 12 of the following poem, you should hold onto the word "although" longer than if it occurred elsewhere in the line. But do not lower your voice on it: it is part of the clause that follows in the next stanza.

THE MAN HE KILLED

shocked at cruelty of war

Had he and I but met
By some old ancient inn,
We should have sat us down to wet
Right many a nipperkin!°   half-pint cup

But ranged as infantry,   5
And staring face to face,
I shot at him as he at me,
And killed him in his place.

I shot him dead because—
Because he was my foe,   *reason for killing* 10
Just so: my foe of course he was;
That's clear enough; although

He thought he'd 'list, perhaps,   *desperation can make a*
Off-hand-like—just as I—   *person do things.*
Was out of work—had sold his traps—   *joined army* 15
No other reason why.   *b/c out of work*

enemy—friend in other circumstance

Yes; quaint and curious war is!
You shoot a fellow down
You'd treat, if met where any bar is,   *friendly*
Or help to half-a-crown.   *helping* 20

Thomas Hardy (1840–1928)

QUESTIONS

1. Vocabulary: *traps* (15).
2. In informational prose the repetition of a word like "because" (9–10) would be an error. What purpose does the repetition serve here? Why does the

speaker repeat to himself his "clear" reason for killing a man (10–11)? The word "although" (12) gets more emphasis than it ordinarily would because it comes not only at the end of a line but at the end of a stanza. What purpose does this emphasis serve? Can the redundancy of "old ancient" (2) be poetically justified?

3. Someone has defined poetry as "the expression of elevated thought in elevated language." Comment on the adequacy of this definition in the light of Hardy's poem.

To aid us in the understanding of a poem, we may ask ourselves a number of questions about it. One of the most important is *Who is the speaker and what is the occasion?* A cardinal error of some readers is to assume always that the speaker is the poet himself. A far safer course is to assume always that the speaker is someone other than the poet himself. For even when the poet does speak directly and express his own thoughts and emotions, he does so ordinarily as a representative human being rather than as an individual who lives at a particular address, dislikes dill pickles, and favors blue neckties. We must always be cautious about identifying anything in a poem with the biography of the poet. Like the novelist and the playwright, he is fully justified in changing actual details of his own experience to make the experience of the poem more universal. We may well think of every poem, therefore, as being to some degree *dramatic,* that is, the utterance of a fictional character rather than of the poet himself. Many poems are expressly dramatic.

In "The Man He Killed" the speaker is a soldier; the occasion is his having been in battle and killed a man—obviously for the first time in his life. We can tell a good deal about him. He is not a career soldier: he enlisted only because he was out of work. He is a workingman: he speaks a simple and colloquial language ("nipperkin," "'list," "off-hand-like," "traps"), and he has sold the tools of his trade—he may have been a tinker or plumber. He is a friendly, kindly sort who enjoys a neighborly drink of ale in a bar and will gladly lend a friend a half crown when he has it. He has known what it is to be poor. In any other circumstances he would have been horrified at taking a human life. He has been given pause as it is. He is trying to figure it out. But he is not a deep thinker and thinks he has supplied a reason when he has only supplied a name: "I killed the man . . . because he was my foe." The critical question, of course, is *Why was the man his "foe"?* Even the speaker is left unsatisfied by his answer, though he is not analytical enough to know what is wrong with it. Obviously this poem is expressly dramatic. We need know nothing about Thomas Hardy's life (he was never a soldier and never killed a man) to realize that the poem is dramatic. The internal evidence of the poem tells us so.

A second important question that we should ask ourselves upon reading any poem is *What is the central purpose of the poem?** The purpose may be to tell a story, to reveal human character, to impart a vivid impression of a scene, to express a mood or an emotion, or to convey to us vividly some idea or attitude. Whatever the purpose is, we must determine it for ourselves and define it mentally as precisely as possible. Only then can we fully understand the function and meaning of the various details in the poem, by relating them to this central purpose. Only then can we begin to assess the value of the poem and determine whether it is a good one or a poor one. In "The Man He Killed" the central purpose is quite clear: it is to make us realize more keenly the irrationality of war. The puzzlement of the speaker may be our puzzlement. But even if we are able to give a more sophisticated answer than his as to why men kill each other, we ought still to have a greater awareness, after reading the poem, of the fundamental irrationality in war that makes men kill who have no grudge against each other and who might under different circumstances show each other considerable kindness.

IS MY TEAM PLOUGHING

is life going on, now that I'm dead

"Is my team ploughing,
  That I was used to drive
And hear the harness jingle
  When I was man alive?"

a ind. life is brief yet life in general is eternal

Aye, the horses trample,   5
  The harness jingles now;
No change though you lie under
  The land you used to plough.

"Is football playing
  Along the river shore,   10
With lads to chase the leather,
  Now I stand up no more?"

Aye, the ball is flying,
  The lads play heart and soul;

---

*Our only reliable evidence of the poem's purpose, of course, is the poem itself. External evidence, when it exists, though often helpful, may also be misleading. Some critics have objected to the use of such terms as "purpose" and "intention" altogether; we cannot know, they maintain, what was *attempted* in the poem; we can know only what was *done*. Philosophically this position is impeccable. Yet it is possible to make inferences about what was attempted, and such inferences furnish a convenient and helpful way of talking about poetry.

The goal stands up, the keeper   15
    Stands up to keep the goal.

"Is my girl happy,
    That I thought hard to leave,
And has she tired of weeping
    As she lies down at eve?"   20

Aye, she lies down lightly,
    She lies not down to weep:
Your girl is well contented.
    Be still, my lad, and sleep.

"Is my friend hearty,   25
    Now I am thin and pine;
And has he found to sleep in
    A better bed than mine?"

Yes, lad, I lie easy,
    I lie as lads would choose;   30
I cheer a dead man's sweetheart,
    Never ask me whose.

               A. E. Housman (1859–1936)

QUESTIONS

1. What is meant by "whose" in line 32?
2. Is Housman cynical in his observation of human nature and human life?
3. The word "sleep" in the concluding stanzas suggests three different meanings. What are they? How many meanings are suggested by the word "bed"?

    Once we have answered the question *What is the central purpose of the poem?* we can consider another question, equally important to full understanding: *By what means is that purpose achieved?* It is important to distinguish means from ends. A student on an examination once used the poem "Is my team ploughing" as evidence that A. E. Housman believed in immortality, because in it a man speaks from the grave. This is as much a misconstruction as to say that Thomas Hardy in "The Man He Killed" joined the army because he was out of work. The purpose of Housman's poem is to communicate poignantly a certain truth about human life: life goes on after our deaths pretty much as it did before—our dying does not disturb the universe. This purpose is achieved by means of a fanciful dramatic framework in which a dead man converses with his still-living friend. The framework tells us nothing about whether Housman believed in immortality (as a matter of fact, he did not). It is simply an effective means by which we *can* learn how Housman felt a man's death affected the life he left behind. The question *By what means is the purpose of the poem achieved?* is partially answered by describing the poem's dramatic framework, if it has any. The complete answer requires an accounting of various resources of communication that we will discuss in the rest of this book.

The most important preliminary advice we can give for reading poetry is to maintain always, while reading it, the utmost mental alertness. The most harmful idea one can get about poetry is that its purpose is to soothe and relax and that the best place to read it is lying in a hammock with a cool drink beside one and low music in the background. One *can* read poetry lying in a hammock but only if he refuses to put his mind in the same attitude as his body. Its purpose is not to soothe and relax but to arouse and awake, to shock one into life, to make one more alive. Poetry is not a substitute for a sedative.

An analogy can be drawn between reading poetry and playing tennis. Both offer great enjoyment if the game is played hard. A good tennis player must be constantly on the tip of his toes, concentrating on his opponent's every move. He must be ready for a drive to the right or a drive to the left, a lob overhead or a drop shot barely over the net. He must be ready for top spin or underspin, a ball that bounces crazily to the left or crazily to the right. He must jump for the high ones and run for the far ones. He will enjoy the game almost exactly in proportion to the effort he puts into it. The same is true of poetry. Great enjoyment is there, but this enjoyment demands a mental effort equivalent to the physical effort one puts into tennis.

The reader of poetry has one advantage over the tennis player. The poet is not trying to win a match. He may expect the reader to stretch for his shots, but he *wants* the reader to return them.

EXERCISE

Most of the poems in this book are accompanied by study questions that are by no means exhaustive. Following is a list of questions that you may apply to any poem. You will not be able to answer many of them until you have read further into the book.

1. Who is the speaker? What kind of person is he?
2. To whom is he speaking? What kind of person is he?
3. What is the occasion?
4. What is the setting in time (hour, season, century, etc.)?

5. What is the setting in place (indoors or out, city or country, land or sea, region, country, hemisphere, etc.)?
6. What is the central purpose of the poem?
7. State the central idea or theme of the poem in a sentence.
8. Discuss the tone of the poem. How is it achieved?
9. a. Outline the poem so as to show its structure and development, or
   b. Summarize the events of the poem.
10. Paraphrase the poem.
11. Discuss the diction of the poem. Point out words that are particularly well chosen and explain why.
12. Discuss the imagery of the poem. What kinds of imagery are used?
13. Point out examples of metaphor, simile, personification, and metonymy and explain their appropriateness.
14. Point out and explain any symbols. If the poem is allegorical, explain the allegory.
15. Point out and explain examples of paradox, overstatement, understatement, and irony. What is their function?
16. Point out and explain any allusions. What is their function?
17. Point out significant examples of sound repetition and explain their function.
18. a. What is the meter of the poem?
    b. Copy the poem and mark its scansion.
19. Discuss the adaptation of sound to sense.
20. Describe the form or pattern of the poem.
21. Criticize and evaluate the poem.

*   *   *

HYLA BROOK

By June our brook's run out of song and speed.
Sought for much after that, it will be found
Either to have gone groping underground
(And taken with it all the Hyla breed
That shouted in the mist a month ago,   5
Like ghost of sleigh bells in a ghost of snow)—
Or flourished and come up in jewelweed,
Weak foliage that is blown upon and bent
Even against the way its waters went.
Its bed is left a faded paper sheet   10
Of dead leaves stuck together by the heat—
A brook to none but who remember long.
This as it will be seen is other far
Than with brooks taken otherwhere in song.
We love the things we love for what they are.   15

Robert Frost (1874–1963)

QUESTIONS

1. Your instructor may occasionally ask you, as a test of your understanding of a poem at its lowest level, or as a means of clearing up misunderstanding, to paraphrase its content. To PARAPHRASE a poem means to restate it in different language, so as to make its prose sense as plain as possible. A paraphrase may be longer or shorter than the poem, but it should contain as far as possible all the ideas in the poem in such a way as to make them clear to a puzzled reader. Figurative language should be reduced when possible to literal language; metaphors should be turned into similes. Though it is neither necessary nor possible to avoid using some words occurring in the original, you should in general use your own language.

The central idea, or THEME, of the above poem is stated in its last line; but this line, despite its simplicity of language, is given full meaning only in the context of the fourteen lines preceding. The poem may be paraphrased as follows:

By June our brook is almost dry. The water no longer flows swiftly or makes a pleasant rippling sound. Soon after that, the water will have disappeared altogether (and with it all the tree toads that made such a racket along the banks a month ago, sounding like ghostly sleighbells in the April mist, which itself looked like the ghost of snow). Either the water will be creeping underground or will have spent itself nourishing the abundant jewelweed, a feeble plant easily bent down by the wind in a direction opposed to the brook's former flow ("against the current" of the now vanished brook). The bed of the brook by this time will be covered with dead leaves matted by the summer heat into the appearance of a faded paper sheet. The brook will be no longer a brook except to people who recall what it was like in mid-spring and earlier. This (the brook as it will then appear) is quite different from the brooks that other poets have celebrated.* But when we truly love things, we cherish them in all their aspects.

A paraphrase is useful only if you understand that it is the barest, most inadequate expression of what the poem really says and is no more equivalent to the poem than a corpse is to a man. Once you have made the paraphrase, you should endeavor to see how far short of the poem it falls and why. If the above paraphrase clarifies the poem for you in any respect, does it also falsify the poem in any way? What features make the poem more appealing, more forceful, and more memorable than the paraphrase?

2. The above paraphrase is more consistent than the poem in its use of verb tenses. Does it gain or lose thereby? Why? What does the paraphrase lose by ignoring most of line 2? Can you think of a different meaning for the phrase "as it will be seen" (13)? Does the paraphrase adequately express the meaning of the final line? How might the paraphrase at this point be further expanded?

---

*The poet is thinking especially of Tennyson's well-known poem "The Brook," with its refrain, "For men may come and men may go, / But I go on forever."

THINK'ST THOU TO SEDUCE ME THEN

Think'st thou to seduce me then with words that have no meaning?
Parrots so can learn to prate, our speech by pieces gleaning;
Nurses teach their children so about the time of weaning.

Learn to speak first, then to woo; to wooing much pertaineth;
He that courts us, wanting art, soon falters when he feigneth,   5
Looks asquint on his discourse, and smiles when he complaineth.

Skillful anglers hide their hooks, fit baits for every season;
But with crooked pins fish thou, as babes do that want reason:
Gudgeons only can be caught with such poor tricks of treason.

Ruth forgive me, if I erred from human heart's compassion,   10
When I laughed sometimes too much to see thy foolish fashion;
But, alas, who less could do that found so good occasion?

Thomas Campion (1567–1620)

QUESTIONS

1. Vocabulary: *feigneth* (5), *gudgeons* (9). Is "fit" (7) an adjective or a verb? Is "Ruth" (10) a common or proper noun? What does "erred" (10) mean in this context?
2. Who is speaking to whom? What is the occasion?
3. What kind of person is the speaker? By what is the speaker offended in the person addressed? Why does the speaker change from "me" (1) to "us" (5)? Does the speaker's attitude undergo any change in stanza 4?

THERE'S BEEN A DEATH
IN THE OPPOSITE HOUSE

There's been a death in the opposite house
As lately as today.
I know it by the numb look
Such houses have alway.

The neighbors rustle in and out,   5
The doctor drives away.
A window opens like a pod,
Abrupt, mechanically;

Somebody flings a mattress out,—
The children hurry by;   10
They wonder if it died on that,—
I used to when a boy.

The minister goes stiffly in
As if the house were his,
And he owned all the mourners now,   15
And little boys besides;

And then the milliner, and the man
Of the appalling trade,
To take the measure of the house.
There'll be that dark parade   20

Of tassels and of coaches soon;
It's easy as a sign,—
The intuition of the news
In just a country town.

Emily Dickinson (1830–1886)

dealer shown
by priest &
mourner
boys!

speaker is out of atmosphere
views scene as too simple

QUESTIONS

1. What can we know about the speaker in the poem?
2. By what signs does the speaker recognize that a death has occurred? Explain them stanza by stanza.
3. Comment on the words "appalling" (18) and "dark" (20).
4. What is the speaker's attitude toward death?

WHEN IN ROME

Marrie dear
the box is full . . .
take
whatever you like
to eat . . .   5

     (an egg
     or soup
     . . . there ain't no meat.)

there's endive there
and   10
cottage cheese . . .

     (whew! if I had some
     black-eyed peas . . .)

there's sardines
on the shelves   15
and such . . .

but
don't
get my anchovies . . .
they cost
too much!   20

     (me get the
     anchovies indeed!
     what she think, she got—
     a bird to feed?)   25

there's plenty in there
to fill you up . . .

     (yes'm. just the
     sight's
     enough!   30

     Hope I lives till I get
     home
     I'm tired of eatin'
     what they eats in Rome . . .)

Mari Evans

QUESTIONS

1. Who are the two speakers? What is the situation? Why are the second speaker's words enclosed in parentheses?
2. What are the attitudes of the two speakers toward one another?
3. What implications have the title and the last two lines?

O WHAT IS THAT SOUND

O what is that sound which so thrills the ear
   Down in the valley drumming, drumming?
Only the scarlet soldiers, dear,
   The soldiers coming.

emphasis of impending doom

O what is that light I see flashing so clear   5
   Over the distance brightly, brightly?
Only the sun on their weapons, dear,
   As they step lightly.

O what are they doing with all that gear,
   What are they doing this morning, this morning?   10

Only their usual manoeuvres, dear,
    Or perhaps a warning.

O why have they left the road down there,
    Why are they suddenly wheeling, wheeling?
Perhaps a change in their orders, dear.   15
    Why are you kneeling?

O haven't they stopped for the doctor's care,
    Haven't they reined their horses, their horses?
Why, they are none of them wounded, dear,
    None of these forces.   20

O is it the parson they want, with white hair, *husband*
    Is it the parson, is it, is it?
No, they are passing his gateway, dear, *wife*
    Without a visit.

O it must be the farmer who lives so near.   25
    It must be the farmer so cunning, so cunning?
They have passed the farmyard already, dear,
    And now they are running.

O where are you going? Stay with me here!
    Were the vows you swore deceiving, deceiving?   30
No, I promised to love you, dear,
    But I must be leaving.   *Shift*

O it's broken the lock and splintered the door, *them*
    O it's the gate where they're turning, turning;
Their boots are heavy on the floor   35
    And their eyes are burning. *violence*

                         W. H. Auden (1907–1973)

soldiers are coming after them

QUESTIONS *war, he is being taken away*

1. Even before it is understood, this *ballad* (see Glossary) manifests considerable power. What are the sources of that power? What aspects of human life are brought into conflict?
2. The first eight stanzas are pretty clearly divided between a male and a female speaker. Which is which? Try to form a consistent hypothesis that takes into account (a) the mounting anxiety of the first speaker, (b) the calm reassurance and final departure of the second speaker, (c) the action of the first speaker indicated in line 16 (how do this speaker's questions after line 16 differ from those before?), and (d) the behavior of the soldiers. (Note: At one point in its publishing history this poem was titled "The Quarry.")
3. Who speaks the final stanza?

MIRROR

[handwritten: way reality is!]

[handwritten: user is not exact]

I am silver and exact. I have no preconceptions.
Whatever I see I swallow immediately
Just as it is, unmisted by love or dislike.
I am not cruel, only truthful—
The eye of a little god, four-cornered.   5
Most of the time I meditate on the opposite wall.
It is pink, with speckles. I have looked at it so long
I think it is a part of my heart. But it flickers.
Faces and darkness separate us over and over.

Now I am a lake. A woman bends over me,   10
Searching my reaches for what she really is.
Then she turns to those liars, the candles or the moon.
I see her back, and reflect it faithfully.
She rewards me with tears and an agitation of hands.
I am important to her. She comes and goes.   15
Each morning it is her face that replaces the darkness.
In me she has drowned a young girl, and in me an old woman
Rises toward her day after day, like a terrible fish.

[handwritten: reality. mirror/ lake reflection]

[handwritten: beauty lies as age]

Sylvia Plath (1932–1963)

QUESTIONS *[handwritten: reality as we perceive it good/bad]*

1. Who is the speaker? Distinguish means from ends.
2. In what ways is the mirror like and unlike a person (stanza 1)? In what ways is it like a lake (stanza 2)?
3. What is the meaning of the last two lines?

A STUDY OF READING HABITS

When getting my nose in a book
Cured most things short of school,
It was worth ruining my eyes
To know I could still keep cool,
And deal out the old right hook   5
To dirty dogs twice my size.   *[handwritten: read]*

Later, with inch-thick specs,
Evil was just my lark:
Me and my cloak and fangs   *[handwritten: folly]*
Had ripping times in the dark.   10
The women I clubbed with sex!
I broke them up like meringues.

Don't read much now: the dude
Who lets the girl down before
The hero arrives, the chap   15
Who's yellow and keeps the store,
Seem far too familiar. Get stewed:
Books are a load of crap.

Philip Larkin (b. 1922)

QUESTIONS

1. The three stanzas delineate three stages in the speaker's life. Describe each.
2. What kind of person is the speaker? What kind of books does he read? May he
   be identified with the poet?
3. Contrast the advice given by the speaker in stanza 3 with the advice given by
   Terence in "Terence, this is stupid stuff" (page 14). Are A. E. Housman and
   Philip Larkin at odds in their attitudes toward drinking and reading? Discuss.

HOW ROSES CAME RED

Roses at first were white,
    Till they could not agree
Whether my Sappho's breast
    Or they more white should be.

But being vanquished quite,
    A blush their cheeks bespread;
Since which (believe the rest)
    The roses first came red.

Robert Herrick (1591–1674)

QUESTION

Distinguish means from end in this poem. Was it written by a naturalist or a
lover?

3. Denotation and Connotation

A primary distinction between the practical use of language and the literary use is that in literature, especially in poetry, a *fuller* use is made of individual words. To understand this, we need to examine the composition of a word.

The average word has three component parts: sound, denotation, and connotation. It begins as a combination of tones and noises, uttered by the lips, tongue, and throat, for which the written word is a notation. But it differs from a musical tone or a noise in that it has a meaning attached to it. The basic part of this meaning is its DENOTATION or denotations: that is, the dictionary meaning or meanings of the word. Beyond its denotations, a word may also have connotations. The CONNOTATIONS are what it suggests beyond what it expresses: its overtones of meaning. It acquires these connotations by its past history and associations, by the way and the circumstances in which it has been used. The word *home*, for instance, by denotation means only a place where one lives, but by connotation it suggests security, love, comfort, and family. The words *childlike* and *childish* both mean "characteristic of a child," but *childlike* suggests meekness, innocence, and wide-eyed wonder, while *childish* suggests pettiness, willfulness, and temper tantrums. If we name over a series of coins: *nickel, peso, lira, shilling, sen, doubloon,* the word *doubloon,* to four out of five readers, will immediately suggest pirates, though one will find nothing about pirates in looking up its meaning in the dictionary. Pirates are part of its connotation.

Connotation is very important in poetry, for it is one of the means by which the poet can concentrate or enrich meaning—say more in fewer words. Consider, for instance, the following short poem:

THERE IS NO FRIGATE LIKE A BOOK

There is no frigate like a book
To take us lands away,
Nor any coursers like a page
Of prancing poetry:
This traverse may the poorest take
Without oppress of toll;
How frugal is the chariot
That bears the human soul!

Emily Dickinson (1830–1886)

In this poem Emily Dickinson is considering the power of a book or of poetry to carry us away, to let us escape from our immediate surroundings into a world of the imagination. To do this she has compared literature to various means of transportation: a boat, a team of horses, a wheeled land vehicle. But she has been careful to choose kinds of transportation and names for them that have romantic connotations. "Frigate" suggests exploration and adventure; "coursers," beauty, spirit, and speed; "chariot," speed and the ability to go through the air as well as on land. (Compare "Swing Low, Sweet Chariot" and the myth of Phaëthon, who tried to drive the chariot of Apollo, and the famous painting of Aurora with her horses, once hung in almost every school.) How much of the meaning of the poem comes from this selection of vehicles and words is apparent if we try to substitute for them, say, *steamship, horses,* and *streetcar.*

QUESTIONS

1. What is lost if *miles* is substituted for "lands" (2) or *cheap* for "frugal" (7)?
2. How is "prancing" (4) peculiarly appropriate to poetry as well as to coursers? Could the poet have without loss compared a book to coursers and poetry to a frigate?
3. Is this account appropriate to all kinds of poetry or just to certain kinds? That is, was the poet thinking of poems like Wilfred Owen's "Dulce et Decorum Est" (page 7) or of poems like Coleridge's "Kubla Khan" (page 267) and Walter de la Mare's "The Listeners" (page 269)?

Just as a word has a variety of connotations, so may it have more than one denotation. If we look up the word *spring* in the dictionary, for instance, we will find that it has between twenty-five and thirty distinguishable meanings: It may mean (1) a pounce or leap, (2) a season of the year, (3) a natural source of water, (4) a coiled elastic wire, and so forth. This variety of denotation, complicated by additional tones of connotation, makes language confusing and difficult to use. Any person using words must be careful to define precisely by context the meanings that he wishes. But the difference between the writer using language to communicate information and the poet is this: the practical writer will always attempt to confine his words to one meaning at a time; the poet will often take advantage of the fact that the word has more than one meaning by using it to mean more than one thing at the same time. Thus when Edith Sitwell in one of her poems writes, "This is the time of the wild spring and the mating of tigers," she uses the word *spring* to denote both a season of the year and a sudden leap (and she uses *tigers* rather than *lambs* or *birds* because it has a connotation of fierceness and wildness that the other two lack).

WHEN MY LOVE SWEARS
THAT SHE IS MADE OF TRUTH

When my love swears that she is made of truth,
I do believe her, though I know she lies,
That she might think me some untutored youth,
Unlearnèd in the world's false subtleties.
Thus vainly thinking that she thinks me young,   5
Although she knows my days are past the best,
Simply I credit her false-speaking tongue;
On both sides thus is simple truth supprest.
But wherefore says she not she is unjust?°   unfaithful
And wherefore say not I that I am old?   10
Oh, love's best habit is in seeming trust,
And age in love loves not to have years told:
Therefore I lie with her and she with me,
And in our faults by lies we flattered be.

William Shakespeare (1564–1616)

QUESTIONS
1. How old is the speaker in the poem? How old is his beloved? What is the nature of their relationship?
2. How is the contradiction in line 2 to be resolved? How is the one in lines 5–6 to be resolved? Who is lying to whom?

3. How do "simply" (7) and "simple" (8) differ in meaning? The words "vainly" (5), "habit" (11), "told" (12), and "lie" (13) all have double meanings. What are they?
4. What is the tone of the poem—that is, the attitude of the speaker toward his situation? Should line 11 be taken as an expression of (a) wisdom, (b) conscious rationalization, or (c) self-deception? In answering these questions, consider both the situation and the connotations of all the important words beginning with "swears" (1) and ending with "flattered" (14).

A frequent misconception of poetic language is that the poet seeks always the most beautiful or noble-sounding words. What he really seeks are the most *meaningful* words, and these vary from one context to another. Language has many levels and varieties, and the poet may choose from them all. His words may be grandiose or humble, fanciful or matter of fact, romantic or realistic, archaic or modern, technical or everyday, monosyllabic or polysyllabic. Usually his poem will be pitched pretty much in one key. The words in Emily Dickinson's "There is no frigate like a book" and those in Thomas Hardy's "The Man He Killed" (page 19) are chosen from quite different areas of language, but both poets have chosen the words most meaningful for their own poetic context. Sometimes a poet may import a word from one level or area of language into a poem composed mostly of words from a different level or area. If he does this clumsily, the result will be incongruous and sloppy. If he does it skillfully, the result will be a shock of surprise and an increment of meaning for the reader. In fact, the many varieties of language open to the poet provide his richest resource. The poet's task is one of constant exploration and discovery. He searches always for the secret affinities of words that allow them to be brought together with soft explosions of meaning.

Distinction of 2

THE NAKED AND THE NUDE

For me, the naked and the nude
(By lexicographers construed
As synonyms that should express
The same deficiency of dress
Or shelter) stand as wide apart   5
As love from lies, or truth from art.

Lovers without reproach will gaze
On bodies naked and ablaze;
The Hippocratic eye will see

In nakedness, anatomy;   10
And naked shines the Goddess when
She mounts her lion among men.

The nude are bold, the nude are sly
To hold each treasonable eye.
While draping by a showman's trick   15
Their dishabille in rhetoric,
They grin a mock-religious grin
Of scorn at those of naked skin.

The naked, therefore, who compete
Against the nude may know defeat;   20
Yet when they both together tread
The briary pastures of the dead,
By Gorgons with long whips pursued,
How naked go the sometime nude!

Robert Graves (b. 1895)

QUESTIONS

1. Vocabulary: *lexicographers* (2), *construed* (2), *Hippocratic* (9), *dishabille* (16), *Gorgons* (23), *sometime* (24).
2. What kind of language is used in lines 2-5? Why? (For example, why is "deficiency" used in preference to *lack?* Purely because of meter?)
3. What is meant by "rhetoric" (16)? Why is the word "dishabille" used in this line instead of some less fancy word?
4. Explain why the poet chose his wording instead of the following alternatives: *brave* for "bold" (13), *clever* for "sly" (13), *clothing* for "draping" (15), *smile* for "grin" (17).
5. What, for the poet, is the difference in connotation between "naked" and "nude"? Try to explain reasons for the difference. If your own sense of the two words differs from that of Graves, state the difference and give reasons to support your sense of them.
6. Explain the reversal in the last line.

The person using language to convey information is largely indifferent to the sound of his words and is hampered by their connotations and multiple denotations. He tries to confine each word to a single exact meaning. He uses, one might say, a fraction of the word and throws the rest away. The poet, on the other hand, tries to use as much of the word as he can. He is interested in sound and uses it to reinforce meaning (see chapter 13). He is interested in connotation and uses it to enrich and convey meaning. And he may use more than one denotation.

The purest form of practical language is scientific language. Scientists need a precise language for conveying information precisely. The fact that words have multiple denotations and various overtones of meaning is a hindrance to them in accomplishing their purpose. Their ideal language would be a language with a one-to-one correspondence between word and meaning; that is, every word would have one meaning only, and for every meaning there would be only one word. Since ordinary language does not fulfill these conditions, they have invented some that do. A statement in one of these languages may look like this:

$$SO_2 + H_2O = H_2SO_3$$

In such a statement the symbols are entirely unambiguous; they have been stripped of all connotation and of all denotations but one. The word *sulfurous,* if it occurred in poetry, might have all kinds of connotations: fire, smoke, brimstone, hell, damnation. But H_2SO_3 means one thing and one thing only: sulfurous acid.

The ambiguity and multiplicity of meanings possessed by words are an obstacle to the scientist but a resource to the poet. Where the scientist wants singleness of meaning, the poet wants richness of meaning. Where the scientist requires and has invented a strictly one-dimensional language, in which every word is confined to one denotation, the poet needs a multidimensional language, and he creates it partly by using a multidimensional vocabulary, in which to the dimension of denotation he adds the dimensions of connotation and sound.

The poet, we may say, plays on a many-stringed instrument. And he sounds more than one note at a time.

The first problem in reading poetry, therefore, or in reading any kind of literature, is to develop a sense of language, a feeling for words. One needs to become acquainted with their shape, their color, and their flavor. There are two ways of doing this: extensive use of the dictionary and extensive reading.

EXERCISES

1. Robert Frost has said that "Poetry is what evaporates from all translations." On the basis of this chapter, can you explain why this statement is true? How much of a word can be translated?
2. Which word in each group has the most "romantic" connotations? (a) horse, nag, steed; (b) king, ruler, tyrant, autocrat; (c) China, Cathay; (d) crow, sparrow, nightingale, catbird; (e) kiss, osculate, buss; (f) Pittsburgh, Birmingham, Samarkand, Podunk; (g) spy, secret agent.

3. Which word in each group has the most favorable connotation? (a) skinny, thin, slender; (b) old-fashioned, out-of-date, obsolete; (c) dwarfish, elfin, pigmy; (d) small, little, petite; (e) doting, loving, amorous; (f) prosperous, rich, moneyed, opulent; (g) revelation, exposure; (h) cur, bitch, dog; (i) scribble, write, indite; (j) brainy, intelligent, smart; (k) famous, notorious.

4. Which word in each group is most emotionally connotative? (a) offspring, children, progeny; (b) brother, sibling.

5. Which of the following is most likely to suggest an off-color remark? (a) pun, (b) play on words, (c) double meaning, (d) *double entendre*.

6. Which of the following should you be least offended at being accused of? (a) having acted foolishly, (b) having acted like a fool.

7. Fill each blank with the word richest in meaning in the given context. Explain.

a. I still had hopes, my latest hours to crown,
   Amidst these humble bowers to lay me down;
   To husband out life's ___taper___ at the close,   *candle, taper*
   And keep the flame from wasting by repose.
                              Goldsmith

b. She was a ___phantom___ of delight   *ghost, phantom,*
   When first she gleamed upon my sight.   *spectre, spook*
                         Wordsworth

c. His sumptuous watch-case, though concealed it lies,
   Like a good conscience, ___solid___ joy supplies.   *perfect, solid,*
                        Edward Young   *thorough*

d. Charmed magic _____ opening on the foam   *casements, windows*
   Of _____ seas, in faery lands forlorn.   *dangerous, perilous*
                              Keats

e. Thou _____ unravished bride of quietness.   *still, yet*
                              Keats

f. I'll _____ the guts into the neighbor room.   *bear, carry,*
                         Shakespeare   *convey, lug*

g. The iron tongue of midnight hath _____   *said, struck,*
      twelve.   *told*
                         Shakespeare

h. In poetry each word reverberates like the note of a
      well-tuned _____ and always leaves   *banjo, guitar,*
      behind it a multitude of vibrations.   *lyre*
                         Joubert

i. Sweet are the uses of adversity,
   Which like the toad, ugly and venomous,
   Wears yet a _____ jewel in his head.   *costly, high-priced,*
                       Shakespeare   *precious*

j. Care on thy maiden brow shall put
A wreath of wrinkles, and thy foot
Be shod with pain: not silken dress
But toil shall _____ thy loveliness.

clothe, tire,
                                        C. Day Lewis   *weary*

8. Ezra Pound has defined great literature as being "simply language charged
with meaning to the utmost possible degree." Would this be a good definition
of poetry? The word "charged" is roughly equivalent to *filled.* Why is
"charged" a better word in Pound's definition? What do its associations with
storage batteries, guns, and dynamite suggest about poetry?

*   *   *

RICHARD CORY

Whenever Richard Cory went down town,
We people on the pavement looked at him:
He was a gentleman from sole to crown,
Clean favored, and imperially slim.

And he was always quietly arrayed,   5
And he was always human when he talked;
But still he fluttered pulses when he said,
"Good-morning," and he glittered when he walked.

And he was rich—yes, richer than a king—
And admirably schooled in every grace: 10
In fine, we thought that he was everything
To make us wish that we were in his place.

So on we worked, and waited for the light,
And went without the meat, and cursed the bread;
And Richard Cory, one calm summer night,   15
Went home and put a bullet through his head.

                        Edwin Arlington Robinson (1869–1935)

QUESTIONS

1. In how many senses is Richard Cory a gentleman?
2. The word "crown" (3), meaning the top of the head, is familiar to you from
"Jack and Jill," but why does Robinson use the unusual phrase "from sole to
crown" instead of the common *from head to foot* or *from top to toe?*
3. List the words that express or suggest the idea of aristocracy or royalty.
4. Try to explain why the poet chose his wording rather than the following

alternatives: *sidewalk* for "pavement" (2), *good-looking* for "Clean favored" (4), *thin* for "slim" (4), *dressed* for "arrayed" (5), *courteous* for "human" (6), *wonderfully* for "admirably" (10), *trained* for "schooled" (10), *manners* for "every grace" (10), *in short* for "in fine" (11). What other examples of effective diction do you find in the poem?

5. Why is "Richard Cory" a good name for the character in this poem?

6. This poem is a good example of how ironic contrast (see chapter 7) generates meaning. The poem makes no direct statement about life; it simply relates an incident. What larger meanings about life does it suggest?

7. A leading American critic has said of this poem: "In 'Richard Cory' . . . we have a superficially neat portrait of the elegant man of mystery; the poem builds up deliberately to a very cheap surprise ending; but all surprise endings are cheap in poetry, if not, indeed, elsewhere, for poetry is written to be read not once but many times."* Do you agree with this evaluation? Discuss.

NAMING OF PARTS

To-day we have naming of parts. Yesterday,
We had daily cleaning. And to-morrow morning,
We shall have what to do after firing. But to-day,
To-day we have naming of parts. Japonica
Glistens like coral in all of the neighboring gardens,   5
    And to-day we have naming of parts.

This is the lower sling swivel. And this
Is the upper sling swivel, whose use you will see,
When you are given your slings. And this is the piling swivel,
Which in your case you have not got. The branches   10
Hold in the gardens their silent, eloquent gestures,
    Which in our case we have not got.

This is the safety-catch, which is always released
With an easy flick of the thumb. And please do not let me
See anyone using his finger. You can do it quite easy   15
If you have any strength in your thumb. The blossoms
Are fragile and motionless, never letting anyone see
    Any of them using their finger.

And this you can see is the bolt. The purpose of this
Is to open the breech, as you see. We can slide it   20
Rapidly backwards and forwards: we call this
Easing the spring. And rapidly backwards and forwards
The early bees are assaulting and fumbling the flowers:
    They call it easing the Spring.

---

*Yvor Winters, *Edwin Arlington Robinson* (Norfolk, Conn.: New Directions, 1946), p. 52.

They call it easing the Spring: it is perfectly easy 25
If you have any strength in your thumb: like the bolt,
And the breech, and the cocking-piece, and the point of balance,
Which in our case we have not got; and the almond-blossom
Silent in all of the gardens and the bees going backwards and forwards,
    For to-day we have naming of parts. 30

Henry Reed (b. 1914)

QUESTIONS

1. Who is the speaker (or who are the speakers) in the poem, and what is the situation?
2. What basic contrasts are represented by the trainees and by the gardens?
3. What is it that the trainees "have not got" (28)? How many meanings have the phrases "easing the Spring" (22) and "point of balance" (27)?
4. What differences in language and rhythm do you find between the lines concerning "naming of parts" and those describing the gardens?
5. Does the repetition of certain phrases throughout the poem have any special function or is it done only to create a kind of refrain?
6. What statement does the poem make about war as it affects men and their lives?

JUDGING DISTANCES

Not only how far away, but the way that you say it
Is very important. Perhaps you may never get
The knack of judging a distance, but at least you know
How to report on a landscape: the central sector,
The right of arc and that, which we had last Tuesday, 5
    And at least you know

That maps are of time, not place, so far as the army
Happens to be concerned—the reason being,
Is one which need not delay us. Again, you know
There are three kinds of tree, three only, the fir and the poplar, 10
And those which have bushy tops to; and lastly
    That things only seem to be things.

A barn is not called a barn, to put it more plainly,
Or a field in the distance, where sheep may be safely grazing.
You must never be over-sure. You must say, when reporting: 15
At five o'clock in the central sector is a dozen
Of what appear to be animals; whatever you do,
    Don't call the bleeders *sheep.*

I am sure that's quite clear; and suppose, for the sake of example,
The one at the end, asleep, endeavors to tell us   20
What he sees over there to the west, and how far away,
After first having come to attention. There to the west,
On the fields of summer the sun and the shadows bestow
    Vestments of purple and gold.

The still white dwellings are like a mirage in the heat,   25
And under the swaying elms a man and a woman
Lie gently together. Which is, perhaps, only to say
That there is a row of houses to the left of arc,
And that under some poplars a pair of what appear to be humans
    Appear to be loving.   30

Well that, for an answer, is what we might rightly call
Moderately satisfactory only, the reason being,
Is that two things have been omitted, and those are important.
The human beings, now: in what direction are they,
And how far away, would you say? And do not forget   35
    There may be dead ground in between.

There may be dead ground in between; and I may not have got
The knack of judging a distance; I will only venture
A guess that perhaps between me and the apparent lovers,
(Who, incidentally, appear by now to have finished,)   40
At seven o'clock from the houses, is roughly a distance
    Of about one year and a half.

Henry Reed (b. 1914)

QUESTIONS

1. In what respect are maps "of time, not place" (7) in the army?
2. Though they may be construed as belonging to the same speaker, there are
   two speaking voices in this poem. Identify each and put quotation marks
   around the lines spoken by the second voice.
3. Two kinds of language are used in this poem—army "officialese" and the
   language of human experience. What are the characteristics of each? What is
   the purpose of each? Which is more precise?
4. The word "bleeders" (18)—that is, "bloody creatures"—is British profanity.
   To which of the two kinds of language does it belong? Or is it perhaps a third
   kind of language?
5. As in "Naming of Parts" (these two poems are part of a series of four with the
   general title "Lessons of War") the two kinds of language used might possibly
   be called "unpoetic" and "poetic." Is the "unpoetic" language *really* unpoetic?
   In other words, is its use inappropriate in these two poems? Explain.
6. The phrase "dead ground" (36) takes on symbolic meaning in the last stanza.

What is its literal meaning? What is its symbolic meaning? What does the second speaker mean by saying that the distance between himself and the lovers is "about one year and a half" (42)? In what respect is the contrast between the recruits and the lovers similar to that between the recruits and the gardens in "Naming of Parts"? What meanings are generated by the former contrast?

BEING HERDED PAST THE PRISON'S HONOR FARM

The closer I come to their huge black-and-white sides, the less
Room there is in the world for anything but Holsteins.
I thought I could squeeze past them, but I'm stuck now
Among them, dwarfed in my car, while they plod gigantically
To pasture ahead of me, beside me, behind me, cow eyes   5
As big as eightballs staring down at another prisoner.

They seem enormously pregnant, bulging with mash and alfalfa,
But their low-slung sacks and rawboned high-rise rumps look insur-
Mountable for any bull. One side-swipes my fender
And gives it a cud-slow look. What fingers would dare   10
Milk those veiny bags? Not mine. I'm cowed. My hands
On the steering wheel are squeezing much too tight to be trusted.

They all wear numbers clipped to their ears. They're going to feed
Behind barbed wire like a work-gang or, later, like solitaries
Stalled in concrete, for the milk of inhuman kindness.   15
They clomp muddily forward. Now splatting his boots down
Like cowflops, the tall black numbered trusty cowpoke tells me
Exactly where I can go, steering me, cutting me out of the herd.

David Wagoner (b. 1926)

QUESTIONS

1. Why did the poet choose to write about Holsteins rather than Jerseys or Guernseys? Why did he make the "cowpoke" (17) black rather than tanned, brown, or white?
2. Explain why the poet chose his wording rather than the following possible alternatives: *guided* for "Herded" (title), *nearer* for "closer" (1), *walk* for "plod" (4), *cueballs* instead of "eightballs" (6), *swollen* for "pregnant" (7), *snail-slow* for "cud-slow" (10), *scared* for "cowed" (11), *hermits* for "solitaries" (14), *stopped* for "stalled" (15), *trod* for "clomp" (16), *putting* for "splatting" (16), *snowshoes* instead of "cowflops" (17), *reliable* for "trusty" (17), *gives me*

good directions for "tells me / Exactly where I can go" (17–18), *getting* for "cutting" (18). Comment on the phrase "the milk of inhuman kindness" (15).
3. How many kinds of "prisoners" are referred to in the poem? Is there any suggestion of the speaker's attitude toward each?

CROSS

My old man's a white old man
And my old mother's black.
If ever I cursed my white old man
I take my curses back.

If ever I cursed my black old mother   5
And wished she were in hell,
I'm sorry for that evil wish
And now I wish her well.

My old man died in a fine big house.
My ma died in a shack.   10
I wonder where I'm gonna die,
Being neither white nor black?

Langston Hughes (1902–1967)

QUESTIONS

1. What different denotations does the title have? Explain.
2. The language in this poem, such as "old man" (1, 3, 9), "ma" (10), and "gonna" (11), is plain, and even colloquial. Is it appropriate to the subject? Why?

BASE DETAILS

If I were fierce, and bald, and short of breath,
   I'd live with scarlet Majors at the Base,
And speed glum heroes up the line to death.
   You'd see me with my puffy petulant face,
Guzzling and gulping in the best hotel,   5
   Reading the Roll of Honor. "Poor young chap,"
I'd say—"I used to know his father well;
   Yes, we've lost heavily in this last scrap."
And when the war is done and youth stone dead,
I'd toddle safely home and die—in bed.   10

Siegfried Sassoon (1886–1967)

1. Vocabulary: *petulant* (4).
2. In what two ways may the title be interpreted? (Both words have two pertinent meanings.) What applications has "scarlet" (2)? What is the force of "fierce" (1)? Try to explain why the poet chose his wording rather than the following alternatives: *fleshy* for "puffy" (4), *eating and drinking* for "guzzling and gulping" (5), *battle* for "scrap" (8), *totter* for "toddle" (10).
3. Who evidently is the speaker? (The poet, a British captain in World War I, was decorated for bravery on the battlefield.) Does he mean what he says? What is the purpose of the poem?

THE CAREFUL ANGLER

> The careful angler chose his nook
> At morning by the lilied brook,
> And all the noon his rod he plied
> By that romantic riverside.
> Soon as the evening hours decline
> Tranquilly he'll return to dine,
> And, breathing forth a pious wish,
> Will cram his belly full of fish.

Robert Louis Stevenson (*1850–1894*)

QUESTION

At what point in the poem does the kind of connotative language used by the poet abruptly change? Explain the change. What does it do to the tone of the poem?

4. Imagery

Experience comes to us largely through the senses. My experience of a spring day, for instance, may consist partly of certain emotions I feel and partly of certain thoughts I think, but most of it will be a cluster of sense impressions. It will consist of *seeing* blue sky and white clouds, budding leaves and daffodils; of *hearing* robins and bluebirds singing in the early morning; of *smelling* damp earth and blossoming hyacinths; and of *feeling* a fresh wind against my cheek. The poet seeking to express his experience of a spring day must therefore provide a selection of the sense impressions he has. Like Shakespeare (page 10), he must give the reader "daisies pied" and "lady-smocks all silver-white" and "merry larks" and the song of the cuckoo and maidens bleaching their summer smocks. Without doing so he will probably fail to evoke the emotions that accompanied his sensations. The poet's language, therefore, must be more *sensuous* than ordinary language. It must be more full of imagery.

IMAGERY may be defined as the representation through language of sense experience. Poetry appeals directly to our senses, of course, through its music and rhythms, which we actually hear when it is read aloud. But indirectly it appeals to our senses through imagery, the representation to the imagination of sense experience. The word *image* perhaps most often suggests a mental picture, something seen in the mind's eye—and *visual* imagery is the kind of imagery that occurs most frequently in poetry. But an image may also represent a sound; a smell; a taste; a tactile experience, such as hardness, wetness, or cold; an internal sensation, such as hunger, thirst, or nausea; or movement or tension in the muscles or joints. If we wished to be scientific, we could extend this list further, for psychologists no longer confine themselves to five or even six senses, but for purposes of discussing poetry the above classification should ordinarily be sufficient.

MEETING AT NIGHT

The gray sea and the long black land; — *sight*
And the yellow half-moon large and low;
And the startled little waves that leap
In fiery ringlets from their sleep,
As I gain the cove with pushing prow,   5
And quench its speed i' the slushy sand.

Then a mile of warm sea-scented beach; *smell   feeling*
Three fields to cross till a farm appears;
A tap at the pane, the quick sharp scratch *sound*
And blue spurt of a lighted match, *warmth*   10
And a voice less loud, through its joys and fears,
Than the two hearts beating each to each!

Robert Browning (1812–1889)

"Meeting at Night" is a poem about love. It makes, one might say, a number of statements about love: being in love is a sweet and exciting experience; when one is in love everything seems beautiful, and the most trivial things become significant; when one is in love one's sweetheart seems the most important object in the world. But the poet actually *tells* us none of these things directly. He does not even use the word *love* in his poem. His business is to communicate experience, not information. He does this largely in two ways. First, he presents us with a specific situation, in which a lover goes to meet his sweetheart. Second, he describes the lover's journey so vividly in terms of sense impressions that the reader not only sees and hears what the lover saw and heard but also shares his anticipation and excitement.

Every line in the poem contains some image, some appeal to the senses: the gray sea, the long black land, the yellow half-moon, the startled little waves with their fiery ringlets, the blue spurt of the lighted match—all appeal to our sense of sight and convey not only shape but also color and motion. The warm sea-scented beach appeals to the senses of both smell and touch. The pushing prow of the boat on the slushy sand, the tap at the pane, the quick scratch of the match, the low speech of the lovers, and the sound of their hearts beating—all appeal to the sense of hearing.

PARTING AT MORNING

> Round the cape of a sudden came the sea,
> And the sun looked over the mountain's rim:
> And straight was a path of gold for him,
> And the need of a world of men for me.

Robert Browning (1812–1889)

QUESTIONS

1. This poem is a sequel to "Meeting at Night." "Him" (3) refers to the sun. Does the last line mean that the lover needs the world of men or that the world of men needs the lover? Or both?
2. Does the sea *actually* come suddenly around the cape or *appear* to? Why does Browning mention the *effect* before its *cause* (the sun looking over the mountain's rim)?
3. Do these two poems, taken together, suggest any larger truths about love? Browning, in answer to a question, said that the second part is the man's confession of "how fleeting is the belief (implied in the first part) that such raptures are self-sufficient and enduring—as for the time they appear."

The sharpness and vividness of any image will ordinarily depend on how specific it is and on the poet's use of effective detail. The word *hummingbird,* for instance, conveys a more definite image than does *bird,* and *ruby-throated hummingbird* is sharper and more specific still. For a vivid representation, however, it is not necessary that something be completely described. One or two especially sharp and representative details will ordinarily serve, allowing the reader's imagination to fill in the rest. Tennyson in "The Eagle" (page 5) gives only one detail about the eagle itself—that he clasps the crag with "crooked hands"—but this detail is an effective and memorable one. Robinson tells us that Richard Cory (page 39) was "clean favored," "slim," and "quietly arrayed," but the detail that really brings Cory before us is that he "glittered when he walked." Browning, in "Meeting at Night," calls up a whole scene with "A tap at the pane, the quick sharp scratch / And blue spurt of a lighted match."

Since imagery is a peculiarly effective way of evoking vivid experience, and since it may be used to convey emotion and suggest ideas as well as to cause a mental reproduction of sensations, it is an invaluable resource of the poet. In general, the poet will seek concrete or image-bearing words in preference to abstract or non-image-bearing words. We cannot evaluate a poem, however, by the amount or quality of its imagery alone. Sense impression is only one of the elements of experience. A poet may attain his ends by other means. We should never judge any single element of a poem except in reference to the total intention of that poem.

✻   ✻   ✻

A LATE AUBADE

<pre>
You could be sitting now in a carrel
Turning some liver-spotted page,
Or rising in an elevator-cage
Toward Ladies' Apparel.

You could be planting a raucous bed   5
Of salvia, in rubber gloves,
Or lunching through a screed of someone's loves
With pitying head,

Or making some unhappy setter
Heel, or listening to a bleak   10
Lecture on Schoenberg's serial technique.
Isn't this better?

Think of all the time you are not
Wasting, and would not care to waste,
Such things, thank God, not being to your taste.   15
Think what a lot

Of time, by woman's reckoning,
You've saved, and so may spend on this,
You who had rather lie in bed and kiss
Than anything.   20

It's almost noon, you say? If so,
Time flies, and I need not rehearse
The rosebuds-theme of centuries of verse.
If you must go,
</pre>

Wait for a while, then slip downstairs   25
And bring us up some chilled white wine,
And some blue cheese, and crackers, and some fine
Ruddy-skinned pears.

Richard Wilbur (b. 1921)

QUESTIONS

1. Vocabulary: *Aubade* (see Glossary), *carrel* (1), *screed* (7), *Schoenberg* (11).
2. Who is the speaker? What is the situation? What plea is the speaker making?
3. As lines 22–23 suggest, this poem treats an age-old theme of poetry. What is it? In what respects is this an original treatment of it? Though line 23 is general in reference, it alludes specifically to a famous poem by Robert Herrick (see page 82). In what respects are these two poems similar? In what respects are they different?
4. What clues are there in the poem as to the characters and personalities of the two people involved?
5. How does the last stanza provide a fitting conclusion to the poem?

ON MOONLIT HEATH AND LONESOME BANK

On moonlit heath and lonesome bank
    The sheep beside me graze;
And yon the gallows used to clank
    Fast by the four cross ways.

A careless shepherd once would keep   5
    The flocks by moonlight there,
And high amongst the glimmering sheep
    The dead man stood on air.

They hang us now in Shrewsbury jail:
    The whistles blow forlorn,   10
And trains all night groan on the rail
    To men that die at morn.

There sleeps in Shrewsbury jail to-night,
    Or wakes, as may betide,
A better lad, if things went right,   15
    Than most that sleep outside.

And naked to the hangman's noose
    The morning clocks will ring
A neck God made for other use
    Than strangling in a string.   20

And sharp the link of life will snap,
　　And dead on air will stand
Heels that held up as straight a chap
　　As treads upon the land.

execution

So here I'll watch the night and wait   25
　　To see the morning shine,
When he will hear the stroke of eight
　　And not the stroke of nine;

And wish my friend as sound a sleep
　　As lads' I did not know,   30
That shepherded the moonlit sheep
　　A hundred years ago.

　　　　　　　　　　　　　A. E. Housman (1859–1936)

QUESTIONS

1. Vocabulary: *heath* (1).
2. Housman explains in a note to lines 5–6 that "Hanging in chains was called keeping sheep by moonlight." Where is this idea repeated?
3. What is the speaker's attitude toward his friend? Toward other young men who have died by hanging? What is the purpose of the reference to the young men hanged "A hundred years ago"?
4. Discuss the kinds of imagery present in the poem and their role in the development of the dramatic situation.
5. Discuss the use of language in stanza 5.

A NARROW FELLOW IN THE GRASS

A narrow fellow in the grass
Occasionally rides;
You may have met him. Did you not,
His notice sudden is:

The grass divides as with a comb,   5
A spotted shaft is seen,
And then it closes at your feet
And opens further on.

He likes a boggy acre,
A floor too cool for corn,   10
Yet when a boy, and barefoot,
I more than once at noon

Have passed, I thought, a whip-lash
Unbraiding in the sun,
When, stooping to secure it, 15
It wrinkled, and was gone.

Several of nature's people
I know, and they know me;
I feel for them a transport
Of cordiality; 20

But never met this fellow,
Attended or alone,
Without a tighter breathing
And zero at the bone.

Emily Dickinson (*1830–1886*)

QUESTIONS

1. The subject of this poem is never named. What is it? How does the imagery identify it?
2. The last two lines might be paraphrased as "without being frightened." Why is Dickinson's wording more effective?
3. Who is the speaker?

LIVING IN SIN

She had thought the studio would keep itself;
no dust upon the furniture of love.
Half heresy, to wish the taps less vocal,
the panes relieved of grime. A plate of pears,
a piano with a Persian shawl, a cat 5
stalking the picturesque amusing mouse
had risen at his urging.
Not that at five each separate stair would writhe
under the milkman's tramp; that morning light
so coldly would delineate the scraps 10
of last night's cheese and three sepulchral bottles;
that on the kitchen shelf among the saucers
a pair of beetle-eyes would fix her own—
envoy from some village in the moldings . . .
Meanwhile, he, with a yawn, 15
sounded a dozen notes upon the keyboard,
declared it out of tune, shrugged at the mirror,
rubbed at his beard, went out for cigarettes;
while she, jeered by the minor demons,

pulled back the sheets and made the bed and found   20
a towel to dust the table-top,
and let the coffee-pot boil over on the stove. *household*
By evening she was back in love again,   *live for loving*
though not so wholly but throughout the night
she woke sometimes to feel the daylight coming   25
like a relentless milkman up the stairs.

day was as predictable as the milkman.

Adrienne Rich (b. 1929)

QUESTIONS

1. Explain the grammatical structure and meaning of the sentence in lines 4–7.
   What are its subject and verb? To whom or what does "his" (7) refer? What
   kind of life do its images conjure up?
2. On what central contrast is the poem based? What is its central mood or
   emotion?
3. Discuss the various kinds of imagery used and their function in conveying the
   experience of the poem.

THOSE WINTER SUNDAYS

Sundays too my father got up early   *father goes*
and put his clothes on in the blueblack cold,   *thru pain*
then with cracked hands that ached
from labor in the weekday weather made   *family →*
banked fires blaze. No one ever thanked him.   *comfort*   5

I'd wake and hear the cold splintering, breaking.
When the rooms were warm, he'd call,
and slowly I would rise and dress,
fearing the chronic angers of that house,

Speaking indifferently to him,   *father not*   10
who had driven out the cold   *appreciated*
and polished my good shoes as well.   *in the home*
What did I know, what did I know
of love's austere and lonely offices?

choses   *Robert Hayden (1913–1980)*

QUESTIONS

1. Vocabulary: *offices* (14).
2. What kind of imagery is central to the poem? How is this imagery related to
   the emotional concerns of the poem?
3. How do the subsidiary images relate to the central images?

4. From what point in time does the speaker view the subject matter of the poem? What has happened to him in the interval?

SPRING

Nothing is so beautiful as spring—
    When weeds, in wheels, shoot long and lovely and lush;
    Thrush's eggs look little low heavens, and thrush
Through the echoing timber does so rinse and wring
The ear, it strikes like lightnings to hear him sing;   5
    The glassy peartree leaves and blooms, they brush
    The descending blue; that blue is all in a rush
With richness; the racing lambs too have fair their fling.

What is all this juice and all this joy?
    A strain of the earth's sweet being in the beginning   10
In Eden garden.—Have, get, before it cloy,

    Before it cloud, Christ, lord, and sour with sinning,
Innocent mind and Mayday in girl and boy,
    Most, O maid's child, thy choice and worthy the winning.

                   Gerard Manley Hopkins (1844–1889)

QUESTIONS

1. The first line makes an abstract statement. How is this statement brought to carry conviction?
2. The sky is described as being "all in a rush / With richness" (7–8). In what other respects is the poem "rich"?
3. The author was a Catholic priest as well as a poet. To what two things does he compare the spring in lines 9–14? In what ways are the comparisons appropriate?

TO AUTUMN

Season of mists and mellow fruitfulness,
    Close bosom-friend of the maturing sun;
Conspiring with him how to load and bless
    With fruit the vines that round the thatch-eves run;
To bend with apples the mossed cottage-trees,   5
    And fill all fruit with ripeness to the core;
      To swell the gourd, and plump the hazel shells
With a sweet kernel; to set budding more,
    And still more, later flowers for the bees,
    Until they think warm days will never cease,   10
      For summer has o'er-brimmed their clammy cells.

[handwritten: autumn is beautiful yet deceiving winter but then spring]

Who hath not seen thee oft amid thy store?
　　Sometimes whoever seeks abroad may find
Thee sitting careless on a granary floor, *[handwritten: autumn]*
　　Thy hair soft-lifted by the winnowing wind;
Or on a half-reaped furrow sound asleep, 　　　　　15
　　Drowsed with the fume of poppies, while thy hook *[handwritten: doesn't always occur at same time/circumstance]*
　　　　Spares the next swath and all its twinèd flowers:
And sometimes like a gleaner thou dost keep
　　Steady thy laden head across a brook; 　　　　　20
　　Or by a cider-press, with patient look,
　　　　Thou watchest the last oozings hours by hours.

Where are the songs of Spring? Ay, where are they?
　　Think not of them, thou hast thy music too,— *[handwritten: you are beautiful too]*
While barred clouds bloom the soft-dying day, 　　25
　　And touch the stubble-plains with rosy hue; *[handwritten: oxymoron w/ a line 2 opposition literally]*
Then in a wailful choir the small gnats mourn
　　Among the river sallows, borne aloft
　　　　Or sinking as the light wind lives or dies;
And full-grown lambs loud bleat from hilly bourn; 　30
　　Hedge-crickets sing; and now with treble soft *[handwritten: beautiful death]*
The red-breast whistles from a garden-croft;
　　And gathering swallows twitter in the skies.

　　　　　　　　　　　　　John Keats (1795–1821)

[handwritten: autumn is an abstract object experienced it like us]

QUESTIONS

1. Vocabulary: *hook* (17), *barred* (25), *sallows* (28), *bourn* (30), *croft* (32).
2. How many kinds of imagery do you find in the poem? Give examples of each.
3. Are the images arranged haphazardly or are they carefully organized? In answering this question, consider: (a) With what aspect of autumn is each stanza particularly concerned? (b) What kind of imagery is dominant in each stanza? (c) What time of the season is presented in each stanza? (d) Is there any progression in time of day?
4. What is Autumn personified as in stanza 2? Is there any suggestion of personification in the other two stanzas?
5. Although the poem is primarily descriptive, what attitude toward transience and passing beauty is implicit in it?

[handwritten: doesn't feel freedom closed in due to coldness of warmth - shed clothes]

[handwritten: wind = changing climates]

1- to provide imaginative pleasure
2- imagery - abstract concrete
3- emotional intensity
4- say much in brief compass

5. Figurative Language 1

METAPHOR, PERSONIFICATION, METONYMY

Poetry provides the one permissible way
of saying one thing and meaning another.

ROBERT FROST

special way of saying somethings

Let us assume that your brother has just come in out of a rainstorm and you say to him, "Well, you're a pretty sight! Got slightly wet, didn't you?" And he replies, "Wet? I'm drowned! It's raining cats and dogs, and my raincoat's like a sieve!"

It is likely that you and your brother understand each other well enough, and yet if you examine this conversation literally, that is to say unimaginatively, you will find that you have been speaking nonsense. Actually you have been speaking figuratively. You have been saying less than what you mean, or more than what you mean, or the opposite of what you mean, or something other than what you mean. You did not mean that your brother was a pretty sight but that he was a wretched sight. You did not mean that he got slightly wet but that he got very wet. Your brother did not mean that he got drowned but that he got drenched. It was not raining cats and dogs; it was raining water. And your brother's raincoat is so unlike a sieve that not even a baby would confuse them.

If you are familiar with Molière's play *Le Bourgeois Gentilhomme,* you will remember how delighted M. Jourdain was to discover that he had been speaking prose all his life. Many people might be equally surprised to learn that they have been speaking a kind of subpoetry all their lives. The difference between their figures of speech and the poet's is that theirs are probably worn and trite, the poet's fresh and original.

On first examination, it might seem absurd to say one thing and mean another. But we all do it and with good reason. We do it because we can say what we want to say more vividly and forcefully by figures than we can by saying it directly. And we can say more by figurative statement than we can by literal statement. Figures of speech are another way of adding extra dimensions to language. We shall examine their usefulness more particularly later in this chapter.

Broadly defined, a FIGURE OF SPEECH is any way of saying something other than the ordinary way, and some rhetoricians have classified as many as 250 separate figures. For our purposes, however, a figure of speech is more narrowly definable as a way of saying one thing and meaning another, and we need be concerned with no more than a dozen. FIGURATIVE LANGUAGE—language using figures of speech—is language that cannot be taken literally (or should not be taken literally only).

METAPHOR and SIMILE are both used as a means of comparing things that are essentially unlike. The only distinction between them is that in simile the comparison is *expressed* by the use of some word or phrase, such as *like, as, than, similar to, resembles,* or *seems;* in metaphor the comparison is *implied*—that is, the figurative term is *substituted for* or *identified with* the literal term.

THE GUITARIST TUNES UP

With what attentive courtesy he bent
Over his instrument;
Not as a lordly conqueror who could
Command both wire and wood,
But as a man with a loved woman might,
Inquiring with delight
What slight essential things she had to say
Before they started, he and she, to play.

Frances Cornford (1886–1960)

QUESTION

Explore the comparison. Does it principally illuminate the guitarist or the lovers or both? What one word brings its two terms together?

THE HOUND

Life the hound
Equivocal
Comes at a bound
Either to rend me
Or to befriend me.   5
I cannot tell

don't know when life will be good or bad

The hound's intent
Till he has sprung
At my bare hand
With teeth or tongue.   10
Meanwhile I stand
And wait the event.

Robert Francis (b. 1901)

QUESTION

What does "equivocal" (2) mean? Show how this is the key word in the poem.
What is the effect of placing it on a line by itself?

Metaphors may take one of four forms, depending on whether the
literal and figurative terms are respectively *named* or *implied*. In the first
form of metaphor, as in simile, both the literal and figurative terms are
named. In Francis's poem, for example, the literal term is "life" and the
figurative term is "hound." In the second form, the literal term is *named*
and the figurative term is *implied.*

BEREFT

Where had I heard this wind before
Change like this to a deeper roar?
What would it take my standing there for,
Holding open a restive door,
Looking downhill to a frothy shore?   5
Summer was past and day was past.
Somber clouds in the west were massed.
Out in the porch's sagging floor
Leaves got up in a coil and hissed,
Blindly struck at my knee and missed.   *fall* 10
Something sinister in the tone
Told me my secret must be known:
Word I was in the house alone
Somehow must have gotten abroad,
Word I was in my life alone,   15
Word I had no one left but God.

Robert Frost (1874–1963)

reassuring always have God

QUESTIONS

1. Describe the situation precisely. What time of day and year is it? Where is the speaker? What is happening to the weather?
2. To what are the leaves in lines 9–10 compared?
3. The word "hissed" (9) is onomatopoetic (see page 187). How is its effect reinforced in the lines following?
4. Though lines 9–10 present the clearest example of the second form of metaphor, there are others. To what is the wind ("it") compared in line 3? Why is the door (4) "restive" and what does this do (figuratively) to the door? To what is the speaker's "life" compared (15)?
5. What is the tone of the poem? How reassuring is the last line?

In the third form of metaphor, the literal term is *implied* and the figurative term is *named*. In the fourth form, both the literal *and* figurative terms are *implied*. The following poem exemplifies both types:

IT SIFTS FROM LEADEN SIEVES

It sifts from leaden sieves, *wired mesh*
It powders all the wood.
It fills with alabaster wool
The wrinkles of the road.

It makes an even face   5
Of mountain and of plain—
Unbroken forehead from the east
Unto the east again.

It reaches to the fence,
It wraps it rail by rail   10
Till it is lost in fleeces;
It deals celestial veil

To stump and stack and stem—   *wire*
A summer's empty room—
Acres of joints where harvests were,   15
Recordless,° but for them.   unrecorded

It ruffles wrists of posts
As ankles of a queen,
Then stills its artisans like ghosts,
Denying they have been.   20

Emily Dickinson (1830–1886)

QUESTIONS

1. This poem consists essentially of a series of metaphors having the same literal term, identified only as "It." What is "It"?
2. In several of these metaphors the figurative term is named—"alabaster wool" (3), "fleeces" (11), "celestial veil" (12). In two of them, however, the figurative term as well as the literal term is left unnamed. To what is "It" compared in lines 1–2? In lines 17–18?
3. Comment on the additional metaphorical expressions or complications contained in "leaden sieves" (1), "alabaster wool" (3), "even face" (5), "unbroken forehead" (7), "a summer's empty room" (14), "artisans" (19).

Metaphors of the fourth form, as one might guess, are comparatively rare. An extended example, however, is provided by Dickinson's "I like to see it lap the miles" (page 196).

PERSONIFICATION consists in giving the attributes of a human being to an animal, an object, or a concept. It is really a subtype of metaphor, an implied comparison in which the figurative term of the comparison is always a human being. When Sylvia Plath makes a mirror speak and think (page 30), she is personifying an object. When Keats describes autumn as a harvester "sitting careless on a granary floor" or "on a half-reaped furrow sound asleep" (page 55), he is personifying a concept. Personifications differ in the degree to which they ask the reader actually to visualize the literal term in human form. In Keats's comparison we are asked to make a complete identification of autumn with a human being. In Sylvia Plath's, though the mirror speaks and thinks, we continue to visualize it as a mirror; similarly, in Frost's "Bereft" (page 58), the "restive" door remains in appearance a door tugged by the wind. In Browning's reference to "the startled little waves" (page 47), a personification is barely suggested; we would make a mistake if we tried to visualize the waves in human form or even, really, to think of them as having human emotions.*

Closely related to personification is APOSTROPHE, which consists in addressing someone absent or dead or something nonhuman as if that person or thing were present and alive and could reply to what is being

---

*The various figures of speech blend into each other, and it is sometimes difficult to classify a specific example as definitely metaphor or symbol, symbolism or allegory, understatement or irony, irony or paradox. Often a given example may exemplify two or more figures at once. In "The Guitarist Tunes Up" (page 57), "wire and wood" are metonymies (see page 62) for a guitar and are personified as subjects, slaves, or soldiers who could be commanded by a lordly conquerer. In "A bird came down the walk" (page 11), when the bird glances around with eyes that look "like frightened beads," the beads function as part of a simile and are personified as something that can be "frightened." The important consideration in reading poetry is not that we classify figures definitely but that we construe them correctly.

said. The speaker in A. E. Housman's "To an Athlete Dying Young" (page 284) apostrophizes a dead runner. William Blake apostrophizes a tiger throughout his famous poem (page 264) but does not otherwise personify it. Keats apostrophizes as well as personifies autumn (page 54). Personification and apostrophe are both ways of giving life and immediacy to one's language, but since neither requires great imaginative power on the part of the poet—apostrophe especially does not—they may degenerate into mere mannerisms and are to be found as often in bad and mediocre poetry as in good. We need to distinguish between their effective use and their merely conventional use.

DR. SIGMUND FREUD DISCOVERS
THE SEA SHELL

Science, that simple saint, cannot be bothered
Figuring what anything is for:
Enough for her devotions that things are
And can be contemplated soon as gathered.

She knows how every living thing was fathered,   5
She calculates the climate of each star,
She counts the fish at sea, but cannot care
Why any one of them exists, fish, fire or feathered.

Why should she? Her religion is to tell
By rote her rosary of perfect answers.   10
Metaphysics she can leave to man:
She never wakes at night in heaven or hell   *doesn't question*
                                                 existence
Staring at darkness. In her holy cell
There is no darkness ever: the pure candle   *time goes on*
Burns, the beads drop briskly from her hand.   15   *discovery*

Who dares to offer Her the curled sea shell!
She will not touch it!—knows the world she sees
Is all the world there is! Her faith is perfect!   *She (science)*
                                                    doesn't
And still he offers the sea shell . . .   *question*

                                     What surf
Of what far sea upon what unknown ground   20
Troubles forever with that asking sound?
What surge is this whose question never ceases?

Archibald MacLeish (1892–1982)

QUESTIONS

1. Vocabulary: *metaphysics* (11).
2. This poem employs an extended personification. List the ways in which science is appropriately compared to a saint. In what way is its faith "perfect" (18)?
3. Who is "he" in line 19?
4. Who was Sigmund Freud, and what discoveries did he make about human nature?
5. What does the sea shell represent?

PACK, CLOUDS, AWAY

Pack, clouds, away; and welcome, day!
With night we banish sorrow.
Sweet air, blow soft; mount, lark, aloft
To give my love good morrow.
Wings from the wind to please her mind,   5
Notes from the lark I'll borrow;
Bird, prune thy wing, nightingale, sing,
To give my love good morrow.
    To give my love good morrow,
    Notes from them all I'll borrow.   10

Wake from thy nest, robin redbreast!
Sing, birds, in every furrow;
And from each bill let music shrill
Give my fair love good morrow.
Black-bird and thrush in every bush,   15
Stare, linnet, and cock-sparrow,
You pretty elves, amongst yourselves
Sing my fair love good morrow.
    To give my love good morrow,
    Sing, birds, in every furrow.   20

Thomas Heywood (c. 1575–1641)

QUESTIONS

1. Vocabulary: *prune* (7), *stare* (16). Could this poem be called an *aubade?*
2. Count the apostrophes in the poem. Why are they effective? Would the poem be damaged if lines 10 and 20 were interchanged? Why?
3. Describe the rime-patterns of the poem. Does the frequency of the rimes serve a poetic function, or are they merely decorative?

SYNECDOCHE (the use of the part for the whole) and METONYMY (the use of something closely related for the thing actually meant) are alike in that both substitute some significant detail or aspect of an experience for the experience itself. Thus, Shakespeare uses synecdoche when he says that the cuckoo's song is unpleasing to a "married ear" (page 10), for he means a married *man*. Robert Graves uses synecdoche in "The Naked and the Nude" (page 35) when he refers to a doctor as a "Hippocratic eye," and T. S. Eliot uses it in "The Love Song of J. Alfred Prufrock" when he refers to a crab or lobster as "a pair of ragged claws" (page 247). Shakespeare uses metonymy when he says that the yellow cuckoo-buds "paint the meadows with delight" (page 10), for he means with bright color, which produces delight. Robert Frost uses metonymy in "Out, Out—" (page 116) when he describes an injured boy holding up his cut hand "as if to keep / The life from spilling," for literally he means to keep the blood from spilling. In each case, however, there is a gain in vividness and meaning. Eliot, by substituting for the crab that part which seizes its prey, tells us something important about the crab and makes us see it more vividly. Shakespeare, by referring to bright color as "delight," evokes not only the visual effect but the emotional response it arouses. Frost tells us both that the boy's hand is bleeding and that his life is in danger.

Many synecdoches and metonymies, of course, like many metaphors, have become so much a part of the language that they no longer strike us as figurative; such is the case with *redhead* for a red-haired person, *wheel* for a bicycle, and *salt* and *tar* for sailor. Such figures are referred to as dead metaphors or dead figures. Synecdoche and metonymy are so much alike that it is hardly worth while to distinguish between them, and the latter term is increasingly coming to be used for both. In this book metonymy will be used for both figures—that is, for any figure in which a part or something closely related is substituted for the thing literally meant.

A HUMMINGBIRD

A route of evanescence *vanish*
With a revolving wheel;
A resonance of emerald,
A rush of cochineal; *red*
And every blossom on the bush
Adjusts its tumbled head,—
The mail from Tunis, probably,
An easy morning's ride.

Emily Dickinson (1830–1886)

1. Vocabulary: *evanescence* (1), *cochineal* (4). "Tunis" (7), on the north coast of Africa, is literally quite distant from Amherst, Massachusetts, where the poet lived, but as a symbol for remoteness it gets its main force from Shakespeare's *Tempest* (II, i, 246–48), where the next heir to the throne of Naples is described as "She that is Queen of Tunis; she that dwells / Ten leagues beyond man's life; she that from Naples / Can have no note, unless the sun were post— / The man i' th' moon's too slow."
2. Identify and explain three metonymies and a metaphor in lines 1–4.
3. Account fully for the vividness of the poem.

We said at the beginning of this chapter that figurative language often provides a more effective means of saying what we mean than does direct statement. What are some of the reasons for that effectiveness?

First, figurative language affords us imaginative pleasure. Imagination might be described in one sense as that faculty or ability of the mind that proceeds by sudden leaps from one point to another, that goes up a stair by leaping in one jump from the bottom to the top rather than by climbing up one step at a time.* The mind takes delight in these sudden leaps, in seeing likenesses between unlike things. We have probably all taken pleasure in staring into a fire and seeing castles and cities and armies in it, or in looking into the clouds and shaping them into animals or faces, or in seeing a man in the moon. We name our plants and flowers after fancied resemblances: jack-in-the-pulpit, babies'-breath, Queen Anne's lace. Figures of speech are therefore satisfying in themselves, providing us with a source of pleasure in the exercise of the imagination.

Second, figures of speech are a way of bringing additional imagery into verse, of making the abstract concrete, of making poetry more sensuous. When MacLeish personifies science (page 61), he gives body and form to what had previously been only a concept. When Emily Dickinson compares poetry to prancing coursers (page 33), she objectifies imaginative and rhythmical qualities by presenting them in visual terms. When Robert Browning compares the crisping waves to "fiery ringlets" (page 47), he starts with one image and transforms it into three. Figurative language is a way of multiplying the sense appeal of poetry.

Third, figures of speech are a way of adding emotional intensity to otherwise merely informative statements and of conveying attitudes along with information. If we say, "So-and-so is a rat" or "My feet are

---

*It is also the faculty of mind that is able to "picture" or "image" absent objects as if they were present. It was with imagination in this sense that we were concerned in the chapter on imagery.

killing me," our meaning is as much emotional as informative. When Thomas Hardy compares "tangled bine-stems" to "strings of broken lyres" (page 281), he not only draws an exact visual comparison but also conjures up a feeling of despondency through the suggestion of discarded instruments no longer capable of making music. When Wilfred Owen compares a soldier caught in a gas attack to a man drowning under a green sea (page 8), he conveys a feeling of despair and suffocation as well as a visual image.

Fourth, figures of speech are a means of concentration, a way of saying much in brief compass. Like words, they may be multidimensional. Consider, for instance, the merits of comparing life to a candle, as Shakespeare does in a passage from *Macbeth* (page 118). Life is like a candle in that it begins and ends in darkness; in that while it burns, it gives off light and energy, is active and colorful; in that it gradually consumes itself, gets shorter and shorter; in that it can be snuffed out at any moment; in that it is brief at best, burning only for a short duration. Possibly your imagination can suggest other similarities. But at any rate, Macbeth's compact metaphorical description of life as a "brief candle" suggests certain truths about life that would require dozens of words to state in literal language. At the same time it makes the abstract concrete, provides imaginative pleasure, and adds a degree of emotional intensity.

Obviously one of the necessary abilities for reading poetry is the ability to interpret figurative language. Every use of figurative language involves a risk of misinterpretation, though the risk is well worth taking. For the person who can translate the figure, the dividends are immense. Fortunately all people have imagination to some degree, and imagination can be cultivated. By practice one's ability to interpret figures of speech can be increased.

EXERCISE

Identify each of the following quotations as literal or figurative. If figurative, explain what is being compared to what and explain the appropriateness of the comparison. EXAMPLE: "Talent is a cistern; genius is a fountain." ANSWER: A metaphor. Talent = cistern; genius = fountain. Talent exists in finite supply; it can be used up. Genius is inexhaustible, ever renewing.

1. O tenderly the haughty day
   Fills his blue urn with fire.   *Emerson*

2. It is with words as with sunbeams—the more they are condensed, the deeper they burn.   *Robert Southey*

3. Joy and Temperance and Repose
   Slam the door on the doctor's nose.   *Anonymous*

4. The pen is mightier than the sword. *Edward Bulwer-Lytton*

5. The strongest oaths are straw
To the fire i' the blood. *Shakespeare*

6. The Cambridge ladies . . . live in furnished souls. *e. e. cummings*

7. The green lizard and the golden snake,
Like unimprisoned flames, out of their trance awake. *Shelley*

8. Dorothy's eyes, with their long brown lashes, looked very much like her
mother's. *Laetitia Johnson*

9. Was this the face that launched a thousand ships? *Marlowe*

10. What should such fellows as I do crawling between earth and heaven?
Shakespeare

11. Love's feeling is more soft and sensible
Than are the tender horns of cockled snails. *Shakespeare*

12. The tawny-hided desert crouches watching her. *Francis Thompson*

13. . . . Let us sit upon the ground
And tell sad stories of the death of kings. *Shakespeare*

14. See, from his [Christ's, on the cross] head, his hands, his side
Sorrow and love flow mingled down. *Isaac Watts*

15. Now half [of the departing guests] to the setting moon are gone,
And half to the rising day. *Tennyson*

16. I do not know whether my present poems are better than the earlier ones.
But this is certain: they are much sadder and sweeter, like pain dipped in
honey. *Heinrich Heine*

17. . . . clouds. . . . Shepherded by the slow, unwilling wind. *Shelley*

18. Let us eat and drink, for tomorrow we shall die. *Isaiah 22:13*

19. Let us eat and drink, for tomorrow we may die.
Common misquotation of the above

*   *   *

THE SILKEN TENT

> She is as in a field a silken tent
> At midday when a sunny summer breeze
> Has dried the dew and all its ropes relent,
> So that in guys it gently sways at ease,
> And its supporting central cedar pole,   5
> That is its pinnacle to heavenward

And signifies the sureness of the soul,
Seems to owe naught to any single cord,
But strictly held by none, is loosely bound
By countless silken ties of love and thought   10
To everything on earth the compass round,
And only by one's going slightly taut
In the capriciousness of summer air
Is of the slightest bondage made aware.

Robert Frost (1874–1963)

QUESTIONS

1. A poet may use a variety of metaphors and similes in developing his subject
   or may, as Frost does here, develop a single figure at length (this poem is an
   excellent example of EXTENDED or SUSTAINED SIMILE). What are the advantages
   of each type of development?
2. Explore the similarities between the two things compared.

Stop

METAPHORS

I'm a riddle in nine syllables,
An elephant, a ponderous house,
A melon strolling on two tendrils.
O red fruit, ivory, fine timbers!
This loaf's big with its yeasty rising.
Money's new-minted in this fat purse.
I'm a means, a stage, a cow in calf.
I've eaten a bag of green apples,
Boarded the train there's no getting off.

Sylvia Plath (1932–1963)

QUESTIONS

1. Like its first metaphor, this poem is a riddle to be solved by identifying the
   literal terms of its metaphors. After you have identified the speaker ("riddle,"
   "elephant," "house," "melon," "stage," "cow"), identify the literal meanings
   of the related metaphors ("syllables," "tendrils," "fruit," "ivory," "timbers,"
   "loaf," "yeasty rising," "money," "purse," "train"). How is line 8 to be inter-
   preted?
2. How does the form of the poem relate to its content?

TOADS

Why should I let the toad *work*
    Squat on my life?
Can't I use my wit as a pitchfork
    And drive the brute off?

Six days of the week it soils   5
    With its sickening poison—
Just for paying a few bills!
    That's out of proportion.

Lots of folk live on their wits:
    Lecturers, lispers,   10
Losels,° loblolly-men,° louts—   scoundrels; bumpkins
    They don't end as paupers;

Lots of folk live up lanes
    With fires in a bucket,
Eat windfalls and tinned sardines—   15
    They seem to like it.

Their nippers° have got bare feet,   children
    Their unspeakable wives
Are skinny as whippets—and yet
    No one actually *starves*.   20

Ah, were I courageous enough
    To shout *Stuff your pension!*
But I know, all too well, that's the stuff
    That dreams are made on;

For something sufficiently toad-like   25
    Squats in me, too;
Its hunkers° are heavy as hard luck,   haunches
    And cold as snow,

And will never allow me to blarney
    My way to getting   30
The fame and the girl and the money
    All at one sitting.

I don't say, one bodies the other
    One's spiritual truth;
But I do say it's hard to lose either,   35
    When you have both.

Philip Larkin (b. 1922)

QUESTIONS

1. How many "toads" are described in the poem? Where is each located? How are they described? What are the antecedents of the pronouns "one" and "the other / one" (33-34) respectively?
2. What characteristics have the people mentioned in stanza 3 in common? Those mentioned in stanzas 4-5?
3. Explain the pun in stanza 6 and the literary allusion it leads into. (If you don't recognize it, check Shakespeare's *Tempest*, Act IV, Scene 1, lines 156-58.)
4. The first "toad" is explicitly identified as "work" (1). The literal term for the second "toad" is not named. Why not? What do you take it to be?
5. What kind of person is the speaker? What are his attitudes toward work?

A VALEDICTION: FORBIDDING MOURNING

As virtuous men pass mildly away,
   And whisper to their souls to go,
While some of their sad friends do say,
   The breath goes now, and some say, no:

So let us melt, and make no noise,
   No tear-floods, nor sigh-tempests move;
'Twere profanation of our joys
   To tell the laity our love.

Moving of th' earth brings harms and fears,
   Men reckon what it did and meant,
But trepidation of the spheres,
   Though greater far, is innocent.

Dull sublunary lovers' love
   (Whose soul is sense) cannot admit
Absence, because it doth remove
   Those things which elemented it.

But we by a love so much refined,
   That ourselves know not what it is,
Inter-assurèd of the mind,
   Care less, eyes, lips, and hands to miss.

Our two souls therefore, which are one,
   Though I must go, endure not yet
A breach, but an expansion,
   Like gold to airy thinness beat.

If they be two, they are two so
   As stiff twin compasses are two;

Thy soul the fixed foot, makes no show
To move, but doth, if th' other do.

And though it in the center sit,
Yet when the other far doth roam,   30
It leans, and hearkens after it,
And grows erect, as that comes home.

Such wilt thou be to me, who must
Like th' other foot, obliquely run;
Thy firmness makes my circle just,   35
And makes me end, where I begun.

John Donne (1572–1631)

QUESTIONS

1. Vocabulary: *valediction* (title), *mourn* (title), *profanation* (7), *laity* (8), *trepidation* (11), *innocent* (12), *sublunary* (13), *elemented* (16). Line 11 is a reference to the spheres of the Ptolemaic cosmology, whose movements caused no such disturbance as does a movement of the earth—that is, an earthquake.
2. Is the speaker in the poem about to die? Or about to leave on a journey? (The answer may be found in a careful analysis of the simile in the last three stanzas.)
3. The poem is organized around a contrast of two kinds of lovers: the "laity" (8) and, as their implied opposite, the "priesthood." Are these terms literal or metaphorical? What is the essential difference between their two kinds of love? How, according to the speaker, does their behavior differ when they must separate from each other? What is the motivation of the speaker in this "valediction"?
4. Find and explain three similes and one metaphor used to describe the parting of true lovers. The figure in the last three stanzas is one of the most famous in English literature. Demonstrate its appropriateness by obtaining a drawing compass or by using two pencils to imitate the two legs.
5. What kind of language is used in the poem? Is the language consonant with the figures of speech?

TO HIS COY MISTRESS

Had we but world enough, and time,
This coyness, lady, were no crime.
We would sit down, and think which way
To walk, and pass our long love's day.
Thou by the Indian Ganges' side   5
Shouldst rubies find; I by the tide
Of Humber would complain. I would
Love you ten years before the Flood,

And you should, if you please, refuse
Till the conversion of the Jews.
My vegetable love should grow   10
Vaster than empires, and more slow;
An hundred years should go to praise
Thine eyes, and on thy forehead gaze;
Two hundred to adore each breast,   15
But thirty thousand to the rest;
An age at least to every part,
And the last age should show your heart.
For, lady, you deserve this state,
Nor would I love at lower rate.   20
   But at my back I always hear
Time's wingèd chariot hurrying near;
And yonder all before us lie
Deserts of vast eternity.
Thy beauty shall no more be found,   25
Nor, in thy marble vault, shall sound
My echoing song; then worms shall try
That long-preserved virginity,
And your quaint honor turn to dust,
And into ashes all my lust: 30
The grave's a fine and private place,
But none, I think, do there embrace.
   Now therefore, while the youthful hue
Sits on thy skin like morning dew,
And while thy willing soul transpires   35
At every pore with instant fires,
Now let us sport us while we may,
And now, like amorous birds of prey,
Rather at once our time devour
Than languish in his slow-chapped power.   40
Let us roll all our strength and all
Our sweetness up into one ball,
And tear our pleasures with rough strife
Thorough° the iron gates of life.   through
Thus, though we cannot make our sun   45
Stand still, yet we will make him run.

Andrew Marvell (1621–1678)

QUESTIONS

1. Vocabulary: *coy* (title), *Humber* (7), *transpires* (35). "Mistress" (title) has the
now archaic meaning of *sweetheart;* "slow-chapped" (40) derives from *chap,*
meaning *jaw.*

2. What is the speaker urging his sweetheart to do? Why is she being "coy"?
3. Outline the speaker's argument in three sentences that begin with the words *If, But,* and *Therefore.* Is the argument valid?
4. Explain the appropriateness of "vegetable love" (11). What simile in the third section contrasts with it and how? What image in the third section contrasts with the distance between the Ganges and the Humber? Of what would the speaker be "complaining" by the Humber (7)?
5. Explain the figures in lines 22, 24, and 40 and their implications.
6. Explain the last two lines. For what is "sun" a metonymy?
7. Is this poem principally about love or about time? If the latter, what might making love represent? What philosophy is the poet advancing here?

WEEP YOU NO MORE, SAD FOUNTAINS

Weep you no more, sad fountains;
   What need you flow so fast?
Look how the snowy mountains
   Heaven's sun doth gently waste.
But my sun's heavenly eyes   5
     View not your weeping,
     That now lies sleeping
Softly, now softly lies
     Sleeping.

Sleep is a reconciling,   10
   A rest that peace begets.
Doth not the sun rise smiling
   When fair at even he sets?
Rest you then, rest, sad eyes,
     Melt not in weeping   15
     While she lies sleeping
Softly, now softly lies
     Sleeping.

Anonymous (c. 1603)

QUESTIONS

1. Are *fountains* (1), *sun* (4), *sun* (5), and *sleeping* (7, 9) respectively literal or metaphorical? Explain.
2. What figures of speech are used in lines 12, 14, and 15?
3. To what do the pronouns *your* (6) and *that* (7) respectively refer? Is *peace* (11) the subject or object of *begets?*
4. Explain the situation and the argument of the poem.

LOVELIEST OF TREES

Loveliest of trees, the cherry now
Is hung with bloom along the bough,
And stands about the woodland ride
Wearing white for Eastertide.

Now, of my threescore years and ten,   5
Twenty will not come again,
And take from seventy springs a score,
It only leaves me fifty more.

And since to look at things in bloom
Fifty springs are little room,   10
About the woodlands I will go
To see the cherry hung with snow.

A. E. Housman (1859–1936)

QUESTIONS

1. Very briefly, this poem presents a philosophy of life. In a sentence, what is it?
2. How old is the speaker? Why does he assume that his life will be seventy years in length? What is surprising about the words "only" (8) and "little" (10)?
3. A good deal of ink has been spilt over whether "snow" (12) is literal or figurative. What do you say? Justify your answer.

DREAM DEFERRED

What happens to a dream deferred?

Does it dry up
like a raisin in the sun?
Or fester like a sore—
And then run?   5
Does it stink like rotten meat?
Or crust and sugar over—
like a syrupy sweet?

Maybe it just sags
like a heavy load.   10

Or does it explode?

Langston Hughes (1902–1967)

1. Of the six images, five are similes. Which is a metaphor? Comment on its position and its effectiveness.
2. Since the dream could be any dream, the poem is general in its implication. What happens to your understanding of it on learning that its author was a black American?

DEATH STANDS ABOVE ME

Death stands above me, whispering low
I know not what into my ear;
Of his strange language all I know
Is, there is not a word of fear.

Walter Savage Landor (1775–1864)

QUESTIONS

1. To what degree is Death personified, and what is the effect of this personification? What is implied by the poet's not knowing what is said in Death's "strange language"?
2. Define as precisely as possible the poet's attitude toward the possibility of some kind of future life.

6. Figurative Language 2

SYMBOL, ALLEGORY

[handwritten: ONE MUST MAKE THEIR OWN DECISIONS.]

THE ROAD NOT TAKEN

Two roads diverged in a yellow wood, *[handwritten: autumn]*
And sorry I could not travel both *[handwritten: so won't make a mistake]*
And be one traveler, long I stood *[handwritten: which one?]*
And looked down one as far as I could
To where it bent in the undergrowth; *[handwritten: wants to see]* 5

Then took the other, as just as fair, *[handwritten: appear future]*
And having perhaps the better claim, *[handwritten: equal]*
Because it was grassy and wanted wear; *[handwritten: takes the risk]*
Though as for that the passing there
Had worn them really about the same, 10

And both that morning equally lay *[handwritten: needed wear]*
In leaves no step had trodden black. *[handwritten: often, later]*
Oh, I kept the first for another day!
Yet knowing how way leads on to way,
I doubted if I should ever come back. *[handwritten: Lost? can't turn around]* 15

I shall be telling this with a sigh *[handwritten: feels made wrong choice]*
Somewhere ages and ages hence:
Two roads diverged in a wood, and I—
I took the one less traveled by,
And that has made all the difference. 20

[handwritten: path in life, doubts his choice]
[handwritten: easy way out?]
[handwritten: wondering about road]

Robert Frost (1874–1963)

[handwritten: who? To whom? Tone? motivation? Type of person?]

1. Does the speaker feel that he made the wrong choice in taking the road "less traveled by"? If not, why will he sigh? What does he regret?
2. Why will the choice between two roads that seem very much alike make such a big difference many years later?

A SYMBOL may be roughly defined as something that means *more* than what it is. "The Road Not Taken," for instance, concerns a choice made between two roads by a person out walking in the woods. He would like to explore both roads. He tells himself that he will explore one and then come back and explore the other, but he knows that he shall probably be unable to do so. By the last stanza, however, we realize that the poet is talking about something more than the choice of paths in a wood, for such a choice would be relatively unimportant, while this choice is one that will make a great difference in the speaker's life and that he will remember with a sigh "ages and ages hence." We must interpret his choice of a road as a symbol for any choice in life between alternatives that appear almost equally attractive but will result through the years in a large difference in the kind of experience one knows.

Image, metaphor, and symbol shade into each other and are sometimes difficult to distinguish. In general, however, an image means only what it is; the figurative term of a metaphor means something other than what it is; and a symbol means what it is and something more too.* If I say that a shaggy brown dog was rubbing its back against a white picket fence, I am talking about nothing but a dog (and a picket fence) and am therefore presenting an image. If I say, "Some dirty dog stole my wallet at the party," I am not talking about a dog at all and am therefore using a metaphor. But if I say, "You can't teach an old dog new tricks," I am talking not only about dogs but about living creatures of any species and am therefore speaking symbolically. Images, of course, do not cease to be images when they become incorporated in metaphors or symbols. If we are discussing the sensuous qualities of "The Road Not Taken" we should refer to the two leaf-strewn roads in the yellow wood as an image; if we are discussing the significance of the poem, we talk about them as symbols.

Symbols vary in the degree of identification and definition given them

---

* This account does not hold for nonliterary symbols such as the letters of the alphabet and algebraic signs (the symbol ∞ for infinity or $=$ for equals). Here, the symbol is meaningless except as it stands for something else, and the connection between the sign and what it stands for is purely arbitrary.

by their authors. Frost in this poem forces us to interpret the choice of roads symbolically by the degree of importance he gives it in the last stanza. Sometimes poets are much more specific in identifying their symbols. Sometimes they do not identify them at all. Consider, for instance, the following poems.

A WHITE ROSE

The red rose whispers of passion,
    And the white rose breathes of love;
Oh, the red rose is a falcon,
    And the white rose is a dove.

But I send you a cream-white rosebud,
    With a flush on its petal tips;
For the love that is purest and sweetest
    Has a kiss of desire on the lips.

          John Boyle O'Reilly (1844–1890)

QUESTIONS

1. Could the poet have made the white rose a symbol of passion and the red rose a symbol of love? Why not?
2. In the second stanza, why does the speaker send a rosebud rather than a rose?

MY STAR

All that I know
    Of a certain star
Is, it can throw
    (Like the angled spar)
Now a dart of red,   5
    Now a dart of blue;
Till my friends have said
    They would fain° see, too,   gladly
My star that dartles the red and the blue!
Then it stops like a bird; like a flower, hangs furled: 10
    They must solace themselves with the Saturn above it.
What matter to me if their star is a world?
    Mine has opened its soul to me; therefore I love it.

          Robert Browning (1812–1889)

In his first two lines O'Reilly indicates so clearly that his red rose is a symbol of physical desire and his white rose a symbol of spiritual attachment that when we get to the metaphor in the third line, we unconsciously substitute passion for the red rose in our minds, knowing without thinking that what O'Reilly is really likening is falcons and passion, not falcons and roses. Similarly in the second stanza, the symbolism of the white rosebud with pink tips is specifically indicated in the last two lines, although, as a matter of fact, it would have been clear from the first stanza. In Browning's poem, on the other hand, there is nothing specific to tell us that Browning is talking about anything other than just a star, and it is only the star's importance to him that makes us suspect that he is talking about something more.

The symbol is the richest and at the same time the most difficult of the poetical figures. Both its richness and its difficulty result from its imprecision. Although the poet may pin down the meaning of his symbol to something fairly definite and precise, as O'Reilly does in "A White Rose," more often the symbol is so general in its meaning that it is able to suggest a great variety of more specific meanings. It is like an opal that flashes out different colors when slowly turned in the light. The choice in "The Road Not Taken," for instance, concerns some choice in life, but what choice? Was it a choice of profession? (Frost took the road "less traveled by" in deciding to become a poet.) A choice of hobby? A choice of mate? It might be any or all or none of these. We cannot determine what particular choice the poet had in mind, if any, and it is not important that we do so. The general meaning of the poem is clear enough. It is an expression of regret that the possibilities of life-experience are so sharply limited. One must live with one mate, have one native country, follow one profession. The speaker in the poem would have liked to explore both roads, but he could explore only one. The person with a craving for life, however satisfied with his own choice, will always long for the realms of experience that had to be passed by. Because the symbol is a rich one, the poem suggests other meanings too. It affirms a belief in the possibility of choice and says something of the nature of choice—how each choice limits the range of possible future choices, so that we make our lives as we go, both freely choosing and being determined by past choices. Though not primarily a philosophical poem, it obliquely comments on the issue of free will versus determinism and indicates the poet's own position. It is able to do all these things, concretely and compactly, by its use of an effective symbol.

"My Star," if we interpret it symbolically, likewise suggests a variety of meanings. It has been most often interpreted as a tribute to Browning's wife, Elizabeth Barrett Browning. As one critic writes, "She shone upon his life like a star of various colors; but the moment the world attempted to pry into the secret of her genius, she shut off the light altogether."* The poem has also been taken to refer to Browning's own peculiar genius, "his gift for seeing in events and things a significance hidden from other men."† A third suggestion is that Browning was thinking of his own peculiar poetic style. He loved harsh, jagged sounds and rhythms and grotesque images; most people of his time found beauty only in the smoother-flowing, melodic rhythms and more conventionally poetic images of his contemporary Tennyson's style, which could be symbolized by Saturn in the poem. The point is not that any one of these interpretations is right or necessarily wrong. We cannot say what the poet had specifically in mind. Literally, the poem is an expression of affection for a particular star in the sky that has a unique beauty and fascination for the poet but in which no one else can see the qualities that the poet sees. If we interpret the poem symbolically, the star is a symbol for anything in life that has unique meanings and value for an individual, which other people cannot see. Beyond this, the meaning is "open." And because the meaning is open, the reader is justified in bringing his own experience to its interpretation. Browning's cherished star might remind him of, for instance, an old rag doll he particularly loved as a child, though its button eyes were off and its stuffing coming out and it had none of the crisp bright beauty of waxen dolls with real hair admired by other children.

Between the extremes represented by "The White Rose" and "My Star" a poem may exercise all degrees of control over the range and meaning of its symbolism. Consider another example.

YOU, ANDREW MARVELL

(unsure about afterlife / good humans but lets enjoy now / can't infringe on inalienable rights)

And here face down beneath the sun
And here upon earth's noonward height
To feel the always coming on
The always rising of the night:

death day / life

To feel creep up the curving east   5
The earthly chill of dusk and slow
Upon those under lands the vast
And ever-climbing shadow grow

*William Lyon Phelps, *Robert Browning: How to Know Him* (Indianapolis: Bobbs-Merrill, 1932), p. 165.

†Quoted from William Clyde DeVane, *A Browning Handbook* (New York: Crofts, 1935), p. 202.

And strange at Ecbatan the trees
Take leaf by leaf the evening strange
The flooding dark about their knees
The mountains over Persia change

And now at Kermanshah the gate
Dark empty and the withered grass
And through the twilight now the late
Few travelers in the westward pass

And Baghdad darken and the bridge
Across the silent river gone
And through Arabia the edge
Of evening widen and steal on

And deepen on Palmyra's street
The wheel rut in the ruined stone
And Lebanon fade out and Crete
High through the clouds and overblown

And over Sicily the air
Still flashing with the landward gulls
And loom and slowly disappear
The sails above the shadowy hulls

And Spain go under and the shore
Of Africa the gilded sand
And evening vanish and no more
The low pale light across that land

Nor now the long light on the sea:
And here face downward in the sun
To feel how swift how secretly
The shadow of the night comes on . . .

10

15

20

25

30

35

Archibald MacLeish (1892–1982)

[handwritten margin note: DEATH is APPROACHING]

[handwritten margin note: BLEAK]

[handwritten note: must concern w/ swift passage of time, enjoy now! if not wasted waiting]

QUESTIONS

1. We ordinarily speak of *nightfall.* Why does MacLeish speak of the "rising" of
   the night? What implicit metaphorical comparison is suggested by phrases
   like "rising of the night" (4), "the flooding dark" (11), "the bridge / Across
   the silent river gone" (17–18), "deepen on Palmyra's street" (21), "Spain go
   under" (29), and so on?
2. Does the comparative lack of punctuation serve any function? What is the
   effect of the repetition of "and" throughout the poem?

3. Ecbatan was founded in 700 B.C. and is associated in history with Cyrus the Great, founder of the Persian Empire, and with Alexander the Great. Kermanshah was another ancient city of Persia. Where are Baghdad, Palmyra, Lebanon, Crete?

On the literal level, "You, Andrew Marvell" is about the coming on of night. The poet, lying at noon full length in the sun somewhere in the United States,* pictures in his mind the earth's shadow, halfway around the world, moving silently westward over Persia, Syria, Crete, Sicily, Spain, Africa, and finally the Atlantic—approaching swiftly, in fact, the place where he himself lies. But the title of the poem tells us that, though particularly concerned with the passage of a day, it is more generally concerned with the swift passage of time; for the title is an allusion to a famous poem on this subject by Andrew Marvell ("To His Coy Mistress," page 70) and especially to two lines of that poem:

> But at my back I always hear
> Time's wingèd chariot hurrying near.

Once we are aware of this larger concern of the poem, two symbolical levels of interpretation open to us. Marvell's poem is primarily concerned with the swift passing of man's life; and the word *night*, we know, from our experience with other literature, is a natural and traditional metaphor or symbol for death. The poet, then, is thinking not only about the passing of a day but about the passing of his life. He is at present "upon earth's noonward height"—in the full flush of manhood—but he is acutely conscious of the declining years ahead and of "how swift how secretly" his death comes on.

If we are to account fully for all the data of the poem, however, a third level of interpretation is necessary. What has dictated the poet's choice of geographical references? The places named, of course, progress from east to west; but they have a further linking characteristic. Ecbatan, Kermanshah, Baghdad, and Palmyra are all ancient or ruined cities, the relics of past empires and crumbled civilizations. Lebanon, Crete, Sicily, Spain, and North Africa are places where civilization once flourished more vigorously than it does at present. On a third level, then, the poet is concerned, not with the passage of a day nor with the passage of a lifetime, but with the passage of historical epochs. The poet's own coun-

---

*MacLeish has identified the fixed location of the poem as Illinois on the shore of Lake Michigan.

try—the United States—now shines "upon earth's noonward height" as a favored nation in the sun of history, but its civilization, too, will pass.

Meanings ray out from a symbol, like the corona around the sun or like connotations around a richly suggestive word. But the very fact that a symbol may be so rich in its meanings makes it necessary that we use the greatest tact in its interpretation. Though Browning's "My Star" might, because of personal associations, make us think of a rag doll, still we should not go around telling people that in this poem Browning uses the star to symbolize a rag doll, for this interpretation is private, idiosyncratic, and narrow. The poem allows it but does not itself suggest it. Moreover, we should never assume that because the meaning of a symbol is more or less open, we may make it mean anything we choose. We would be wrong, for instance, in interpreting the choice in "The Road Not Taken" as some choice between good and evil, for the poem tells us that the two roads are much alike and that both lie "in leaves no step had trodden black." Whatever the choice is, it is a choice between two goods. Whatever our interpretation of a symbolical poem, it must be tied firmly to the facts of the poem. We must not let loose of the string and let our imaginations go ballooning up among the clouds. Because the symbol is capable of adding so many dimensions to a poem, it is a peculiarly effective resource of the poet, but it is also peculiarly susceptible of misinterpretation by the incautious reader.

Accurate interpretation of the symbol requires delicacy, tact, and good sense. The reader must keep his balance while walking a tightrope between too little and too much—between underinterpretation and overinterpretation. If he falls off, however, it is much more desirable that he fall off on the side of too little. The reader who reads "The Road Not Taken" as being only about a choice between two roads in a wood has at least gotten part of the experience that the poem communicates, but the reader who reads into it anything he chooses might as well discard the poem and simply daydream.

Above all, we should avoid the disease of seeing symbols everywhere, like a man with hallucinations, whether there are symbols there or not. It is better to miss a symbol now and then than to walk constantly among shadows and mirages.

TO THE VIRGINS, TO MAKE MUCH OF TIME

> Gather ye rosebuds while ye may,
>   Old Time is still a-flying;
> And this same flower that smiles today
>   Tomorrow will be dying.

The glorious lamp of heaven, the Sun,   5
   The higher he's a-getting,
The sooner will his race be run,
   And nearer he's to setting.

That age is best which is the first,
   When youth and blood are warmer;   10
But being spent, the worse, and worst
   Times still succeed the former.

Then be not coy, but use your time;
   And while ye may, go marry;
For having lost but once your prime,   15
   You may forever tarry.

Robert Herrick (1591–1674)

QUESTIONS

1. The first two stanzas might be interpreted literally if the third and fourth stanzas did not force us to interpret them symbolically. What do the rosebuds symbolize (stanza 1)? What does the course of a day symbolize (stanza 2)? Does the poet fix the meaning of the rosebud symbol in the last stanza or merely name *one* of its specific meanings?
2. How does the title help us interpret the meaning of the symbol? Why did Herrick use "virgins" instead of *maidens?*
3. Why is such haste necessary in gathering the rosebuds? True, the blossoms die quickly, but they are replaced by others. Who *really* is dying?
4. What are the "worse, and worst" times (11)? Why?
5. Why did the poet use his wording rather than the following alternatives: *blooms* for "smiles" (3), *course* for "race" (7), *used* for "spent" (11), *spend* for "use" (13)?

ALLEGORY is a narrative or description that has a second meaning beneath the surface one. Although the surface story or description may have its own interest, the author's major interest is in the ulterior meaning. When Pharaoh in the Bible, for instance, has a dream in which seven fat kine are devoured by seven lean kine, the story does not really become significant until Joseph interprets its allegorical meaning: that Egypt is to enjoy seven years of fruitfulness and prosperity followed by seven years of famine. Allegory has been defined sometimes as an extended metaphor and sometimes as a series of related symbols. But it is usually distinguishable from both of these. It is unlike extended metaphor in that it involves a *system* of related comparisons rather than one comparison drawn out. It differs from symbolism in that it puts less emphasis on the images for their own sake and more on their ulterior meanings. Also, these meanings are more fixed. In allegory usually there is a one-to-one correspondence between the details and a single set of ulterior meanings. In complex allegories the details may have more than one meaning, but these meanings tend to be definite. Meanings do not ray out from allegory as they do from a symbol.

Allegory is less popular in modern literature than it was in medieval and Renaissance writing, and it is much less often found in short poems than in long works such as *The Faerie Queene, Everyman,* and *Pilgrim's Progress.* It has sometimes, especially with political allegory, been used to disguise meaning rather than reveal it (or, rather, to disguise it from some people while revealing it to others). Though less rich than the symbol, allegory is an effective way of making the abstract concrete and has occasionally been used effectively even in fairly short poems.

REDEMPTION

Having been tenant long to a rich Lord,
    Not thriving, I resolvèd to be bold,
    And make a suit unto him, to afford
A new small-rented lease and cancel the old.
In heaven at his manor I him sought: 5
    They told me there that he was lately gone
    About some land which he had dearly bought
Long since on earth, to take possession.
I straight returned, and knowing his great birth,
    Sought him accordingly in great resorts;   10
    In cities, theaters, gardens, parks, and courts:
At length I heard a ragged noise and mirth
    Of thieves and murderers; there I him espied,
Who straight, "Your suit is granted," said, and died.

George Herbert (1593–1633)

QUESTIONS

1. Vocabulary: *suit* (3, 14), *afford* (3), *dearly* (7).
2. On the surface this poem tells about a business negotiation between a tenant landholder and his landlord. What clues indicate that the poem really concerns something deeper?
3. Who is the "rich Lord"? Who is the tenant? What is the old lease? What is the new one? Where does the tenant find his Lord? What is the significance of his suit being granted just as the landlord dies?
4. What are the implications of the landlord's having gone to take possession of

some land which he "had dearly bought / Long since on earth"? In what senses (on both levels of meaning) is the landlord of "great birth"? What is "a ragged noise and mirth / Of thieves and murderers"?

EXERCISE

Determine whether "sleep," in the following poems, is literal, metaphorical, symbolical, or other. In each case explain and justify your answer.

1. "On moonlit heath and lonesome bank," page 50, line 13.
2. "On moonlit heath and lonesome bank," line 29.
3. "Dulce et Decorum Est," page 7, line 5.
4. "Terence, this is stupid stuff," page 14, line 8.
5. "Is my team ploughing," page 21, lines 24, 27.
6. "Meeting at Night," page 47, line 4.
7. "Weep ye no more, sad fountains," page 72, lines 7, 9, 16, 18.
8. "Reveille," page 85, line 24.
9. "Ulysses," page 87, line 5.
10. "Stopping by Woods on a Snowy Evening," page 128, line 16.

*   *   *

REVEILLE

Wake: the silver dusk returning
  Up the beach of darkness brims,
And the ship of sunrise burning
  Strands upon the eastern rims.

Wake: the vaulted shadow shatters,   5
  Trampled to the floor it spanned,
And the tent of night in tatters
  Straws the sky-pavilioned land.

Up, lad, up, 'tis late for lying:
  Hear the drums of morning play;   10
Hark, the empty highways crying
  "Who'll beyond the hills away?"

Towns and countries woo together,
  Forelands beacon, belfries call;
Never lad that trod on leather   15
  Lived to feast his heart with all.

Up, lad: thews that lie and cumber
  Sunlit pallets never thrive;

Morns abed and daylight slumber
Were not meant for man alive.   20

Clay lies still, but blood's a rover;
Breath's a ware that will not keep.
Up, lad: when the journey's over
There'll be time enough to sleep.

A. E. Housman (1859-1936)

QUESTIONS

1. Are *Reveille* (title) and *drums* (10) literal or metaphorical? Explain.
2. Explain the metaphors in lines 1-4, 5-8, and 22. What figure of speech predominates in lines 11-14?
3. Identify and explain the metonymies in lines 15, 17, 21, and 22.
4. What symbolical meanings have *journey* (23) and *sleep* (24)?
5. What philosophy does the poem express?

FIRE AND ICE

Some say the world will end in fire,
Some say in ice.
From what I've tasted of desire
I hold with those who favor fire.
But if it had to perish twice,
I think I know enough of hate
To say that for destruction ice
Is also great
And would suffice.

Robert Frost (1874-1963)

QUESTIONS

1. Who are "Some"? To what two theories do lines 1-2 refer?
2. What do "fire" and "ice" respectively symbolize? What two meanings has "the world"?
3. The poem ends with an *understatement* (see chapter 7). How does it affect the tone of the poem?

THE SICK ROSE

O Rose, thou art sick!
The invisible worm
That flies in the night,
In the howling storm,

Has found out thy bed
Of crimson joy,
And his dark secret love
Does thy life destroy.

William Blake (1757–1827)

QUESTIONS

1. As in Browning's "My Star," the meaning of the symbolism in this poem is
left fairly open. The poem might be interpreted as being only about a rose
which has been attacked on a stormy night by a cankerworm. But the conno-
tations of certain words and details are so powerful as to suggest that more is
meant: "sick" (applied to a flower), "invisible," "night," "howling storm,"
"bed of crimson joy," "dark secret love." Can you suggest specific meanings
for the rose and the worm? What broad boundaries of meaning must any
specific interpretations observe? Can the poem be read as about the overcom-
ing of something evil by something good?
2. Besides being a symbol, the rose is to some degree personified. What words or
details of the poem contribute to this personification?

ULYSSES

It little profits that an idle king,
By this still hearth, among these barren crags,
Matched with an agèd wife, I mete and dole
Unequal laws unto a savage race,
That hoard, and sleep, and feed, and know not me.   5
I cannot rest from travel; I will drink
Life to the lees. All times I have enjoyed
Greatly, have suffered greatly, both with those
That loved me, and alone; on shore, and when
Through scudding drifts the rainy Hyades   10
Vext the dim sea. I am become a name;
For always roaming with a hungry heart
Much have I seen and known,—cities of men
And manners, climates, councils, governments,
Myself not least, but honored of them all;   15
And drunk delight of battle with my peers,
Far on the ringing plains of windy Troy.
I am a part of all that I have met;
Yet all experience is an arch wherethrough
Gleams that untraveled world, whose margin fades   20
For ever and for ever when I move.
How dull it is to pause, to make an end,
To rust unburnished, not to shine in use!

As though to breathe were life! Life piled on life
Were all too little, and of one to me   25
Little remains; but every hour is saved
From that eternal silence, something more,
A bringer of new things; and vile it were
For some three suns to store and hoard myself,
And this grey spirit yearning in desire   30
To follow knowledge like a sinking star,
Beyond the utmost bound of human thought.

This is my son, mine own Telemachus,
To whom I leave the scepter and the isle—
Well-loved of me, discerning to fulfil   35
This labor, by slow prudence to make mild
A rugged people, and through soft degrees
Subdue them to the useful and the good.
Most blameless is he, centered in the sphere
Of common duties, decent not to fail   40
In offices of tenderness, and pay
Meet adoration to my household gods,
When I am gone. He works his work, I mine.

There lies the port; the vessel puffs her sail:
There gloom the dark, broad seas. My mariners,   45
Souls that have toiled, and wrought, and thought with me—
That ever with a frolic welcome took
The thunder and the sunshine, and opposed
Free hearts, free foreheads—you and I are old;
Old age hath yet his honor and his toil.   50
Death closes all; but something ere the end,
Some work of noble note, may yet be done,
Not unbecoming men that strove with Gods.
The lights begin to twinkle from the rocks;
The long day wanes; the slow moon climbs; the deep   55
Moans round with many voices. Come, my friends,
'Tis not too late to seek a newer world.
Push off, and sitting well in order smite
The sounding furrows; for my purpose holds
To sail beyond the sunset, and the baths   60
Of all the western stars, until I die.
It may be that the gulfs will wash us down;
It may be we shall touch the Happy Isles,
And see the great Achilles, whom we knew.
Though much is taken, much abides; and though   65
We are not now that strength which in old days
Moved earth and heaven, that which we are, we are:

One equal temper of heroic hearts,
Made weak by time and fate, but strong in will
To strive, to seek, to find, and not to yield.   70

Alfred, Lord Tennyson (1809–1892)

QUESTIONS

1. Vocabulary: *lees* (7), *Hyades* (10), *meet* (42).
2. Ulysses, king of Ithaca, is a legendary Greek hero, a major figure in Homer's *Iliad*, the hero of Homer's *Odyssey*, and a minor figure in Dante's *Divine Comedy*. After ten years at the siege of Troy, Ulysses set sail for home but, having incurred the wrath of the god of the sea, he was subjected to storms and vicissitudes and was forced to wander for another ten years, having many adventures and seeing most of the Mediterranean world before again reaching Ithaca, his wife, and his son. Once back home, according to Dante, he still wished to travel and "to follow virtue and knowledge." In Tennyson's poem, Ulysses is represented as about to set sail on a final voyage from which he will not return. Locate Ithaca on a map. Where exactly, in geographical terms, does Ulysses intend to sail (59–64)? (The Happy Isles were the Elysian fields, or Greek paradise; Achilles was another Greek prince, the hero of the *Iliad*, who was killed at the siege of Troy.)
3. Ulysses' speech is divided into three sections. What is the topic or purpose of each section? To whom, specifically, is the third section addressed? To whom, would you infer, are sections 1 and 2 addressed? Where do you visualize Ulysses as standing during his speech?
4. Characterize Ulysses. What kind of person is he as Tennyson represents him?
5. What does Ulysses symbolize? What way of life is being recommended? Find as many evidences as you can that Ulysses' desire for travel represents something more than mere wanderlust and wish for adventure.
6. Give two symbolical implications of the westward direction of Ulysses' journey.
7. Interpret lines 18–21 and 26–29. What is symbolized by "the thunder and the sunshine" (48)? What do the two metonymies in line 49 stand for? What metaphor is implied in line 23?

CURIOSITY

may have killed the cat; more likely
the cat was just unlucky, or else curious
to see what death was like, having no cause
to go on licking paws, or fathering
litter on litter of kittens, predictably.   5

Nevertheless, to be curious
is dangerous enough. To distrust
what is always said, what seems,
to ask odd questions, interfere in dreams,

leave home, smell rats, have hunches 10
do not endear cats to those doggy circles
where well-smelt baskets, suitable wives, good lunches
are the order of things, and where prevails
much wagging of incurious heads and tails.

Face it. Curiosity 15
will not cause us to die—
only lack of it will.
Never to want to see
the other side of the hill
or that improbable country 20
where living is an idyll
(although a probable hell)
would kill us all.
Only the curious
have, if they live, a tale 25
worth telling at all.

Dogs say cats love too much, are irresponsible,
are changeable, marry too many wives,
desert their children, chill all dinner tables
with tales of their nine lives. 30
Well, they are lucky. Let them be
nine-lived and contradictory,
curious enough to change, prepared to pay
the cat price, which is to die
and die again and again, 35
each time with no less pain.
A cat minority of one
is all that can be counted on
to tell the truth. And what cats have to tell
on each return from hell 40
is this: that dying is what the living do,
that dying is what the loving do,
and that dead dogs are those who do not know
that dying is what, to live, each has to do.

Alastair Reid (b. 1926)

QUESTIONS

1. On the surface this poem is a dissertation on cats. What deeper comments
   does it make? Of what are cats and dogs, in this poem, symbols?
2. In what different senses are the words "death," "die," and "dying" here used?
3. Compare and contrast this poem in meaning and manner with "Ulysses."

LOVE SONG: I AND THOU

Nothing is plumb, level or square:
 the studs are bowed, the joists
are shaky by nature, no piece fits
 any other piece without a gap
or pinch, and bent nails   5
 dance all over the surfacing
like maggots. By Christ
 I am no carpenter, I built
the roof for myself, the walls
 for myself, the floors   10
for myself, and got
 hung up in it myself. I
danced with a purple thumb
 at this house-warming, drunk
with my prime whiskey: rage.   15
 Oh I spat rage's nails
into the frame-up of my work:
 it held. It settled plumb,
level, solid, square and true
 for that one moment. Then   20
it screamed and went on through
 skewing as wrong the other way.
God damned it. This is hell,
 but I planned it, I sawed it,
I nailed it, and I   25
 will live in it until it kills me.
I can nail my left palm
 to the left-hand cross-piece but
I can't do everything myself.
 I need a hand to nail the right,   30
a help, a love, a you, a wife.

Alan Dugan (b. 1923)

QUESTIONS

1. What clues are there that this house is not literal? What does it stand for?
2. Why does the speaker swear "By Christ" rather than *By God* (7)? Where else in the poem is Christ alluded to? What parallels and differences does the speaker see between himself and Christ?
3. "God damned it" (23) at first sounds like another curse, but the past tense makes its meaning more precise. What are the implications of lines 24–26? What implications are added in the phrase "by nature" (3)? What meanings has "prime" (15)?

4. What is the meaning of the last three lines? (Note: *I and Thou* is the title of a very influential book by the Jewish theologian Martin Buber. Briefly, it argues that, though suffering is inescapable, human life becomes meaningful as man forms "I–Thou" relationships, as opposed to "I–It" relationships—that is, as one becomes deeply involved with and committed to other human beings in relationships of love and concern.)

A HOLE IN THE FLOOR

The carpenter's made a hole
In the parlor floor, and I'm standing
Staring down into it now
At four o'clock in the evening,
As Schliemann stood when his shovel   5
Knocked on the crowns of Troy.

A clean-cut sawdust sparkles
On the grey, shaggy laths,
And here is a cluster of shavings
From the time when the floor was laid.   10
They are silvery-gold, the color
Of Hesperian apple-parings.

Kneeling, I look in under
Where the joists go into hiding.
A pure street, faintly littered   15
With bits and strokes of light,
Enters the long darkness
Where its parallels will meet.

The radiator-pipe
Rises in middle distance   20
Like a shuttered kiosk, standing
Where the only news is night.
Here it's not painted green
As it is in the visible world.

For God's sake, what am I after?   25
Some treasure, or tiny garden?
Or that untrodden place,
The house's very soul,
Where time has stored our footbeats
And the long skein of our voices?   30

Not these, but the buried strangeness
Which nourishes the known:
That spring from which the floor-lamp

Drinks now a wilder bloom,
Inflaming the damask love-seat   35
And the whole dangerous room.

Richard Wilbur (b. 1921)

QUESTIONS

1. Vocabulary: *laths* (8), *Hesperian* (12), *joists* (14), *kiosk* (21), *skein* (30).
2. Heinrich Schliemann (5), an archaeologist, discovered and excavated the ruins of ancient Troy. In Greek mythology a tree bearing golden apples, a wedding gift to Hera, was guarded by three nymphs called the Hesperides. What meanings are combined in the adjective "Hesperian" (12)? What do these two allusions add to the poem?
3. The first four stanzas are mainly descriptive, the fifth transitional. What associations prompt the questions in this stanza?
4. Of what does the house become a symbol in the sixth stanza? What does the region beneath the house symbolize? What do the words "nourishes," "spring," "wilder bloom," "inflaming," "love-seat," and "dangerous" suggest about its qualities? Comment on each.

SUN AND MOON

A strong man, a fair woman,
Bound fast in love,
Parted by ordered heaven,   *dEATH*
Punishment prove.°   undergo

He suffers gnawing fires: 5
She in her frost
Beams in his sight, but dies
When he seems lost.

Not till the poles are joined
Shall the retreat   10
Of fierce brother from lost sister
End, and they meet.

Jay Macpherson (b. 1931)

QUESTIONS

1. In what ways are the personifications of sun and moon as man and woman, and brother and sister, appropriate?
2. In what senses have they been parted "by ordered heaven"? Explain their punishment.
3. When will they "meet" (12)?

FAME

See, as the prettiest graves will do in time,
Our poet's wants the freshness of its prime:
Spite of the sexton's browsing horse, the sods
Have struggled through its binding osier-rods;
Headstone and half-sunk footstone lean awry,
Wanting the brick-work promised by-and-by;
How the grey lichens, plate o'er plate,
Have softened down the crisp-cut name and date!

Robert Browning (1812–1889)

EXERCISE

In what respects are the following poems alike? In what respects are they essentially different?

DUST OF SNOW

The way a crow
Shook down on me
The dust of snow
From a hemlock tree

Has given my heart
A change of mood
And saved some part
Of a day I had rued.

Robert Frost (1874–1963)

SOFT SNOW

I walked abroad in a snowy day;
I asked the soft snow with me to play;
She played and she melted in all her prime,
And the winter called it a dreadful crime.

William Blake (1757–1827)

7. Figurative Language 3

PARADOX, OVERSTATEMENT, UNDERSTATEMENT, IRONY

esop tells the tale of a traveler who sought refuge with a Satyr on a bitter winter night. On entering the Satyr's lodging, he blew on his fingers, and was asked by the Satyr what he did it for. "To warm them up," he explained. Later, on being served with a piping hot bowl of porridge, he blew also on it, and again was asked what he did it for. "To cool it off," he explained. The Satyr thereupon thrust him out of doors, for he would have nothing to do with a man who could blow hot and cold with the same breath.

A PARADOX is an apparent contradiction that is nevertheless somehow true. It may be either a situation or a statement. Aesop's tale of the traveler illustrates a paradoxical situation. As a figure of speech, paradox is a statement. When Alexander Pope wrote that a literary critic of his time would "damn with faint praise," he was using a verbal paradox, for how can a man damn by praising?

When we understand all the conditions and circumstances involved in a paradox, we find that what at first seemed impossible is actually entirely plausible and not strange at all. The paradox of the cold hands and hot porridge is not strange to a man who knows that a stream of air directed upon an object of different temperature will tend to bring that object closer to its own temperature. And Pope's paradox is not strange when we realize that *damn* is being used figuratively, and that Pope means only that a too reserved praise may damage an author with the public almost as much as adverse criticism. In a paradoxical statement the contradiction usually stems from one of the words being used figuratively or in more than one sense.

The value of paradox is its shock value. Its seeming impossibility startles the reader into attention and, thus, by the fact of its apparent absurdity, it underscores the truth of what is being said.

MY LIFE CLOSED TWICE

My life closed twice before its close;
It yet remains to see
If Immortality unveil
A third event to me,

So huge, so hopeless to conceive,
As these that twice befell.
Parting is all we know of heaven,
And all we need of hell.

Emily Dickinson (1830–1886)

QUESTIONS

1. Do lines 2–6 mean: (a) I do not know yet whether there is a life after death—a continued existence in heaven and hell or (b) I do not know yet whether my entry into heaven or hell—whichever place I go—will be as "huge" an event as two events that have already happened to me during my life? Or both?
2. The poem sets forth two or possibly three paradoxes: (a) that the speaker's life closed twice before its close; (b) (if we accept the second alternative above) that death and entry into immortality may possibly be "lesser" events than two not extraordinary occurrences that happened during the speaker's lifetime; (c) that parting from a loved one is *both* heaven and hell. Resolve (that is, explain) each of these paradoxes.

Overstatement, understatement, and verbal irony form a continuous series, for they consist, respectively, of saying more, saying less, and saying the opposite of what one really means.

OVERSTATEMENT, or *hyperbole,* is simply exaggeration, but exaggeration in the service of truth. It is not the same as a fish story. If you say, "I'm starved!" or "You could have knocked me over with a feather!" or "I'll die if I don't pass this course!" you do not expect to be believed; you are merely adding emphasis to what you really mean. (And if you say, "There were literally millions of people at the dance!" you are merely piling one overstatement on top of another, for you really mean that

"There were figuratively millions of people at the dance," or, literally, "The dance hall was very crowded.") Like all figures of speech, overstatement may be used with a variety of effects. It may be humorous or grave, fanciful or restrained, convincing or unconvincing. When Tennyson says of his eagle (page 5) that it is "*Close* to the sun in lonely lands," he says what appears to be literally true, though we know from our study of astronomy that it is not. When Wordsworth reports of his daffodils in "I wandered lonely as a cloud" that they "stretched *in never-ending line*" along the margin of a bay, he too reports faithfully a visual appearance. When Frost says, at the conclusion of "The Road Not Taken" (page 75),

> I shall be telling this with a sigh
> Somewhere *ages and ages hence,*

we are scarcely aware of the overstatement, so quietly is the assertion made. Unskillfully used, however, overstatement may seem strained and ridiculous, leading us to react as Gertrude does to the player-queen's speeches in *Hamlet:* "The lady doth protest too much."

It is paradoxical that one can emphasize a truth either by overstating it or by understating it. UNDERSTATEMENT, or saying less than one means, may exist in what one says or merely in how one says it. If, for instance, upon sitting down to a loaded dinner plate, you say, "This looks like a good bite," you are actually stating less than the truth; but if you say, with Artemus Ward, that a man who holds his hand for half an hour in a lighted fire will experience "a sensation of excessive and disagreeable warmth," you are stating what is literally true but with a good deal less force than the situation might seem to warrant.

A RED, RED ROSE

O my Luve's like a red, red rose,
 That's newly sprung in June;
O my Luve's like the melodie
 That's sweetly play'd in tune.

As fair art thou, my bonnie lass,   5
 So deep in luve am I;
And I will love thee still, my Dear,
 Till a'° the seas gang° dry.   all; go

Till a' the seas gang dry, my Dear,
 And the rocks melt wi' the sun: 10
I will love thee still, my Dear,
 While the sands o' life shall run.

And fare thee weel, my only Luve!
And fare thee weel, a while!
And I will come again, my Luve,   15
Tho' it were ten thousand mile!

Attributed to *Robert Burns* (*1759–1796*)

THE ROSE FAMILY

The rose is a rose,
And was always a rose.
But the theory now goes
That the apple's a rose,
And the pear is, and so's   5
The plum, I suppose.
The dear only knows
What will next prove a rose.
You, of course, are a rose—
But were always a rose.   10

Robert Frost (*1874–1963*)

QUESTION

Burns and Frost use the same metaphor in paying tribute to their loved ones;
otherwise their methods are opposed. Burns begins with a couple of convention-
ally poetic similes and proceeds to a series of overstatements. Frost begins with
literal and scientific fact (the apple, pear, plum, and rose all belong to the same
botanical family, the Rosaceae), and then slips in his metaphor so casually and
quietly that the assertion has the effect of understatement. What is the function
of "of course" and "but" in the last two lines?

Like paradox, *irony* has meanings that extend beyond its use merely
as a figure of speech.

VERBAL IRONY, saying the opposite of what one means, is often con-
fused with sarcasm and with satire, and for that reason it may be well to
look at the meanings of all three terms. SARCASM and SATIRE both imply
ridicule, one on the colloquial level, the other on the literary level. Sar-
casm is simply bitter or cutting speech, intended to wound the feelings (it
comes from a Greek word meaning to tear flesh). Satire is a more formal
term, usually applied to written literature rather than to speech and ordi-
narily implying a higher motive: it is ridicule (either bitter or gentle) of
human folly or vice, with the purpose of bringing about reform or at least
of keeping other people from falling into similar folly or vice. Irony, on

the other hand, is a literary device or figure that may be used in the service of sarcasm or ridicule or may not. It is popularly confused with sarcasm and satire because it is so often used as their tool; but irony may be used without either sarcastic or satirical intent, and sarcasm and satire may exist (though they do not usually) without irony. If, for instance, one of the members of your class raises his hand on the discussion of this point and says, "I don't understand," and your instructor replies, with a tone of heavy disgust in his voice, "Well, I wouldn't expect *you* to," he is being sarcastic but not ironical; he means exactly what he says. But if, after you have done particularly well on an examination, your instructor brings your test papers into the classroom saying, "Here's some *bad* news for you: you all got A's and B's!" he is being ironical but not sarcastic. Sarcasm, we may say, is cruel, as a bully is cruel: it intends to give hurt. Satire is both cruel and kind, as a surgeon is cruel and kind: it gives hurt in the interest of the patient or of society. Irony is neither cruel nor kind: it is simply a device, like a surgeon's scalpel, for performing any operation more skillfully.

Though verbal irony always implies the opposite of what is said, it has many gradations, and only in its simplest forms does it mean *only* the opposite of what is said. In more complex forms it means both what is said and the opposite of what is said, at once, though in different ways and with different degrees of emphasis. When Terence's critic, in "Terence, this is stupid stuff" (page 14) says, "*Pretty* friendship 'tis to rhyme / Your friends to death before their time" (11–12), we may substitute the literal *sorry* for "pretty" with little or no loss of meaning. When Terence speaks in reply, however, of the pleasure of drunkenness—"And down in *lovely* muck I've lain, / Happy till I woke again" (35–36)—we cannot substitute *loathsome* for "lovely" without considerable loss of meaning, for, while muck is actually extremely unpleasant to lie in, it may *seem* lovely to an intoxicated person. Thus two meanings—one the opposite of the other—operate at once.

Like all figures of speech, verbal irony runs the danger of being misunderstood. With irony the risks are perhaps greater than with other figures, for if metaphor is misunderstood, the result may be simply bewilderment; but if irony is misunderstood, the reader goes away with exactly the opposite idea from what the user meant to convey. The results of misunderstanding if, for instance, you ironically called someone a villain, might be calamitous. For this reason the user of irony must be very skillful in its use, conveying by an altered tone or by a wink of the eye or pen, that he is speaking ironically; and the reader of literature must be always alert to recognize the subtle signs that irony is intended.

No matter how broad or obvious the irony, there will always be in any large audience, a number who will misunderstand. The humorist Artemus Ward used to protect himself against these people by writing at the bottom of his newspaper column, "This is writ ironical." But irony is most delightful and most effective when it is subtlest. It sets up a special understanding between writer and reader that may add either grace or force. If irony is too obvious, it sometimes seems merely crude. But if effectively used, it, like all figurative language, is capable of adding extra dimensions to meaning.

WHAT SOFT, CHERUBIC CREATURES

What soft, cherubic creatures
These gentlewomen are.
One would as soon assault a plush
Or violate a star.

Such dimity convictions,   5
A horror so refined
Of freckled human nature,
Of deity ashamed—

It's such a common glory,
A fisherman's degree.   10
Redemption, brittle lady,
Be so ashamed of thee.

Emily Dickinson (1830–1886)

QUESTIONS

1. In what sense (or senses) is the word "gentlewomen" used? What qualities are attributed to them in the first seven lines? What are "dimity convictions" (*dimity* was a thin, crisp cotton cloth fashionable for women's dresses)?
2. For whom is "Redemption" (11) a metonymy? What is the meaning of "common" (9) and of "degree" (10)? What "common glory" is referred to, and why is it a "fisherman's degree"? What is "freckled human nature" (7)? How are the gentlewomen "ashamed" of deity?
3. How is the judgment implied on the "gentlewomen" in the first half of the poem reversed in the second half? Which half is ironical?
4. Does Luke 9:26 help you with any of these questions?

The term *irony* always implies some sort of discrepancy or incongruity. In verbal irony the discrepancy is between what is said and what is meant. In other forms the discrepancy may be between appearance and reality or between expectation and fulfillment. These other forms of irony are, on the whole, more important resources for the poet than is verbal irony. Two types are especially important.

In DRAMATIC IRONY* the discrepancy is not between what the speaker says and what he means but between what the speaker says and what the author means. The speaker's words may be perfectly straightforward, but the author, by putting these words in a particular speaker's mouth, may be indicating to the reader ideas or attitudes quite opposed to those the speaker is voicing. This form of irony is more complex than verbal irony and demands a more complex response from the reader. It may be used not only to convey attitudes but also to illuminate character, for the author who uses it is indirectly commenting not only upon the value of the ideas uttered but also upon the nature of the person who utters them. Such comment may be harsh, gently mocking, or sympathetic.

THE CHIMNEY SWEEPER

When my mother died I was very young,
And my father sold me while yet my tongue
Could scarcely cry "'weep! 'weep! 'weep! 'weep!"
So your chimneys I sweep, and in soot I sleep.

There's little Tom Dacre, who cried when his head,   5
That curled like a lamb's back, was shaved; so I said,
"Hush, Tom! never mind it, for, when your head's bare,
You know that the soot cannot spoil your white hair."

And so he was quiet, and that very night,
As Tom was asleeping, he had such a sight!   10
That thousands of sweepers, Dick, Joe, Ned, and Jack,
Were all of them locked up in coffins of black.

And by came an Angel who had a bright key,
And he opened the coffins and set them all free;

*The term *dramatic irony*, which stems from Greek tragedy, often connotes something more specific and perhaps a little different from what I am developing here. It is used of a speech or an action in a story which has much greater significance to the audience than to the character who speaks or performs it, because of possession by the audience of knowledge the character does not have, as when the enemies of Ulysses, in the *Odyssey*, wish good luck and success to a man who the reader knows is Ulysses himself in disguise, or as when Oedipus, in the play by Sophocles, bends every effort to discover the murderer of Laius so that he may avenge the death, not knowing, as the audience does, that Laius is the man whom he himself once slew. I have appropriated the term for a perhaps slightly different situation, because no other suitable term exists. Both uses have the common characteristic—that the author conveys to the reader something different, or at least something more, than the character himself intends.

Then down a green plain leaping, laughing, they run,   15
And wash in a river, and shine in the sun.

Then naked and white, all their bags left behind,
They rise upon clouds and sport in the wind;
And the Angel told Tom, if he'd be a good boy,
He'd have God for his father, and never want joy.   20

And so Tom awoke, and we rose in the dark,
And got with our bags and our brushes to work.
Though the morning was cold, Tom was happy and warm;
So if all do their duty they need not fear harm.

William Blake (1757–1827)

QUESTIONS

1. In the eighteenth century small boys, sometimes no more than four or five years old, were employed to climb up the narrow chimney flues and clean them, collecting the soot in bags. Such boys, sometimes sold to the master sweepers by their parents, were miserably treated by their masters and often suffered disease and physical deformity. Characterize the boy who speaks in this poem. How do his and the poet's attitudes toward his lot in life differ? How, especially, are the meanings of the poet and the speaker different in lines 3, 7–8, and 24?
2. The dream in lines 11–20, besides being a happy dream, is capable of allegorical interpretations. Point out possible significances of the sweepers' being "locked up in coffins of black" and the Angel's releasing them with a bright key to play upon green plains.

A third type of irony is IRONY OF SITUATION. This occurs when there is a discrepancy between the actual circumstances and those that would seem appropriate or between what one anticipates and what actually comes to pass. If a man and his second wife, on the first night of their honeymoon, are accidentally seated at the theater next to the man's first wife, we should call the situation ironical. When, in O. Henry's famous short story "The Gift of the Magi" a poor young husband pawns his most prized possession, a gold watch, in order to buy his wife a set of combs for her hair for Christmas, and his wife sells her most prized possession, her long brown hair, in order to buy a fob for her husband's watch, we call the situation ironical. When King Midas, in the famous fable, is granted his fondest wish, that anything he touch turn to gold, and then finds that he cannot eat because even his food turns to gold, we call the situation ironical. When Coleridge's Ancient Mariner finds himself in the middle of the ocean with "Water, water, everywhere" but not a "drop to drink," we call the situation ironical. In each case the circumstances are not what would seem appropriate or what we would expect.

Dramatic irony and irony of situation are powerful devices for the poet, for, like symbol, they enable him to suggest meanings without stating them—to communicate a great deal more than he says. We have seen one effective use of irony of situation in "Richard Cory" (page 39). Another is in "Ozymandias," which follows.

Irony and paradox may be trivial or powerful devices, depending on their use. At their worst they may degenerate into mere mannerism and mental habit. At their best they may greatly extend the dimensions of meaning in a work of literature. Because irony and paradox are devices that demand an exercise of critical intelligence, they are particularly valuable as safeguards against sentimentality.

OZYMANDIAS

I met a traveler from an antique land
Who said: Two vast and trunkless legs of stone
Stand in the desert . . . Near them, on the sand,
Half sunk, a shattered visage lies, whose frown,
And wrinkled lip, and sneer of cold command,   5
Tell that its sculptor well those passions read
Which yet survive, stamped on these lifeless things,
The hand that mocked them, and the heart that fed;
And on the pedestal these words appear:
"My name is Ozymandias, king of kings;   10
Look on my works, ye Mighty, and despair!"
Nothing beside remains. Round the decay
Of that colossal wreck, boundless and bare
The lone and level sands stretch far away.

Percy Bysshe Shelley (1792–1822)

QUESTIONS

1. "Survive" (7) is a transitive verb with "hand" and "heart" as direct objects. Whose hand? Whose heart? What figure of speech is exemplified in "hand" and "heart"?
2. Characterize Ozymandias.
3. Ozymandias was an ancient Egyptian tyrant. This poem was first published in 1817. Of what is Ozymandias a *symbol*? What contemporary reference might the poem have had in Shelley's time?
4. What is the theme of the poem and how is it "stated"?

Identify each of the following quotations as literal or figurative. If figurative, identify the figure as paradox, overstatement, understatement, or irony and explain the use to which it is put (emotional emphasis, humor, satire, etc.).

1. Poetry is a language that tells us, through a more or less emotional reaction, something that cannot be said.   *Edwin Arlington Robinson*

2. Have not the Indians been kindly and justly treated? Have not the temporal things, the vain baubles and filthy lucre of this world, which were too apt to engage their worldly and selfish thoughts, been benevolently taken from them? And have they not instead thereof, been taught to set their affections on things above?   *Washington Irving*

3. A man who could make so vile a pun would not scruple to pick a pocket.   *John Dennis*

4. Last week I saw a woman flayed, and you will hardly believe how much it altered her person for the worse.   *Swift*

5. . . . Where ignorance is bliss,
   'Tis folly to be wise.   *Thomas Gray*

6. All night I made my bed to swim; with my tears I dissolved my couch.   *Psalms 6:6*

7. Believe him, he has known the world too long,
   And seen the death of much immortal song.   *Pope*

8. Give me my Romeo: and, when he shall die,
   Take him and cut him out in little stars,
   And he will make the face of heaven so fine
   That all the world will be in love with night,
   And pay no worship to the garish sun.   *Juliet, in Shakespeare*

9. Immortality will come to such as are fit for it; and he who would be a great soul in the future must be a great soul now.   *Emerson*

10. Whoe'er their crimes for interest only quit,
    Sin on in virtue, and good deeds *commit*.   *Edward Young*

*   *   *

TO ALTHEA, FROM PRISON

> When love with unconfinèd wings
> Hovers within my gates,
> And my divine Althea brings
> To whisper at the grates;

When I lie tangled in her hair   5
    And fettered to her eye,
The birds that wanton in the air
    Know no such liberty.

When flowing cups run swiftly round
    With no allaying Thames,   10
Our careless heads with roses bound,
    Our hearts with loyal flames;
When thirsty grief in wine we steep,
    When healths and draughts go free,
Fishes that tipple in the deep   15
    Know no such liberty.

When, like committed linnets, I
    With shriller throat shall sing
The sweetness, mercy, majesty,
    And glories of my King;   20
When I shall voice aloud how good
    He is, how great should be,
Enlargèd winds that curl the flood
    Know no such liberty.

Stone walls do not a prison make,   25
    Nor iron bars a cage;
Minds innocent and quiet take
    That for an hermitage;
If I have freedom in my love
    And in my soul am free,   30
Angels alone, that soar above,
    Enjoy such liberty.

Richard Lovelace (1618–1658)

QUESTIONS

1. Vocabulary: *wanton* (7), *allaying* (10), *committed* (17), *enlargèd* (23).
2. Richard Lovelace was a Cavalier poet, a loyal follower of Charles I who because of his royalist sympathies was imprisoned by Parliament in the Gatehouse at Westminster in 1642, a few months before the outbreak of the English Civil War. What is the central paradox of the poem? To whom are healths being drunk in stanza 2 and songs or poems being "sung" in stanza 3?
3. Each of the first three stanzas names a different pleasure which the poet may enjoy even though in prison. What are they? Each stanza also develops and intensifies the central paradox by suggesting some further kind of "confinement" (besides physical) which is not inconsistent with "liberty." What? Each

of the four stanzas ends, in its last two lines, with a comparison. Show how each of these is especially appropriate to its stanza.

4. Explain the image in lines 1–2. What is the subject of "brings" (3)? "Thames" (10) is a metonymy; what does it mean?

BATTER MY HEART, THREE-PERSONED GOD

Batter my heart, three-personed God, for you
As yet but knock, breathe, shine, and seek to mend;
That I may rise and stand, o'erthrow me; and bend
Your force to break, blow, burn, and make me new.
I, like an usurped town, to another due,   5
Labor to admit you, but oh, to no end;
Reason, your viceroy in me, me should defend,
But is captived, and proves weak or untrue.
Yet dearly I love you and would be loved fain,°   gladly
But am betrothed unto your enemy;   10
Divorce me, untie or break that knot again,
Take me to you, imprison me, for I
Except° you enthrall me, never shall be free,   unless
Nor ever chaste, except you ravish me.

John Donne (1572–1631)

QUESTIONS

1. In this sonnet (No. 14 in a group called "Holy Sonnets") Donne addresses God in a series of metaphors and paradoxes. What is the paradox in the first quatrain? To what is the "three-personed God" metaphorically compared? To what is Donne compared? Can the first three verbs of the parallel lines 2 and 4 be taken as addressed to specific "persons" of the Trinity (Father, Son, Holy Spirit)? If so, to which are "knock" and "break" addressed? "breathe" and "blow"? "shine" and "burn"? (What concealed pun helps in the attribution of the last pair? What etymological pun in the attribution of the second?)
2. To what does Donne compare himself in the second quatrain? To what is God compared? Who is the usurper? What role does Reason play in this political metaphor, and why is it a weak one?
3. To what does Donne compare himself in the sestet (lines 9–14)? To what does he compare God? Who is the "enemy" (10)? Resolve the paradox in lines 12–13 by explaining the double meaning of "enthrall." Resolve the paradox in line 14 by explaining the double meaning of "ravish."
4. Sum up the meaning of the poem in a sentence.

LOVE POEM

My clumsiest dear, whose hands shipwreck vases,
At whose quick touch all glasses chip and ring,

Whose palms are bulls in china, burs in linen, *clumsy*
And have no cunning with any soft thing

Except all ill-at-ease fidgeting people: 5
The refugee uncertain at the door
You make at home; deftly you steady
The drunk clambering on his undulant floor.

Unpredictable dear, the taxi drivers' terror,
Shrinking from far headlights pale as a dime   10
Yet leaping before red apoplectic streetcars—
Misfit in any space. And never on time.

A wrench in clocks and the solar system. Only
With words and people and love you move at ease.
In traffic of wit expertly manoeuvre   15
And keep us, all devotion, at your knees.

yet clumsy in the eyes of love

Forgetting your coffee spreading on our flannel,
Your lipstick grinning on our coat,
So gayly in love's unbreakable heaven
Our souls on glory of spilt bourbon float.   20

Be with me, darling, early and late. Smash glasses—
I will study wry music for your sake.
For should your hands drop white and empty
All the toys of the world would break.

if you die joy gone

John Frederick Nims (b. 1914)

QUESTIONS

1. Overstatement is the traditional language of love poetry. Point out examples
   here. How does this poem differ from traditional love poems?
2. What is the meaning of the last two lines?

INCIDENT

Once riding in old Baltimore
   Heart-filled, head-filled with glee,
I saw a Baltimorean
   Keep looking straight at me.

Now I was eight and very small,   5
   And he was no whit bigger,
And so I smiled, but he poked out
   His tongue, and called me, "Nigger."

I saw the whole of Baltimore
    From May until December;   10
Of all the things that happened there
    That's all that I remember.

Countee Cullen (1903–1946)

QUESTION

What accounts for the effectiveness of the last stanza? Comment on the title. Is it in key with the meaning of the poem?

FORMAL APPLICATION

"The poets apparently want to rejoin the human race." TIME

I shall begin by learning to throw
the knife, first at trees, until it sticks
in the trunk and quivers every time;

next from a chair, using only wrist
and fingers, at a thing on the ground,   5
a fresh ant hill or a fallen leaf;

then at a moving object, perhaps
a pieplate swinging on twine, until
I pot it at least twice in three tries.

Meanwhile, I shall be teaching the birds   10
that the skinny fellow in sneakers
is a source of suet and bread crumbs,

first putting them on a shingle nailed
to a pine tree, next scattering them
on the needles, closer and closer   15

to my seat, until the proper bird,
a towhee, I think, in black and rust
and gray, takes tossed crumbs six feet away.

Finally, I shall coordinate
conditioned reflex and functional   20
form and qualify as Modern Man.

You see the splash of blood and feathers
and the blade pinning it to the tree?
It's called an "Audubon Crucifix."

The phrase has pleasing (even pious)   25
connotations, like *Arbeit Macht Frei,*
"Molotov Cocktail," and *Enola Gay.*

Donald W. Baker (b. 1923)

QUESTIONS

1. This poem has an epigraph: a quotation following the title which relates to
   the theme of the poem or provides the stimulus which gave rise to its writing.
   How is this poem related to its epigraph? Who is the speaker?
2. What meanings has the title?
3. *Arbeit Macht Frei* (26) ("Labor liberates") was the slogan of the German Nazi
   Party. "Molotov Cocktail" (27), a homemade hand grenade named after Sta-
   lin's foreign minister, was widely used during the Spanish Civil War and
   World War II. *Enola Gay* (27) was the American plane that dropped the first
   atom bomb on Hiroshima. In what ways are the connotations of these
   phrases—and of "Audubon Crucifix" (24)—"pleasing" (25)?
4. What different kinds of irony operate in this poem? Discuss.

THE UNKNOWN CITIZEN

doesn't ever have a name

(To JS/07/M/378 This Marble Monument Is Erected by the State)

He was found by the Bureau of Statistics to be
One against whom there was no official complaint,
And all the reports on his conduct agree
That, in the modern sense of an old-fashioned word, he was a saint,
For in everything he did he served the Greater Community.   5
Except for the War till the day he retired
He worked in a factory and never got fired,
But satisfied his employers, Fudge Motors Inc.
Yet he wasn't a scab or odd in his views,
For his Union reports that he paid his dues,   10
(Our report on his Union shows it was sound)
And our Social Psychology workers found
That he was popular with his mates and liked a drink.
The Press are convinced that he bought a paper every day
And that his reactions to advertisements were normal in every way. 15
Policies taken out in his name prove that he was fully insured,
And his Health-card shows he was once in hospital but left it cured.
Both Producers Research and High-Grade Living declare
He was fully sensible to the advantages of the Installment Plan
And had everything necessary to the Modern Man,   20
A phonograph, a radio, a car and a frigidaire.

Our researchers into Public Opinion are content
That he held the proper opinions for the time of year;
When there was peace, he was for peace; when there was war, he went.
He was married and added five children to the population, 25
Which our Eugenist says was the right number for a parent of his generation,
And our teachers report that he never interfered with their education.
Was he free? Was he happy? The question is absurd:
Had anything been wrong, we should certainly have heard.

                                        W. H. Auden (1907–1973)

QUESTIONS

1. Vocabulary: *scab* (9), *Eugenist* (26).
2. Explain the allusion and the irony in the title. Why was the citizen "unknown"?
3. This obituary of an unknown state "hero" was apparently prepared by a functionary of the state. Give an account of the citizen's life and character from Auden's own point of view.
4. What trends in modern life and social organization does the poem satirize?

DEPARTMENTAL

An ant on the tablecloth
Ran into a dormant moth
Of many times his size.
He showed not the least surprise.
His business wasn't with such. 5
He gave it scarcely a touch,
And was off on his duty run.
Yet if he encountered one
Of the hive's enquiry squad
Whose work is to find out God 10
And the nature of time and space,
He would put him onto the case.
Ants are a curious race;
One crossing with hurried tread
The body of one of their dead 15
Isn't given a moment's arrest—
Seems not even impressed.
But he no doubt reports to any
With whom he crosses antennae,
And they no doubt report 20
To the higher up at court.

Then word goes forth in Formic:
"Death's come to Jerry McCormic,
Our selfless forager Jerry.
Will the special Janizary   25
Whose office it is to bury
The dead of the commissary
Go bring him home to his people.
Lay him in state on a sepal.
Wrap him for shroud in a petal.   30
Embalm him with ichor of nettle.
This is the word of your Queen."
And presently on the scene
Appears a solemn mortician;
And taking formal position   35
With feelers calmly atwiddle,
Seizes the dead by the middle,
And heaving him high in air,
Carries him out of there.
No one stands round to stare.   40
It is nobody else's affair.

It couldn't be called ungentle.
But how thoroughly departmental.

Robert Frost (1874-1963)

QUESTIONS

1. Vocabulary: *dormant* (2), *Formic* (22), *Janizary* (25), *commissary* (27), *sepal* (29), *ichor* (31).
2. The poem is ostensibly about ants. Is it ultimately about ants? Give reasons to support your view that it is or is not.
3. What is the author's attitude toward the "departmental" organization of ant society? How is it indicated? Could this poem be described as "gently satiric"? If so, in what sense?
4. Compare and contrast this poem with "The Unknown Citizen" in content and manner.

MR. Z

Taught early that his mother's skin was the sign of error,
He dressed and spoke the perfect part of honor;
Won scholarships, attended the best schools,
Disclaimed kinship with jazz and spirituals;
Chose prudent, raceless views for each situation,   5

Or when he could not cleanly skirt dissension,
Faced up to the dilemma, firmly seized
Whatever ground was Anglo-Saxonized.

In diet, too, his practice was exemplary:
Of pork in its profane forms he was wary;   10
Expert in vintage wines, sauces and salads,
His palate shrank from cornbread, yams and collards.

He was as careful whom he chose to kiss:
His bride had somewhere lost her Jewishness,
But kept her blue eyes; an Episcopalian   15
Prelate proclaimed them matched chameleon.
Choosing the right addresses, here, abroad,
They shunned those places where they might be barred;
Even less anxious to be asked to dine
Where hosts catered to kosher accent or exotic skin.   ·   20

And so he climbed, unclogged by ethnic weights,
An airborne plant, flourishing without roots.
Not one false note was struck—until he died:
His subtly grieving widow could have flayed
The obit writers, ringing crude changes on a clumsy phrase: 25
"One of the most distinguished members of his race."

                                        M. Carl Holman (b. 1919)

QUESTIONS

1. Vocabulary: *profane* (10), *kosher* (20), *exotic* (20), *ethnic* (21), *obit* (25).
2. Explain Mr. Z's motivation and the strategies he used to achieve his goal.
3. What is the author's attitude toward Mr. Z? Is he satirizing him or the society that produced him? Why does he not give Mr. Z a name?
4. What judgments on Mr. Z are implied by the metaphors in lines 16 and 22? Explain them.
5. What kind of irony is operating in the last line? As you reread the poem, where else do you detect ironic overtones?
6. What is Mr. Z's color?

MY LAST DUCHESS

FERRARA

That's my last duchess painted on the wall,
Looking as if she were alive. I call
That piece a wonder, now; Fra Pandolf's hands
Worked busily a day, and there she stands.

Will't please you sit and look at her? I said   5
"Fra Pandolf" by design, for never read
Strangers like you that pictured countenance,
The depth and passion of its earnest glance,
But to myself they turned (since none puts by
The curtain I have drawn for you, but I)   10
And seemed as they would ask me, if they durst,
How such a glance came there; so, not the first
Are you to turn and ask thus. Sir, 'twas not
Her husband's presence only, called that spot
Of joy into the Duchess' cheek; perhaps   15
Fra Pandolf chanced to say, "Her mantle laps
Over my lady's wrist too much," or, "Paint
Must never hope to reproduce the faint
Half-flush that dies along her throat." Such stuff
Was courtesy, she thought, and cause enough   20
For calling up that spot of joy. She had
A heart—how shall I say?—too soon made glad,
Too easily impressed; she liked whate'er
She looked on, and her looks went everywhere.
Sir, 'twas all one! My favor at her breast,   25
The dropping of the daylight in the West,
The bough of cherries some officious fool
Broke in the orchard for her, the white mule
She rode with round the terrace—all and each
Would draw from her alike the approving speech,   30
Or blush, at least. She thanked men—good! but thanked
Somehow—I know not how—as if she ranked
My gift of a nine-hundred-years-old name   *[condescending]*
With anybody's gift. Who'd stoop to blame   *[attitude]*   35
This sort of trifling? Even had you skill
In speech—which I have not—to make your will
Quite clear to such an one, and say, "Just this
Or that in you disgusts me; here you miss,
Or there exceed the mark"—and if she let
Herself be lessoned so, nor plainly set   *[she had been   40
Her wits to yours, forsooth, and made excuse—   unfaithful]*
E'en then would be some stooping; and I choose
Never to stoop. Oh, sir, she smiled, no doubt,
Whene'er I passed her; but who passed without
Much the same smile? This grew; I gave commands;   45
Then all smiles stopped together. There she stands
As if alive. Will 't please you rise? We'll meet
The company below, then. I repeat,
The Count your master's known munificence

*[she has lose
nothing to
of drags him (cuss)
down
he his nose]*

Is ample warrant that no just pretense   50
Of mine for dowry will be disallowed;
Though his fair daughter's self, as I avowed
At starting, is my object. Nay, we'll go
Together down, sir. Notice Neptune, though,
Taming a sea-horse, thought a rarity,   55
Which Claus of Innsbruck cast in bronze for me!

Robert Browning (*1812–1889*)

QUESTIONS

1. Vocabulary: *officious* (27), *munificence* (49).
2. Ferrara is in Italy. The time is during the Renaissance, probably the sixteenth century. To whom is the Duke speaking? What is the occasion? Are the Duke's remarks about his last Duchess a digression, or do they have some relation to the business at hand?
3. Characterize the Duke as fully as you can. How does your characterization differ from the Duke's opinion of himself? What kind of irony is this?
4. Why was the Duke dissatisfied with his last Duchess? Was it sexual jealousy? What opinion do you get of the Duchess's personality, and how does it differ from the Duke's opinion?
5. What characteristics of the Italian Renaissance appear in the poem (marriage customs, social classes, art)? What is the Duke's attitude toward art? Is it insincere?
6. What happened to the Duchess? Should we have been told?

EARTH

"A planet doesn't explode of itself," said drily
The Martian astronomer, gazing off into the air—
"That they were able to do it is proof that highly
Intelligent beings must have been living there."

John Hall Wheelock (*1886–1978*)

8. Allusion

The famous English diplomat and letter writer Lord Chesterfield was once invited to a great dinner given by the Spanish ambassador. At the conclusion of the meal the host rose and proposed a toast to his master, the king of Spain, whom he compared to the sun. The French ambassador followed with a health to the king of France, whom he likened to the moon. It was then Lord Chesterfield's turn. "Your excellencies have taken from me," he said, "all the greatest luminaries of heaven, and the stars are too small for me to make a comparison of my royal master; I therefore beg leave to give your excellencies—Joshua!"*

For a reader familiar with the Bible—that is, for one who recognizes the Biblical allusion—Lord Chesterfield's story will come as a stunning revelation of his wit. For an ALLUSION—a reference to something in history or previous literature—is, like a richly connotative word or a symbol, a means of suggesting far more than it says. The one word "Joshua," in the context of Chesterfield's toast, calls up in the reader's mind the whole Biblical story of how the Israelite captain stopped the sun and the moon in order that the Israelites might finish a battle and conquer their enemies before nightfall.† The force of the toast lies in its extreme economy; it says so much in so little, and it exercises the mind of the reader to make the connection for himself.

---

*Samuel Shellabarger, *Lord Chesterfield and His World* (Boston: Little, Brown, 1951), p. 132.

† Joshua 10:12–14.

The effect of Chesterfield's allusion is chiefly humorous or witty, but allusions may also have a powerful emotional effect. The essayist William Hazlitt writes of addressing a fashionable audience about the lexicographer Samuel Johnson. Speaking of Johnson's great heart and of his charity to the unfortunate, Hazlitt recounted how, finding a drunken prostitute lying in Fleet Street late at night, Johnson carried her on his broad back to the address she managed to give him. The audience, unable to face the picture of the famous dictionary-maker doing such a thing, broke out in titters and expostulations. Whereupon Hazlitt simply said: "I remind you, ladies and gentlemen, of the parable of the Good Samaritan." The audience was promptly silenced.*

Allusions are a means of reinforcing the emotion or the ideas of one's own work with the emotion or ideas of another work or occasion. Because they are capable of saying so much in so little, they are extremely useful to the poet.

"OUT, OUT—"

The buzz-saw snarled and rattled in the yard
And made dust and dropped stove-length sticks of wood,
Sweet-scented stuff when the breeze drew across it.
And from there those that lifted eyes could count
Five mountain ranges one behind the other   5
Under the sunset far into Vermont.
And the saw snarled and rattled, snarled and rattled,
As it ran light, or had to bear a load.
And nothing happened: day was all but done.
Call it a day, I wish they might have said   10
To please the boy by giving him the half hour
That a boy counts so much when saved from work.
His sister stood beside them in her apron
To tell them "Supper." At the word, the saw,
As if to prove saws knew what supper meant,   15
Leaped out at the boy's hand, or seemed to leap—
He must have given the hand. However it was,
Neither refused the meeting. But the hand!
The boy's first outcry was a rueful laugh,
As he swung toward them holding up the hand   20
Half in appeal, but half as if to keep
The life from spilling. Then the boy saw all—

Not going blindly in the accident.

*Jacques Barzun, *Teacher in America* (Boston: Little, Brown, 1945), p. 160.

This is the way life going to be.

Since he was old enough to know, big boy
Doing a man's work, though a child at heart—
He saw all spoiled. "Don't let him cut my hand off—   25
The doctor, when he comes. Don't let him, sister!"
So. But the hand was gone already.
The doctor put him in the dark of ether.
He lay and puffed his lips out with his breath.
And then—the watcher at his pulse took fright.   30
No one believed. They listened at his heart.
Little—less—nothing!—and that ended it.
No more to build on there. And they, since they
Were not the one dead, turned to their affairs.

Robert Frost (1874–1963)

QUESTIONS

1. How does this poem differ from a newspaper account that might have dealt with the same incident?
2. To whom does "they" (33) refer? The boy's family? The doctor and hospital attendants? Casual onlookers? Need we assume that all these people—whoever they are—turned immediately "to their affairs"? Does the ending of this poem seem to you callous or merely realistic? Would a more tearful and sentimental ending have made the poem better or worse?
3. What figure of speech is used in lines 21–22?

   Allusions vary widely in the burden put on them by the poet to convey his meaning. Lord Chesterfield risked his whole meaning on his hearers' recognizing his allusion. Robert Frost in "Out, Out—" makes his meaning entirely clear even for the reader who does not recognize the allusion contained in his title. His theme is the uncertainty and unpredictability of life, which may be accidentally ended at any moment, and the tragic waste of human potentiality which takes place when such premature deaths occur. A boy who is already "doing a man's work" and gives every promise of having a useful life ahead of him is suddenly wiped out. There seems no rational explanation for either the accident or the death. The only comment to be made is, "No more to build on there."
   Frost's title, however, is an allusion to one of the most famous passages in all English literature, and it offers a good illustration of how a poet may use allusion not only to reinforce emotion but also to help define his theme. The passage is that in *Macbeth* in which Macbeth has just been informed of his wife's death. A good many readers will recall the key phrase, "Out, out, brief candle!" with its underscoring of the

tragic brevity and uncertainty of life that can be snuffed out at any moment. For some readers, however, the allusion will summon up the whole passage in act V, scene 5, in which this phrase occurs. Macbeth's words are:

> She should have died hereafter;
> There would have been a time for such a word.
> To-morrow, and to-morrow, and to-morrow
> Creeps in this petty pace from day to day
> To the last syllable of recorded time;   5
> And all our yesterdays have lighted fools
> The way to dusty death. Out, out, brief candle!
> Life's but a walking shadow, a poor player,
> That struts and frets his hour upon the stage
> And then is heard no more. It is a tale   10
> Told by an idiot, full of sound and fury,
> Signifying nothing.

Macbeth's first words underscore the theme of premature death. The boy also "should have died hereafter." The rest of the passage, with its marvelous evocation of the vanity and meaninglessness of life, expresses neither Shakespeare's philosophy nor, ultimately, Frost's, but it is Macbeth's philosophy at the time of his bereavement, and it is likely to express the feelings of us all when such tragic accidents occur. Life does indeed seem cruel and meaningless, a tale told by an idiot, signifying nothing, when human life and potentiality are thus without explanation so suddenly ended.

Allusions vary widely in the number of readers to whom they will be familiar. The poet, in using an allusion as in using a figure of speech, is always in danger of not being understood. In appealing powerfully to one reader, he may lose another reader altogether. But the poet must assume a certain fund of common experience with his readers. He could not even write about the ocean unless he could assume that his readers had seen the ocean or pictures of it. In the same way he will assume a certain common fund of literary experience. He is often justified in expecting a rather wide range of literary experience in his readers, for the people who read poetry for pleasure are generally people of good minds and good education who have read widely. But, obviously, beginning readers will not have this range, just as they will not know the meanings of as many words as will maturer readers. Students ought therefore to be prepared to look up certain allusions, just as they should be eager to look up in their dictionaries the meanings of unfamiliar words. They will find that every increase in knowledge broadens their base for understanding both literature and life.

IN JUST-

                in Just-
                spring   when the world is mud-
                luscious the little
                lame balloonman

                whistles   far   and wee   5

                and eddieandbill come
                running from marbles and
                piracies and it's
                spring

                when the world is puddle-wonderful   10

                the queer
                old balloonman whistles
                far   and   wee
                and bettyandisbel come dancing

                from hop-scotch and jump-rope and   15

                it's
                spring
                and
                    the

                        goat-footed   20

                balloonMan   whistles
                far
                and
                wee

                                    e. e. cummings (*1894–1962*)

QUESTION

Why is the balloonman called "goat-footed"? How does the identification made
by this mythological allusion enrich the meaning of the poem?

ON HIS BLINDNESS

            When I consider how my light is spent
                Ere half my days in this dark world and wide,
                And that one talent which is death to hide
                Lodged with me useless, though my soul more bent

To serve therewith my Maker, and present   5
  My true account, lest he returning chide,
  "Doth God exact day-labor, light denied?"
  I fondly ask. But Patience, to prevent
That murmur, soon replies, "God doth not need
  Either man's work or his own gifts. Who best   10
  Bear his mild yoke, they serve him best. His state
Is kingly: thousands at his bidding speed,
  And post o'er land and ocean without rest;
  They also serve who only stand and wait."

John Milton (1608–1674)

QUESTIONS

1. Vocabulary: *spent* (1), *fondly* (8), *prevent* (8), *post* (13).
2. What two meanings has "talent" (3)? What is Milton's "one talent"?
3. The poem is unified and expanded in its dimensions by a Biblical allusion that Milton's original readers would have recognized immediately. What is it? If you do not know, look up Matthew 25:14–30. In what ways is the situation in the poem similar to that in the parable? In what ways is it different?
4. What is the point of the poem?

GOD IS A DISTANT, STATELY LOVER

  God is a distant, stately lover—
  Woos, as he states us, by his son:
  Verily, a vicarious courtship—
  Miles and Priscilla were such an one,

  But lest the soul, like fair Priscilla,
  Choose the envoy and spurn the groom,
  Vouches, with hyperbolic archness,
  Miles and John Alden were synonym.

Emily Dickinson (1830–1886)

QUESTIONS

1. Vocabulary: *vicarious* (3), *hyperbolic* (7), *archness* (7).
2. In Longfellow's long narrative poem *The Courtship of Miles Standish*—once familiar to every American school child—the widower Miles Standish, Captain of the Plymouth Colony, determines to marry the virtuous Puritan maiden Priscilla. A blunt old soldier with no gift for words, he requests his literate young friend John Alden to make the proposal for him, not knowing John loves her too. Faithful to friendship, but torn by his own love, John makes the proposal and is answered by Priscilla, "Why don't you speak for

yourself, John?" Eventually the two young persons marry. How, in Dickinson's poem, is God like Miles Standish? Who is His "John Alden"? Who is the "Priscilla" whom He woos? How does He insure himself against the kind of defeat Miles Standish suffered?

3. What is Dickinson satirizing in this poem?

AUNT JANE

Aunt Jane, of whom I dreamed the nights it thundered,
was dead at ninety, buried at a hundred.
We kept her corpse a decade, hid upstairs,
where it ate porridge, slept and said its prayers.

And every night before I went to bed
they took me in to worship with the dead.
Christ Lord, if I should die before I wake,
I pray thee Lord my body take.

Alden Nowlan (b. 1933)

want to keep dead
she thinks it
better not to

QUESTION

Resolve the paradox and explain the allusion.

ON THE IDLE HILL OF SUMMER

On the idle hill of summer,
    Sleepy with the flow of streams,
Far I hear the steady drummer
    Drumming like a noise in dreams.

Far and near and low and louder   5
    On the roads of earth go by,
Dear to friends and food for powder,
    Soldiers marching, all to die.

East and west on fields forgotten
    Bleach the bones of comrades slain,   10
Lovely lads and dead and rotten;
    None that go return again.

Far the calling bugles hollo,
    High the screaming fife replies,
Gay the files of scarlet follow: 15
    Woman bore me, I will rise.

A. E. Housman (1859–1936)

women brave?

1. What effect does the sound of the drums, bugles, fifes, and marching soldiers have on the speaker? Is it a single or a mixed effect? Describe it as precisely as possible.
2. What syntactical qualities of the poem combine to put heavy emphasis on the two clauses in the last line? What relevance has the first to the second? (For help, see Job 14:1 and ff.) What does the speaker resolve to do in the last line? In what spirit?
3. "Scarlet" (14) refers to the bright red coats of British army dress uniforms. What figures of speech are involved in this and in "food for powder" (7)?

LEDA AND THE SWAN

A sudden blow: the great wings beating still
Above the staggering girl, her thighs caressed
By the dark webs, her nape caught in his bill,
He holds her helpless breast upon his breast.

How can those terrified vague fingers push   5
The feathered glory from her loosening thighs?
And how can body, laid in that white rush,
But feel the strange heart beating where it lies?

A shudder in the loins engenders there
The broken wall, the burning roof and tower   10
And Agamemnon dead.
                              Being so caught up,
So mastered by the brute blood of the air,
Did she put on his knowledge with his power
Before the indifferent beak could let her drop?

William Butler Yeats (1865–1939)

QUESTIONS

1. What is the connection between Leda and "the broken wall, the burning roof and tower / And Agamemnon dead"? If you do not know, look up the myth of Leda, and, if necessary, the story of Agamemnon.
2. What is the significance of the question asked in the last two lines?

VETERAN SIRENS

The ghost of Ninon would be sorry now
To laugh at them, were she to see them here,

So brave and so alert for learning how
To fence with reason for another year.

Age offers a far comelier diadem   5
Than theirs; but anguish has no eye for grace,
When time's malicious mercy cautions them
To think a while of number and of space.

The burning hope, the worn expectancy,
The martyred humor, and the maimed allure,   10
Cry out for time to end his levity,
And age to soften its investiture;

But they, though others fade and are still fair,
Defy their fairness and are unsubdued;
Although they suffer, they may not forswear   15
The patient ardor of the unpursued.

Poor flesh, to fight the calendar so long;
Poor vanity, so quaint and yet so brave;
Poor folly, so deceived and yet so strong,
So far from Ninon and so near the grave.   20

Edwin Arlington Robinson (1869-1935)

QUESTIONS

1. The poem is based on two allusions, one historical and one mythological. Ninon de Lenclos (1620-1705), mistress of a *salon* in Paris which attracted the most celebrated political and literary figures of her time, is famous for having retained her beauty and charm to an advanced age, and is said to have had lovers until she was seventy. If you do not recognize the allusion in the title, look up "siren" in your dictionary. In what respect is the title ironical?
2. Who are the "veteran sirens" in the poem? How old do you imagine them to be? What do they hope for? How do they "fence with reason" (4)? What is the "far comelier diadem / Than theirs" (5-6) offered them by age? What is the central irony of the poem?
3. Explain the metonymies involved in the words "anguish" (6), "number and space" (8), "flesh" (17), "calendar" (17), "vanity" (18), "folly" (19), "Ninon" (20), "grave" (20). Explain the effectiveness of the phrases "malicious mercy" (7), "worn expectancy" (9), "martyred humor" (10), "maimed allure" (10), "patient ardor of the unpursued" (16).
4. What is the poet's attitude toward the "veteran sirens"?

JOURNEY OF THE MAGI

"A cold coming we had of it,
Just the worst time of the year

For a journey, and such a long journey:
The ways deep and the weather sharp,
The very dead of winter."   5
And the camels galled, sore-footed, refractory,
Lying down in the melting snow.
There were times we regretted
The summer palaces on slopes, the terraces,
And the silken girls bringing sherbet.   10
Then the camel men cursing and grumbling
And running away, and wanting their liquor and women,
And the night-fires going out, and the lack of shelters,
And the cities hostile and the towns unfriendly
And the villages dirty and charging high prices: 15
A hard time we had of it.
At the end we preferred to travel all night,
Sleeping in snatches,
With the voices singing in our ears, saying
That this was all folly.   20

    Then at dawn we came down to a temperate valley,
Wet, below the snow line, smelling of vegetation;
With a running stream and a water-mill beating the darkness,
And three trees on the low sky,
And an old white horse galloped away in the meadow.   25
Then we came to a tavern with vine-leaves over the lintel,
Six hands at an open door dicing for pieces of silver,
And feet kicking the empty wine-skins.
But there was no information, and so we continued
And arrived at evening, not a moment too soon   30
Finding the place; it was (you may say) satisfactory.

    All this was a long time ago, I remember,
And I would do it again, but set down
This set down
This: were we led all that way for   35
Birth or Death? There was a Birth, certainly,
We had evidence and no doubt. I had seen birth and death,
But had thought they were different; this Birth was
Hard and bitter agony for us, like Death, our death.
We returned to our places, these Kingdoms,   40
But no longer at ease here, in the old dispensation,
With an alien people clutching their gods.
I should be glad of another death.

T. S. Eliot (1888-1965)

1. The Biblical account of the journey of the Magi, or wise men, to Bethlehem is given in Matthew 2:1-12 and has since been elaborated by numerous legendary accretions. It has been made familiar through countless pageants and Christmas cards. How does this account differ from the familiar one? Compare it with the Biblical account. What has been added? What has been left out? What is the poet doing? (Lines 1–5 are in quotation marks because they are taken, with very slight modification, from a Christmas sermon [1622] by the Anglican bishop Lancelot Andrewes.)
2. Who is the speaker? Where and when is he speaking? What is the "old dispensation" (41) to which he refers, and why are the people "alien" (42)? Why does he speak of the "Birth" as being "like Death" (39)? Of whose "Birth" and "Death" is he speaking? How does his life differ from the life he lived before his journey? What does he mean by saying that he would be "glad of another death" (43)?
3. This poem was written while the poet was undergoing religious conversion. (Eliot published it in 1927, the year he was confirmed in the Anglican Church.) Could the poem be considered a parable of the conversion experience? If so, how does this account differ from popular conceptions of this experience?
4. How do the images in the second section differ from those of the first? Do any of them suggest connections with the life of Christ?

IN THE GARDEN

In the garden there strayed
A beautiful maid
As fair as the flowers of the morn;
The first hour of her life
She was made a man's wife,
And was buried before she was born.

Anonymous

QUESTION

Resolve the paradox by identifying the allusion.

9. Meaning and Idea

Little Jack Horner
Sat in a corner
Eating a Christmas pie.
He stuck in his thumb
And pulled out a plum
And said, "What a good boy am I!"

Anonymous

The meaning of a poem is the experience it expresses—nothing less. But the reader who, baffled by a particular poem, asks perplexedly, "What does it *mean?*" is usually after something more specific than this. He wants something that he can grasp entirely with his mind. We may therefore find it useful to make a distinction between the TOTAL MEANING of a poem—the experience it communicates (and which can be communicated in no other way)—and its PROSE MEANING—the ingredient that can be separated out in the form of a prose paraphrase. If we make this distinction, however, we must be careful not to confuse the two kinds of meaning. The prose meaning is no more the poem than a plum is a pie or than a prune is a plum.

The prose meaning will not necessarily or perhaps even usually be an idea. It may be a story, it may be a description, it may be a statement of emotion, it may be a presentation of human character, or it may be some combination of these. "O what is that sound" (page 28) tells a story; "The Eagle" (page 5) is primarily descriptive; "A Red, Red Rose" (page 97) is an expression of emotion; "My Last Duchess" (page 112) is an account of human character. None of these poems is directly concerned with ideas. The message-hunter will be baffled and disappointed by poetry of this kind, for he will not find what he is looking for, and he may attempt to read some idea into the poem that is really not there. Yet ideas are also part of human experience, and therefore many poems are concerned, at least partially, with presenting ideas. But with these poems message-hunting is an even more dangerous activity. For the message-hunter is likely to think that the whole object of reading the poem is to find the message—that the idea is really the only important thing in it. Like Little Jack Horner, he will reach in and pluck it out and say, "What a good boy am I!" as if the pie existed for the plum.

The idea in a poem is only part of the total experience it communicates. The value and worth of the poem are determined by the value of the total experience, not by the truth or the nobility of the idea itself. This is not to say that the truth of the idea is unimportant, or that its validity should not be examined and appraised. But a good idea will not make a good poem, nor need an idea with which the reader does not agree ruin one. The good reader of poetry will be a reader receptive to all kinds of experience. He will be able to make that "willing suspension of disbelief" that Coleridge characterized as constituting poetic faith. When one attends a performance of *Hamlet*, one is willing to forget for the time being that such a person as Hamlet never existed and that the events on the stage are fictions. The reader of poetry should also be willing to enter imaginatively, for the time being, into ideas he objectively regards as untrue. It is one way of understanding these ideas better and of enlarging the reader's own experience. The believer in God should be able to enjoy a good poem expressing atheistic ideas, and the atheist a good poem in praise of God. The optimist by temperament should be able to find pleasure in pessimistic poetry, and the pessimist in optimistic poetry. The teetotaler should be able to enjoy "The Rubáiyát of Omar Khayyám," and the winebibber a good poem in praise of austerity. The primary value of a poem depends not so much on the truth of the idea presented as on the power with which it is communicated and on its being made a convincing part of a meaningful total experience. We must feel that the idea has been truly and deeply *felt* by the poet and that he is doing something more than merely moralizing. The plum must be made part of a pie. If the plum is properly combined with other ingredients and if the pie is well baked, it should be enjoyable even for persons who do not care for the brand of plums it is made of. Let us consider, for instance, the following two poems.

BARTER

Life has loveliness to sell,
    All beautiful and splendid things,
Blue waves whitened on a cliff,
    Soaring fire that sways and sings,

And children's faces looking up,   5
Holding wonder like a cup.

Life has loveliness to sell,
    Music like a curve of gold,
Scent of pine trees in the rain,
    Eyes that love you, arms that hold,   10
And for your spirit's still delight,
Holy thoughts that star the night.

Spend all you have for loveliness,
    Buy it and never count the cost;
For one white singing hour of peace   15
    Count many a year of strife well lost,
And for a breath of ecstasy
Give all you have been, or could be.

Sara Teasdale (*1884-1933*)

STOPPING BY WOODS ON A SNOWY EVENING

Whose woods these are I think I know.
His house is in the village though;
He will not see me stopping here
To watch his woods fill up with snow.

My little horse must think it queer   5
To stop without a farmhouse near
Between the woods and frozen lake
The darkest evening of the year.

He gives his harness bells a shake
To ask if there is some mistake.   10
The only other sound's the sweep
Of easy wind and downy flake.

The woods are lovely, dark and deep,
But I have promises to keep,
And miles to go before I sleep,   15
And miles to go before I sleep.

Robert Frost (*1874-1963*)

QUESTIONS

1. How do these two poems differ in idea?
2. What contrasts are suggested between the speaker in the second poem and
   (a) his horse and (b) the owner of the woods?

Both of these poems present ideas, the first more or less explicitly, the second symbolically. Perhaps the best way to get at the idea of the second poem is to ask two questions. First, why does the speaker stop? Second, why does he go on? He stops, we answer, to watch the woods fill up with snow—to observe a scene of natural beauty. He goes on, we answer, because he has "promises" to keep, that is, he has obligations to fulfill. He is momentarily torn between his love of beauty and these other various and complex claims that life has upon him. The small conflict in the poem is symbolical of a larger conflict in life. One part of the sensitive thinking person would like to give up his life to the enjoyment of beauty and art. But another part is aware of larger duties and responsibilities—responsibilities owed, at least in part, to other human beings. The speaker in the poem would like to satisfy both impulses. But when the two come into conflict, he seems to suggest, the "promises" must be given precedence.

The first poem also presents a philosophy but an opposed one. For this poet, beauty is of such supreme value that any conflicting demand should be sacrificed to it. "Spend all you have for loveliness, / Buy it and never count the cost . . . And for a breath of ecstasy / Give all you have been, or could be." The reader, if he is a thinking person, will have to choose between these two philosophies—to commit himself to one or the other—but this commitment should not destroy for him his enjoyment of either poem. If it does, he is reading for plums and not for pies.

Nothing so far said in this chapter should be construed as meaning that the truth or falsity of the idea in a poem is a matter of no importance. *Other things being equal,* the good reader naturally will, and properly should, value more highly the poem whose idea he feels to be maturer and nearer to the heart of human experience. There may be some ideas, moreover, that he feels to be so vicious or so foolish or so beyond the pale of normal human decency as to discredit *by themselves* the poems in which he finds them. A rotten plum may spoil a pie. But a good reader will strive for intellectual flexibility and tolerance, and be able to entertain sympathetically ideas other than his own. He will often like a poem whose idea he disagrees with better than one with an idea he accepts. And, above all, he will not confuse the prose meaning of any poem with its total meaning. He will not mistake plums for pies.

*   *   *

SONG

The year's at the spring,
And day's at the morn;
Morning's at seven;

The hillside's dew-pearled;
The lark's on the wing;
The snail's on the thorn;
God's in his heaven—
All's right with the world!

Robert Browning (1812–1889)

DIRGE

Rough wind, that moanest loud
Grief too sad for song;
Wild wind, when sullen cloud
Knells all the night long;
Sad storm, whose tears are vain,
Bare woods, whose branches strain,
Deep caves and dreary main,—
Wail, for the world's wrong!

Percy Bysshe Shelley (1792–1822)

QUESTIONS

1. In what ways are these two poems alike? In what ways are they different?
2. How would you evaluate the two comments made on the world? Is it possible to justify both? Should you be surprised to learn that the first poet was a tremendous admirer of the second poet?

TO A WATERFOWL

Whither, midst falling dew,
While glow the heavens with the last steps of day,
Far, through their rosy depths, dost thou pursue
Thy solitary way?

Vainly the fowler's eye   5
Might mark thy distant flight to do thee wrong,
As, darkly seen against the crimson sky,
Thy figure floats along.

Seek'st thou the plashy brink
Of weedy lake, or marge of river wide,   10
Or where the rocking billows rise and sink
On the chafed ocean side?

There is a Power whose care
Teaches thy way along that pathless coast—

The desert and illimitable air—   15
    Lone wandering, but not lost.

All day thy wings have fanned,
At that far height, the cold, thin atmosphere,
Yet stoop not, weary, to the welcome land,
    Though the dark night is near.   20

And soon that toil shall end;
Soon shalt thou find a summer home, and rest,
And scream among thy fellows; reeds shall bend,
    Soon, o'er thy sheltered nest.

Thou'rt gone, the abyss of heaven   25
Hath swallowed up thy form; yet, on my heart
Deeply has sunk the lesson thou hast given,
    And shall not soon depart.

He who, from zone to zone,
Guides through the boundless sky thy certain flight,   30
In the long way that I must tread alone,
    Will lead my steps aright.

William Cullen Bryant (1794–1878)

QUESTIONS

1. Vocabulary: *fowler* (5), *desert* (15), *stoop* (19).
2. What figure of speech unifies the poem?
3. Where is the waterfowl flying? Why? What is "that pathless coast" (14)?
4. What "Power" (13) "guides" (30) the waterfowl to its destination? How does
   it do so?
5. What lesson does the poet derive from his observations?

DESIGN

I found a dimpled spider, fat and white,
On a white heal-all, holding up a moth
Like a white piece of rigid satin cloth—
Assorted characters of death and blight
Mixed ready to begin the morning right,   5
Like the ingredients of a witches' broth—
A snow-drop spider, a flower like a froth,
And dead wings carried like a paper kite.

What had that flower to do with being white,
The wayside blue and innocent heal-all?   10

What brought the kindred spider to that height,
Then steered the white moth thither in the night?
What but design of darkness to appall?—
If design govern in a thing so small.

Robert Frost (1874–1963)

QUESTIONS

1. Vocabulary: *characters* (4).
2. The heal-all is a wildflower, usually blue or violet but occasionally white, found blooming along roadsides in the summer. It was once supposed to have healing qualities, hence its name. Of what significance, scientific and poetic, is the fact that the spider, the heal-all, and the moth are all white? Of what poetic significance is the fact that the spider is "dimpled" and "fat" and like a "snow-drop," and that the flower is "innocent" and named "heal-all"?
3. The "argument from design," as it was called, was a favorite eighteenth-century argument for the existence of God. What twist does Frost give the argument? What answer does he suggest to the question in lines 11–13? How comforting is the apparent concession in line 14?
4. Contrast Frost's poem in content and emotional effect with "To a Water-fowl." Is it possible to like both?

WHAT IF A MUCH OF A WHICH OF A WIND

what if a much of a which of a wind
gives the truth to summer's lie;
bloodies with dizzying leaves the sun
and yanks immortal stars awry?
Blow king to beggar and queen to seem   5
(blow friend to fiend:blow space to time)
—when skies are hanged and oceans drowned,
the single secret will still be man

what if a keen of a lean wind flays
screaming hills with sleet and snow: 10
strangles valleys by ropes of thing
and stifles forests in white ago?
Blow hope to terror;blow seeing to blind
(blow pity to envy and soul to mind)
—whose hearts are mountains,roots are trees,   15
it's they shall cry hello to the spring

what if a dawn of a doom of a dream
bites this universe in two,
peels forever out of his grave

and sprinkles nowhere with me and you? 20
Blow soon to never and never to twice
(blow life to isn't:blow death to was)
—all nothing's only our hugest home;
the most who die,the more we live

e. e. cummings (1894–1962)

QUESTIONS

1. What unconventional uses does cummings make of grammar and diction? Can you justify them?
2. All stanzas follow a common syntactical and structural pattern. Describe it.
3. What assertions does the poet make about man in each of the three stanzas?

WHEN SERPENTS BARGAIN FOR THE RIGHT TO SQUIRM

when serpents bargain for the right to squirm
and the sun strikes to gain a living wage—
when thorns regard their roses with alarm
and rainbows are insured against old age

when every thrush may sing no new moon in 5
if all screech-owls have not okayed his voice
—and any wave signs on the dotted line
or else an ocean is compelled to close

when the oak begs permission of the birch
to make an acorn—valleys accuse their 10
mountains of having altitude—and march
denounces april as a saboteur

then we'll believe in that incredible
unanimal mankind(and not until)

e. e. cummings (1894–1962)

QUESTIONS

1. What characteristics do the various activities not engaged in by nature have in common? What qualities of thought and feeling or kinds of behavior ought to replace these activities, in the poet's view?
2. What does the poet imply by calling man an "unanimal" (14)? What is the precise force here of "incredible" (13)?
3. How does the view of man implied in this poem differ from that implied in the preceding poem? Which of the two poems is *satirical* (see page 98)?

THE CAGED SKYLARK

As a dare-gale skylark scanted in a dull cage
   Man's mounting spirit in his bone-house, mean house, dwells—
   That bird beyond the remembering his free fells;
This in drudgery, day-laboring-out life's age.

Though aloft on turf or perch or poor low stage,   5
   Both sing sometimes the sweetest, sweetest spells,
   Yet both droop deadly sometimes in their cells
Or wring their barriers in bursts of fear or rage.

Not that the sweet-fowl, song-fowl, needs no rest—
Why, hear him, hear him babble and drop down to his nest,   10
   But his own nest, wild nest, no prison.

Man's spirit will be flesh-bound when found at best,
But uncumbered: meadow-down is not distressed
   For a rainbow footing it nor he for his bones risen.

                    Gerard Manley Hopkins (*1844–1889*)

QUESTIONS

1. Vocabulary: *scanted* (1), *fells* (3). What meanings of "mean" (2) are appropriate here? "Turf" (5) is a piece of sod placed in a cage.
2. This poem, written by a poet-priest, expresses his belief in the orthodox Roman Catholic doctrine of the resurrection of the body. According to this belief, man's immortal soul, after death, will be ultimately reunited with his body; this body, however, will be a weightless, perfected, glorified body, not the gross imperfect body of mortal life. Express the analogy in the poem as a pair of mathematical statements of proportion (in the form $a:b=c:d$, and $e:f=g:h=i:j$), using the following terms: caged skylark, mortal body, meadow-down, cage, rainbow, spirit-in-life, nest, immortal spirit, wild skylark, resurrected body.
3. Discuss the image of the last two lines as a figure for weightlessness. Why would not a shadow have been equally apt as a rainbow for this comparison?

AUBADE

    I work all day, and get half drunk at night.
    Waking at four to soundless dark, I stare.
    In time the curtain-edges will grow light.
    Till then I see what's really always there:
    Unresting death, a whole day nearer now,   5
    Making all thought impossible but how
    And where and when I shall myself die.
    Arid interrogation: yet the dread

Of dying, and being dead,
Flashes afresh to hold and horrify. 10

The mind blanks at the glare. Not in remorse
—The good not done, the love not given, time
Torn off unused—nor wretchedly because
An only life can take so long to climb
Clear of its wrong beginnings, and may never; 15
But at the total emptiness for ever,
The sure extinction that we travel to
And shall be lost in always. Not to be here,
Not to be anywhere,
And soon; nothing more terrible, nothing more true. 20

This is a special way of being afraid
No trick dispels. Religion used to try,
That vast moth-eaten musical brocade
Created to pretend we never die,
And specious stuff that says *No rational being* 25
Can fear a thing it will not feel, not seeing
That this is what we fear—no sight, no sound,
No touch or taste or smell, nothing to think with,
Nothing to love or link with,
The anaesthetic from which none come round. 30

And so it stays just on the edge of vision,
A small unfocused blur, a standing chill
That slows each impulse down to indecision.
Most things may never happen: this one will,
And realization of it rages out 35
In furnace-fear when we are caught without
People or drink. Courage is no good:
It means not scaring others. Being brave
Lets no one off the grave.
Death is no different whined at than withstood. 40

Slowly light strengthens, and the room takes shape.
It stands plain as a wardrobe, what we know,
Have always known, know that we can't escape,
Yet can't accept. One side will have to go.
Meanwhile telephones crouch, getting ready to ring 45
In locked-up offices, and all the uncaring
Intricate rented world begins to rouse.
The sky is white as clay, with no sun.
Work has to be done.
Postmen like doctors go from house to house. 50

Philip Larkin (b. 1922)

QUESTIONS

1. Vocabulary: *remorse* (11), *specious* (25), *stuff* (25), *anaesthetic* (30).
2. The title of this poem, like that of Richard Wilbur's (page 49), is partially ironical, but the irony arises from a quite different source. What is the irony here?
3. How does the speaker characterize death? Why is 4 A.M. the time when he feels it most intensely?
4. Comment on Larkin's metaphor for religion (23). What are its implications?
5. What is the "specious stuff" characterized by the italicized sentence in lines 25–26?
6. The speaker dismisses courage as a useless remedy for his fear of death (37–40). Is he, then, an utter coward? Does he display *any* kind of courage?
7. Contrast this poem with "The Caged Skylark" in idea and tone. Discuss its merits as a poem.

ARS POETICA

A poem should be palpable and mute
As a globed fruit,

Dumb
As old medallions to the thumb,

Silent as the sleeve-worn stone   5
Of casement ledges where the moss has grown—

A poem should be wordless
As the flight of birds.

                          *

A poem should be motionless in time
As the moon climbs,   10

Leaving, as the moon releases
Twig by twig the night-entangled trees,

Leaving, as the moon behind the winter leaves,
Memory by memory the mind—

A poem should be motionless in time   15
As the moon climbs.

                          *

A poem should be equal to:
Not true.

For all the history of grief
An empty doorway and a maple leaf.   20

For love
The leaning grasses and two lights above the sea—

A poem should not mean
But be.

Archibald MacLeish (*1892–1982*)

QUESTIONS

1. How can a poem be "wordless" (7)? How can it be "motionless in time" (15)?
2. The Latin title, literally translatable as "The Art of Poetry," is a traditional title for works on the philosophy of poetry. What is *this* poet's philosophy of poetry? What does he mean by saying that a poem should not "mean" and should not be "true"?

10. Tone

Tone, in literature, may be defined as the writer's or speaker's attitude toward his subject, his audience, or himself. It is the emotional coloring, or the emotional meaning, of the work and is an extremely important part of the full meaning. In spoken language it is indicated by the inflections of the speaker's voice. If, for instance, a friend tells you, "I'm going to get married today," the facts of the statement are entirely clear. But the emotional meaning of the statement may vary widely according to the tone of voice with which it is uttered. The tone may be ecstatic ("Hooray! I'm going to get married today!"); it may be incredulous ("I can't believe it! I'm going to get married today"); it may be despairing ("Horrors! I'm going to get married today"); it may be resigned ("Might as well face it. I'm going to get married today"). Obviously, a correct interpretation of the tone will be an important part of understanding the full meaning. It may even have rather important consequences. If someone calls you a fool, your interpretation of the tone may determine whether you roll up your sleeves for a fight or walk off with your arm around his shoulder. If a woman says "No" to a proposal of marriage, the man's interpretation of her tone may determine whether he asks her again and wins her or starts going with someone else.

In poetry tone is likewise important. We have not really understood a poem unless we have accurately sensed whether the attitude it manifests is playful or solemn, mocking or reverent, calm or excited. But the correct determination of tone in literature is a much more delicate matter than it is with spoken language, for we do not have the speaker's voice to guide us. We must learn to recognize tone by other means. Almost all the elements of poetry go into indicating its tone: connotation, imagery, and metaphor; irony and understatement; rhythm, sentence construction, and formal pattern. There is therefore no simple formula for recognizing tone. It is an end product of all the elements in a poem. The best we can do is illustrate.

Robert Frost's "Stopping by Woods on a Snowy Evening" (page 128) seems a simple poem, but it has always afforded trouble to beginning readers. A very good student, asked to interpret it, once wrote this: "The poem means that we are forever passing up pleasures to go onward to what we wrongly consider our obligations. We would like to watch the snow fall on the peaceful countryside, but we always have to rush home to supper and other engagements. Frost feels that the average person considers life too short to stop and take time to appreciate true pleasures." This student did a good job in recognizing the central conflict of the poem. He went astray in recognizing its tone. Let's examine why.

In the first place, the fact that the speaker in the poem *does* stop to watch the snow fall in the woods immediately establishes him as a human being with more sensitivity and feeling for beauty than most. He is not one of the people of Wordsworth's sonnet (page 316) who, "getting and spending," have laid waste their powers and lost the capacity to be stirred by nature. Frost's speaker is contrasted with his horse, who, as a creature of habit and an animal without esthetic perception, cannot understand the speaker's reason for stopping. There is also a suggestion of contrast with the "owner" of the woods, who, if he saw the speaker stopping, might be as puzzled as the horse. (Who most truly "profits" from the woods—its absentee owner or the person who can enjoy its beauty?) The speaker goes on because he has "promises to keep." But the word "promises," though it may here have a wry ironic undertone of regret, has a favorable connotation: people almost universally agree that promises ought to be kept. If the poet had used a different term, say, "things to do," or "business to attend to," or "financial affairs to take care of," or "money to make," the connotations would have been quite different. As it is, the tone of the poem tells us that the poet is sympathetic to the speaker, is endorsing rather than censuring his action. Perhaps we may go even further. In the concluding two lines, because of their climactic position, because they are repeated, and because "sleep" in poetry is often used figuratively to refer to death, there is a suggestion of symbolic interpretation: "and many years to live before I die." If we accept this interpretation, it poses a parallel between giving oneself up to contemplation of the woods and dying. The poet's total implication would seem to be that beauty is a distinctively human value that deserves its place in a full life but that to devote one's life to its pursuit, at the expense of other obligations and duties, is tantamount to one's death as a responsible being. The poet therefore accepts the choice the speaker makes, though not without a touch of regret.

Differences in tone, and their importance, can perhaps be studied best in poems with similar content. Consider, for instance, the following pair.

THE VILLAIN

While joy gave clouds the light of stars,
    That beamed where'er they looked;
And calves and lambs had tottering knees,
    Excited, while they sucked;
While every bird enjoyed his song,   5
Without one thought of harm or wrong—
I turned my head and saw the wind,
    Not far from where I stood,
Dragging the corn by her golden hair,
    Into a dark and lonely wood.   10

W. H. Davies (1871–1940)

QUESTIONS

1. Vocabulary: *corn* (9).
2. From what realm of experience is the image in the title and the last two lines taken? What implications does your answer have for the way this image should be taken—that is, for its relation to reality?

APPARENTLY WITH NO SURPRISE

Apparently with no surprise
To any happy flower,
The frost beheads it at its play
In accidental power.

The blond assassin passes on,
The sun proceeds unmoved
To measure off another day
For an approving God.

Emily Dickinson (1830–1886)

QUESTIONS

1. What is the "blond assassin"?
2. What ironies are involved in this poem?

Both of these poems are concerned with nature; both use contrast as their basic organizing principle—a contrast between innocence and evil, joy and tragedy. But in tone the two poems are sharply different. The first is light and fanciful; its tone is one of delight or delighted surprise. The second, though superficially fanciful, is basically grim, almost savage; its tone is one of horror. Let's examine the difference.

In "The Villain" the images of the first six lines all suggest joy and innocence. The last four introduce the sinister. The poet, on turning his head, sees a villain dragging a beautiful maiden toward a dark wood to commit there some unmentionable deed, or so his metaphor tells us. But our response is one not of horror but of delight, for we realize that the poet does not mean us to take his metaphor seriously. He has actually seen only the wind blowing through the wheat and bending its golden tops gracefully toward a shady wood. The beauty of the scene has delighted him, and he has been further delighted by the fanciful metaphor which he has found to express it. The reader shares his delight both in the scene and in the metaphor.

The second poem makes the same contrast of joyful innocence (the "happy flower . . . at its play") with the sinister ("the blond assassin"). The chief difference would seem to be that the villain is this time the frost rather than the wind. But this time the poet, though her metaphor is no less fanciful, is earnest in what she is saying. For the frost actually *does* kill the flower. What makes the horror of the killing even worse is that nothing else in nature is disturbed over it or seems even to notice it. The sun "proceeds unmoved / To measure off another day." Nothing in nature stops or pauses. The flower itself is not surprised. And even God— the God who we have all been told is benevolent and concerned over the least sparrow's fall—seems to approve of what has happened, for He shows no displeasure, and it was He who created the frost as well as the flower. Further irony lies in the fact that the "assassin" (the word's connotations are of terror and violence) is not dark but "blond," or white (the connotations here are of innocence and beauty). The destructive agent, in other words, is among the most exquisite creations of God's handiwork. The poet, then, is shocked at what has happened, and is even more shocked that nothing else in nature is shocked. What has happened seems inconsistent with a rule of benevolence in the universe. In her ironic reference to an "approving God," therefore, the poet is raising a dreadful question: are the forces that created and govern the universe actually benevolent? And if we think that the poet is unduly disturbed over the death of a flower, we may consider that what is true for the flower is true throughout nature. Death—even early or accidental death, in terrible juxtaposition with beauty—is its constant condition; the fate that befalls the flower befalls us all.

These two poems, then, though superficially similar, are basically as different as night and day. And the difference is primarily one of tone.

Accurate determination of tone, therefore, is extremely important, whether in the reading of poetry or the interpretation of a woman's "No." For the experienced reader it will be instinctive and automatic. For the beginning reader it will require study. But beyond the general suggestions for reading that already have been made, no specific instructions can be given. Recognition of tone requires an increasing familiarity with the meanings and connotations of words, alertness to the presence of irony and other figures, and, above all, careful reading. Poetry cannot be read as one would skim a newspaper or a mystery novel looking merely for facts.

EXERCISES

1. Marvell's "To His Coy Mistress" (page 70), Housman's "Loveliest of trees" (page 73), and Herrick's "To the Virgins, to Make Much of Time" (page 82) all treat a traditional poetic theme known as the *carpe diem* ("seize the day") theme. They differ, however, in tone. Characterize the tone of each, and point out the differences in poetic management that account for the difference in tone.

2. Describe and account for the differences in tone between the poems in each of the following pairs:
   a. "A bird came down the walk" (page 11) and "A narrow fellow in the grass" (page 51).
   b. "The Lamb" and "The Tiger" (pages 263–64).
   c. "Spring" (Shakespeare, page 10) and "Spring" (Hopkins, page 54).
   d. "God is a distant, stately lover" (page 120) and "Batter my heart, three-personed God" (page 106).
   e. "Elegy for Alfred Hubbard" (page 145) and "The Mill" (Wilbur, page 314).
   f. "Bredon Hill" and "To an Athlete Dying Young" (pages 283–84).
   g. "When my love swears that she is made of truth" (page 34) and "The Silken Tent" (page 66).
   h. "Virtue" (page 168) and "Mr. Edwards and the Spider" (page 290).
   i. "Song" (Praed, page 163) and "Sestina: Altaforte" (page 296).
   j. "Design" (page 131) and "Some keep the Sabbath going to church" (page 233).
   k. "Pike" (page 285) and "The Truro Bear" (page 295).
   l. "I taste a liquor never brewed" (page 272) and "All day I hear" (page 201).
   m. "Landcrab" (page 259) and "Lion" (page 307).

* * *

THE COMING OF WISDOM WITH TIME

Though leaves are many, the root is one;
Through all the lying days of my youth
I swayed my leaves and flowers in the sun;
Now I may wither into the truth.

William Butler Yeats (1865–1939)

QUESTION

Is the poet exulting over a gain or lamenting over a loss?

SINCE THERE'S NO HELP

Since there's no help, come let us kiss and part;
Nay, I have done, you get no more of me,
And I am glad, yea, glad with all my heart
That thus so cleanly I myself can free;
Shake hands forever, cancel all our vows,   5
And when we meet at any time again,
Be it not seen in either of our brows
That we one jot of former love retain.
Now at the last gasp of Love's latest breath,
When, his pulse failing, Passion speechless lies,   10
When Faith is kneeling by his bed of death,
And Innocence is closing up his eyes,
Now, if thou wouldst, when all have given him over,
From death to life thou mightst him yet recover.

Michael Drayton (1563–1631)

QUESTIONS

1. What difference in tone do you find between the first eight lines and the last six? In which is the speaker more sincere? What differences in rhythm and language help to establish the difference in tone?

2. How many figures are there in the allegorical scene in lines 9–12? What do the pronouns "his" and "him" in lines 10–14 refer to? What is dying? Why? How might the person addressed still restore it from death to life?
3. Define the dramatic situation as precisely as possible, taking into consideration both the man's attitude and the woman's.

FAREWELL TO BARN AND STACK AND TREE

"Farewell to barn and stack and tree,
    Farewell to Severn shore.
Terence, look your last at me,
    For I come home no more.

"The sun burns on the half-mown hill,   5
    By now the blood is dried;
And Maurice amongst the hay lies still
    And my knife is in his side.

"My mother thinks us long away;
    'Tis time the field were mown.   10
She had two sons at rising day,
    To-night she'll be alone.

"And here's a bloody hand to shake,
    And oh, man, here's good-bye;
We'll sweat no more on scythe and rake,   15
    My bloody hands and I.

"I wish you strength to bring you pride,
    And a love to keep you clean,
And I wish you luck, come Lammastide,
    At racing on the green.   20

"Long for me the rick will wait,
    And long will wait the fold,
And long will stand the empty plate,
    And dinner will be cold."

A. E. Housman (1859–1936)

QUESTIONS

1. Vocabulary: *stack* (1), *rick* (21), *fold* (22). The *Severn* (2) is the principal river in the county of Shropshire in the west of England. *Lammastide* (19) was an annual harvest festival held on August 1.
2. Who is speaking to whom? What is the situation?
3. What kind of things does the speaker wish his friend in stanza 5?

4. Explain the effectiveness of the last stanza. What figure of speech does it use throughout?
5. What is the attitude of the poet toward the speaker? How is it conveyed?
6. Though there is no explicit allusion, the poem should remind most readers of a famous Biblical story. How does this association deepen the effect of the poem?

ELEGY FOR ALFRED HUBBARD

Hubbard is dead, the old plumber;
who will mend our burst pipes now,
the tap that has dripped all the summer,
testing the sink's overflow?

No other like him. Young men with knowledge   5
of new techniques, theories from books,
may better his work straight from college,
but who will challenge his squint-eyed looks

in kitchen, bathroom, under floorboards,
rules of thumb which were often wrong;   10
seek as erringly stopcocks in cupboards,
or make a job last half as long?

He was a man who knew the ginnels,
alleyways, streets—the whole district,
family secrets, minor annals,   15
time-honored fictions fused to fact.

Seventy years of gossip muttered
under his cap, his tufty thatch,
so that his talk was slow and clotted,
hard to follow, and too much.   20

As though nothing fell, none vanished,
and time were the maze of Cheetham Hill,
in which the dead—with jobs unfinished—
waited to hear him ring the bell.

For much he never got round to doing,   25
but meant to, when weather bucked up,
or worsened, or when his pipe was drawing,
or when he'd finished this cup.

I thought time, he forgot so often,
had forgotten him but here's Death's pomp   30
over his house, and by the coffin
the son who will inherit his blowlamp,

tools, workshop, cart, and cornet
(pride of Cheetham Prize Brass Band),
and there's his mourning widow, Janet,   35
stood at the gate he'd promised to mend.

Soon he will make his final journey;
shaved and silent, strangely trim,
with never a pause to talk to any-
body: how arrow-like, for him!   40

In St. Mark's church, whose dismal tower
he pointed and painted when a lad,
they will sing his praises amidst flowers
while, somewhere, a cellar starts to flood,

and the housewife banging his front-door knocker   45
is not surprised to find him gone,
and runs for Thwaite, who's a better worker,
and sticks at a job until it's done.

Tony Connor (b. 1930)

QUESTIONS

1. Vocabulary: *annals* (15), *pomp* (30). "Ginnels" (13) are tunnels that punctuate
   rows of houses, giving access to the "backs." "Pointed" (42) means refinishing
   the mortar between bricks.
2. Characterize Hubbard. How does this "elegy" (see Glossary) differ from the
   eulogy that will be said for him in St. Mark's church (41–43)? Compose his
   eulogy.
3. What is the poet's attitude toward his subject?

THE TELEPHONE

"When I was just as far as I could walk
From here today,
There was an hour
All still
When leaning with my head against a flower   5
I heard you talk.
Don't say I didn't, for I heard you say—
You spoke from that flower on the window sill—
Do you remember what it was you said?"

"First tell me what it was you thought you heard."   10

"Having found the flower and driven a bee away,
I leaned my head,

And holding by the stalk,
I listened and I thought I caught the word—
What was it? Did you call me by my name?   15
Or did you say—
Someone said 'Come'—I heard it as I bowed."

"I may have thought as much, but not aloud."

"Well, so I came."

Robert Frost (1874–1963)

QUESTIONS

1. When and where does the above dialogue take place? What is the relationship between the two speakers?
2. How does the title relate to the poem?
3. Characterize the first speaker. Why does he interrupt his narrative to say, "Don't say I didn't" (7)? Why does he not tell her what he heard her say (7–9, 14–16)? Why does he shift to what *"Someone"* said (17)?
4. Characterize the second speaker.
5. What is the poem about? What is its tone?

LOVE IN BROOKLYN

"I love you, Horowitz," he said, and blew his nose.
She splashed her drink. "The hell you say," she said.
Then, thinking hard, she lit a cigarette:
"Not *love*. You don't *love* me. You like my legs,
and how I make your letters nice and all.   5
You drunk your drink too fast. You don't love *me*."

"You wanna bet?" he asked. "You wanna bet?
I loved you from the day they moved you up
from Payroll, last July. I watched you, right?
You sat there on that typing chair you have   10
and swung round like a kid. It made me shake.
Like once, in World War II, I saw a tank
slide through some trees at dawn like it was god.
That's how you make me feel. I don't know why."

She turned towards him, then sat back and grinned,   15
and on the bar stool swung full circle round.
"You think I'm like a tank, you mean?" she asked.
"Some fellers tell me nicer things than that."
But then she saw his face and touched his arm
and softly said "I'm only kidding you."   20

He ordered drinks, the same again, and paid.
A fat man, wordless, staring at the floor.
She took his hand in hers and pressed it hard.
And his plump fingers trembled in her lap.

John Wakeman (b. 1928)

QUESTIONS

1. When and where does the above dialogue take place? What is the relationship between the two speakers?
2. Characterize the first speaker. How does he feel toward the other?
3. Characterize the second speaker. How does she feel toward him? Do her feelings change? If so, how?
4. Contrast this poem in tone with "The Telephone."

ONE DIGNITY DELAYS FOR ALL

One dignity delays for all,
One mitred afternoon.
None can avoid this purple,
None avoid this crown.

Coach it insures, and footmen,   5
Chamber and state and throng;
Bells, also, in the village,
As we ride grand along.

What dignified attendants,
What service when we pause!   10
How loyally at parting
Their hundred hats they raise!

How pomp surpassing ermine
When simple you and I
Present our meek escutcheon   15
And claim the rank to die!

Emily Dickinson (1830–1886)

QUESTIONS

1. Vocabulary: *mitred* (2), *state* (6), *escutcheon* (15).
2. What is the "dignity" that delays for all? What is its nature? What is being described in stanzas 2 and 3?

3. What figures of speech are combined in "our meek escutcheon" (15)? What metaphorically does it represent?

'TWAS WARM AT FIRST LIKE US

'Twas warm at first like us,
Until there crept upon
A chill, like frost upon a glass,
Till all the scene be gone.

The forehead copied stone,   5
The fingers grew too cold
To ache, and like a skater's brook
The busy eyes congealed.

It straightened—that was all,
It crowded cold to cold,   10
It multiplied indifference
As Pride were all it could.

And even when with cords
'Twas lowered like a weight,
It made no signal, nor demurred,   15
But dropped like adamant.

Emily Dickinson (1830–1886)

QUESTIONS

1. Vocabulary: *adamant* (16).
2. What is "It" in the opening line? What is being described in the poem, and between what points in time?
3. How would you describe the tone of this poem? How does it contrast with that of the preceding?

CROSSING THE BAR

Sunset and evening star,
    And one clear call for me!
And may there be no moaning of the bar
    When I put out to sea,

But such a tide as moving seems asleep,   5
    Too full for sound and foam,
When that which drew from out the boundless deep
    Turns again home.

Twilight and evening bell,
   And after that the dark!   10
And may there be no sadness of farewell
   When I embark;

For though from out our bourne of Time and Place
   The flood may bear me far,
I hope to see my Pilot face to face   15
   When I have crossed the bar.

Alfred, Lord Tennyson (1809–1892)

QUESTIONS

1. Vocabulary: *bourne* (13).
2. What two sets of figures does Tennyson use for approaching death? What is the precise moment of death in each set?
3. In troubled weather the wind and waves above the sandbar across a harbor's mouth make a moaning sound. What metaphorical meaning has the "moaning of the bar" here (3)? For what kind of death is the poet wishing? Why does he want "no sadness of farewell" (11)?
4. What is "that which drew from out the boundless deep" (7)? What is "the boundless deep"? To what is it opposed in the poem? Why is "Pilot" (15) capitalized?

THE OXEN

Christmas Eve, and twelve of the clock.
   "Now they are all on their knees,"
An elder said as we sat in a flock
   By the embers in hearthside ease.

We pictured the meek mild creatures where   5
   They dwelt in their strawy pen,
Nor did it occur to one of us there
   To doubt they were kneeling then.

So fair a fancy few would weave
   In these years! Yet, I feel,   10
If someone said on Christmas Eve,
   "Come; see the oxen kneel

"In the lonely barton° by yonder coomb°   farm; valley
   Our childhood used to know,"
I should go with him in the gloom,   15
   Hoping it might be so.

Thomas Hardy (1840–1928)

1. Is the simple superstition referred to in the poem here opposed to, or identified with, religious faith? With what implications for the meaning of the poem?
2. What are "these years" (10) and how do they contrast with the years of the poet's boyhood? What event in intellectual history between 1840 and 1915 (the date of composition of this poem) was most responsible for the change?
3. Both "Crossing the Bar" and "The Oxen" in their last lines use a form of the verb *hope*. By full discussion of tone, establish the precise meaning of hope in each poem. What degree of expectation does it imply? How should the word be handled in reading Tennyson's poem aloud?

LOVE

There's the wonderful love of a beautiful maid,
　　And the love of a staunch true man,
And the love of a baby that's unafraid—
　　All have existed since time began.
But the most wonderful love, the Love of all loves,
　　Even greater than the love for Mother,
Is the infinite, tenderest, passionate love
　　Of one dead drunk for another.

Anonymous

The radical shift in tone makes "Love" come off. If such a shift were unintentional in a poem, what would our view be?

ENGRAVED ON THE COLLAR OF A DOG WHICH I GAVE TO HIS ROYAL HIGHNESS

I am his Highness' dog at Kew;
Pray tell me, sir, whose dog are you?

Alexander Pope (1688–1744)

11. Musical Devices

I t is obvious that poetry makes a greater use of the "music" of language than does language that is not poetry. The poet, unlike the person who uses language to convey only information, chooses words for sound as well as for meaning, and uses the sound as a means of reinforcing meaning. So prominent is this musical quality of poetry that some writers have made it the distinguishing term in their definitions of poetry. Edgar Allan Poe, for instance, describes poetry as "music . . . combined with a pleasurable idea." Whether or not it deserves this much importance, verbal music, like connotation, imagery, and figurative language, is one of the important resources that enable the poet to do something more than communicate mere information. The poet may indeed sometimes pursue verbal music for its own sake; more often, at least in first-rate poetry, it is an adjunct to the total meaning or communication of the poem.

There are two broad ways by which the poet achieves musical quality: by the choice and arrangement of sounds and by the arrangement of accents. In this chapter we will consider one aspect of the first of these.

An essential element in all music is repetition. In fact, we might say that all art consists of giving structure to two elements: repetition and variation. All things we enjoy greatly and lastingly have these two elements. We enjoy the sea endlessly because it is always the same yet always different. We enjoy a baseball game because it contains the same complex combination of pattern and variation. Our love of art, then, is rooted in human psychology. We like the familiar, we like variety, but we like them combined. If we get too much sameness, the result is monotony and tedium; if we get too much variety, the result is bewilderment and confusion. The composer of music, therefore, repeats certain musical tones; repeats them in certain combinations, or chords; and repeats them in certain patterns, or melodies. The poet likewise repeats certain sounds in certain combinations and arrangements, and thus gives organization and structure to his verse. Consider the following short example.

THE TURTLE

> The turtle lives 'twixt plated decks
> Which practically conceal its sex.
> I think it clever of the turtle
> In such a fix to be so fertile.

Ogden Nash (1902-1971)

Here is a little joke, a paradox of animal life to which the author has cleverly drawn our attention. An experiment will show us, however, that much of its appeal lies not so much in what it says as in the manner in which it says it. If, for instance, we recast the verse as prose: "The turtle lives in a shell which almost conceals its sex. It is ingenious of the turtle, in such a situation, to be so prolific," the joke falls flat. Some of its appeal must lie in its metrical form. So now we cast it in unrimed verse:

> Because he lives between two decks,
> It's hard to tell a turtle's gender.
> The turtle is a clever beast
> In such a plight to be so fertile.

Here, perhaps, is *some* improvement, but still the piquancy of the original is missing. Much of that appeal must have consisted in the use of rime—the repetition of sound in "decks" and "sex," "turtle" and "fertile." So we try once more:

> The turtle lives 'twixt plated decks
> Which practically conceal its sex.
> I think it clever of the turtle
> In such a plight to be so fertile.

But for perceptive readers there is still something missing—they may not at first see what—but some little touch that makes the difference between a good piece of verse and a little masterpiece in its kind. And then they see it: "plight" has been substituted for "fix."

But why should "fix" make such a difference? Its meaning is little different from that of "plight"; its only important difference is in sound. But there we are. The final *x* in "fix" catches up the concluding consonant sound in "sex," and its initial f is repeated in the initial consonant sound of "fertile." Not only do these sound recurrences provide a subtle gratification to the ear, but they also give the verse structure; they emphasize and draw together the key words of the piece: "sex," "fix," and "fertile."

The poet may repeat any unit of sound from the smallest to the largest. He may repeat individual vowel and consonant sounds, whole syllables, words, phrases, lines, or groups of lines. In each instance, in a good poem, the repetition will serve several purposes: it will please the ear, it will emphasize the words in which the repetition occurs, and it will give structure to the poem. The popularity and initial impressiveness of such repetitions is evidenced by their becoming in many instances embedded in the language as clichés like "wild and woolly," "first and foremost," "footloose and fancy-free," "penny-wise, pound-foolish," "dead as a doornail," "might and main," "sink or swim," "do or die," "pell-mell," "helter-skelter," "harum-scarum," "hocus-pocus." Some of these kinds of repetition have names, as we will see.

A syllable consists of a vowel sound that may be preceded or followed by consonant sounds. Any of these sounds may be repeated. The repetition of initial consonant sounds, as in "tried and true," "safe and sound," "fish or fowl," "rime or reason," is ALLITERATION. The repetition of vowel sounds, as in "mad as a hatter," "time out of mind," "free and easy," "slapdash," is ASSONANCE. The repetition of final consonant sounds, as in "first and last," "odds and ends," "short and sweet," "a stroke of luck," or Shakespeare's "struts and frets" (page 118) is CONSONANCE.*

Repetitions may be used alone or in combination. Alliteration and assonance are combined in such phrases as "time and tide," "thick and thin," "kith and kin," "alas and alack," "fit as a fiddle," and Edgar Allan Poe's famous line, "The viol, the violet, and the vine." Alliteration and consonance are combined in such phrases as "crisscross," "last but not least," "lone and lorn," "good as gold," Housman's "Malt does more than Milton can" (page 14), "strangling in a string" (page 50) and "fleet foot" (page 284), and e. e. cummings's "blow friend to fiend" and "a doom of a

---

*There is no established terminology for these various repetitions. *Alliteration* is used by some writers to mean any repetition of consonant sounds. *Assonance* has been used to mean the similarity as well as the identity of vowel sounds, or even the similarity of any sounds whatever. *Consonance* has often been reserved for words in which both the initial *and* final consonant sounds correspond, as in *green* and *groan, moon* and *mine*. *Rime* (or rhyme) has been used to mean any sound repetition, including alliteration, assonance, and consonance. In the absence of clear agreement on the meanings of these terms, the terminology chosen here has appeared most useful, with support in usage. Labels are useful in analysis. The student should, however, learn to recognize the devices and, more important, to see their function, without worrying too much over nomenclature.

dream" (page 132). The combination of assonance and consonance is rime.

RIME is the repetition of the accented vowel sound and all succeeding sounds. It is called MASCULINE when the rime sounds involve only one syllable, as in *decks* and *sex* or *support* and *retort*. It is FEMININE when the rime sounds involve two or more syllables, as in *turtle* and *fertile* or *spitefully* and *delightfully*. It is referred to as INTERNAL RIME when one or more riming words are within the line and as END RIME when the riming words are at the *ends* of lines. End rime is probably the most frequently used and most consciously sought sound repetition in English poetry. Because it comes at the end of the line, it receives emphasis as a musical effect and perhaps contributes more than any other musical resource except rhythm and meter to give poetry its musical effect as well as its structure. There exists, however, a large body of poetry that does not employ rime and for which rime would not be appropriate. Also, there has always been a tendency, especially noticeable in modern poetry, to substitute approximate rimes for perfect rimes at the ends of lines. AP-PROXIMATE RIMES include words with any kind of sound similarity, from close to fairly remote. Under approximate rime we include alliteration, assonance, and consonance or their combinations when used at the end of the line; half-rime (feminine rimes in which only half of the word rimes—the accented half, as in *lightly* and *frightful,* or the unaccented half, as in *yellow* and *willow*); and other similarities too elusive to name. "A bird came down the walk" (page 11) and "A narrow fellow in the grass" (page 51), "Dr. Sigmund Freud Discovers the Sea Shell" (page 61), "Toads" (page 68), and "Mr. Z" (page 111), to different degrees, all employ various kinds of approximate end rime.

THAT NIGHT WHEN JOY BEGAN

That night when joy began
Our narrowest veins to flush,
We waited for the flash
Of morning's leveled gun.

But morning let us pass,   5
And day by day relief
Outgrows his nervous laugh,
Grown credulous of peace,

As mile by mile is seen
No trespasser's reproach,   10

And love's best glasses reach
No fields but are his own.

W. H. Auden (1907–1973)

QUESTIONS

1. What has been the past experience with love of the two people in the poem? What is their present experience? What precisely is the tone of the poem?
2. What basic metaphor underlies the poem? Work it out stanza by stanza. What is "the flash of morning's leveled gun"? Does line 10 mean that no trespasser reproaches the lovers or that no one reproaches the lovers for being trespassers? Does "glasses" (11) refer to spectacles, tumblers, mirrors, or field glasses? Point out three personifications.
3. The rime pattern in this poem is intricate and exact. Work it out, considering alliteration, assonance, and consonance.

In addition to the repetition of individual sounds and syllables, the poet may repeat whole words, phrases, lines, or groups of lines. When such repetition is done according to some fixed pattern, it is called a REFRAIN. The refrain is especially common in songlike poetry. Examples are to be found in Shakespeare's "Winter" (page 6) and "Spring" (page 10).

It is not to be thought that we have exhausted the possibilities of sound repetition by giving names to a few of the more prominent kinds. The complete study of possible kinds of sound repetition in poetry would be so complex that it would break down under its own machinery. Some of the subtlest and loveliest effects escape our net of names. In as short a phrase as this from the prose of John Ruskin—"ivy as light and lovely as the vine"—we notice alliteration in *light* and *lovely*, assonance in *ivy*, *light*, and *vine*, and consonance in *ivy* and *lovely*, but we have no name to connect the *v* in *vine* with the *v*'s in *ivy* and *lovely*, or the second *l* in *lovely* with the first *l*, or the final syllables of *ivy* and *lovely* with each other; but these are all an effective part of the music of the line. Also contributing to the music of poetry is the use of related rather than identical sounds, such as *m* and *n* or *p* and *b* or the vowel sounds in *boat*, *boot*, and *book*.

These various musical repetitions, for trained readers, will ordinarily make an almost subconscious contribution to their reading of the poem: readers will feel their effect without necessarily being aware of what has caused it. There is value, however, in occasionally analyzing a poem for these devices in order to increase awareness of them. A few words of caution are necessary. First, the repetitions are entirely a matter of sound; spelling is irrelevant. *Bear* and *pair* are rimes, but *through* and *rough* are not. *Cell* and *sin,* *folly* and *philosophy* alliterate, but *sin* and *sugar, gun* and *gem* do not. Second, alliteration, assonance, consonance, and masculine rime are matters that ordinarily involve only stressed or accented sylla-bles; for only such syllables ordinarily make enough impression on the ear to be significant in the sound pattern of the poem. We should hardly consider *which* and *its* in the second line of "The Turtle," for instance, as an example of assonance, for neither word is stressed enough in the read-ing to make it significant as a sound. Third, the words involved in these repetitions must be close enough together that the ear retains the sound, consciously or subconsciously, from its first occurrence to its second. This distance varies according to circumstances, but for alliteration, asso-nance, and consonance the words ordinarily have to be in the same line or adjacent lines. End rime bridges a longer gap.

GOD'S GRANDEUR

The world is charged with the grandeur of God.
   It will flame out, like shining from shook foil;
   It gathers to a greatness, like the ooze of oil
Crushed. Why do men then now not reck his rod?
Generations have trod, have trod, have trod;   5
   And all is seared with trade; bleared, smeared with toil;
   And wears man's smudge and shares man's smell: the soil
Is bare now, nor can foot feel, being shod.

And for all this, nature is never spent;
   There lives the dearest freshness deep down things;   10
And though the last lights off the black West went
   Oh, morning, at the brown brink eastward, springs—
Because the Holy Ghost over the bent
   World broods with warm breast and with ah! bright wings.

Gerard Manley Hopkins (1844–1889)

QUESTIONS

1. What is the theme of this sonnet?
2. The image in lines 3–4 possibly refers to olive oil being collected in great vats from crushed olives, but the image is much disputed. Explain the simile in line 2 and the symbols in lines 7–8 and 11–12.
3. Explain "reck his rod" (4), "spent" (9), "bent" (13).
4. Using different-colored pencils, encircle and connect examples of allitera-tion, assonance, consonance, and internal rime. Do these help to carry the meaning?

We should not leave the impression that the use of these musical devices is necessarily or always valuable. Like the other resources of poetry, they can be judged only in the light of the poem's total intention. Many of the greatest works of English poetry—for instance, *Hamlet* and *King Lear* and *Paradise Lost*—do not employ end rime. Both alliteration and rime, especially feminine rime, if used excessively or unskillfully, become humorous or silly. If the intention is humorous, the result is delightful; if not, fatal. Shakespeare, who knew how to use all these devices to the utmost advantage, parodied their unskillful use in lines like "The preyful princess pierced and pricked a pretty pleasing prickett" in *Love's Labor's Lost* and

> Whereat with blade, with bloody, blameful blade,
> He bravely broached his boiling bloody breast

in *A Midsummer Night's Dream*. Swinburne parodied his own highly alliterative style in "Nephelidia" with lines like "Life is the lust of a lamp for the light that is dark till the dawn of the day when we die." Used skillfully and judiciously, however, musical devices provide a palpable and delicate pleasure to the ear and, even more important, add dimension to meaning.

EXERCISE

Discuss the various ways in which the following poems make use of refrain:

1. "Winter," page 6.
2. "The Pasture," page 13.
3. "Pack, clouds, away," page 62.
4. "Weep you no more, sad fountains," page 72.
5. "To Althea, from Prison," page 104.
6. "in Just—," page 119.
7. "When I was one-and-twenty," page 214.
8. "Edward," page 217.
9. "Southern Cop," page 265.
10. "Do not go gentle into that good night," page 308.

*   *   *

WITH RUE MY HEART IS LADEN

> With rue my heart is laden
> For golden friends I had,
> For many a rose-lipt maiden
> And many a lightfoot lad.

By brooks too broad for leaping
        The lightfoot boys are laid;
The rose-lipt girls are sleeping
        In fields where roses fade.

A. E. Housman (1859–1936)

QUESTIONS

1. Vocabulary: *rue* (1).
2. What, where, or why are the "brooks too broad for leaping" and the "fields where roses fade"?
3. What are the connotations here of "golden"? Does the use of "golden" (2), "lad" (4), and "girls" (7) remind you of any earlier poem? (If not, see page 304.) How does this submerged allusion enrich the poem?
4. Point out and discuss the contribution to the poem of alliteration, end rime (masculine and feminine), and other repetitions.

WE REAL COOL

The Pool Players.
Seven At The Golden Shovel.

We real cool. We
Left school. We

Lurk late. We
Strike straight. We

Sing sin. We
Thin gin. We

Jazz June. We
Die soon.

Gwendolyn Brooks (b. 1917)

QUESTIONS

1. In addition to end rime, what other musical devices does this poem employ?
2. Try reading this poem with the pronouns at the beginning of the lines instead of at the end. What is lost?
3. English teachers in a certain urban school were criticized recently for having their students read this poem: it was said to be immoral. Was the criticism justified? Why or why not?

SHOE SHOP

I shut the door on the racket
Of rush hour traffic,
Inhale the earthy, thick
Perfume of leather and pipe tobacco.

The place might be a barbershop   5
Where the air gets lathered with gossip.
You can almost hear the whippersnap
Of the straightedge on the razor strop.

It might be a front for agitators,
But there's no back room. A rabble   10
Of boots and shoes lies tumbled
In heaps like a hoard of potatoes.

The cobbler, broad as a blacksmith,
Turns a shoe over his pommel,
Pummels the sole, takes the nail   15
He's bit between his teeth,

And drives it into the heel. Hunched
At his workbench, he pays the old shoe
More attention than me. "Help you?"
He grunts, as if the man held a grudge   20

Against business. He gives my run-over
Loafer a look. "Plastic," he spits.
"And foreign-made. Doubt I can fix it."
I could be holding a dead gopher.

"The Europeans might make good shoes,   25
But I never see them. Cut the price.
Advertise! Never mind the merchandise.
You buy yourself a pair, brand new,

"The welt will be cardboard
Where it ought to be leather.   30
There's nothing to hold the shoe together."
He stows my pair in a cupboard.

"And all of them tan with acid.
The Mexicans make fancy boots, but they cure
Their leather in cow manure. Wear   35
Them out in the rain once. Rancid?

"I had a guy bring me a pair.
Wanted me to get rid of the stink.

Honest to God. I hate to think
My customers are crazy, but I swear."   40

He curses factories, inflation,
And I welcome the glow of conspiracy.
Together we plot, half seriously,
A counter industrial revolution.

His pride's been steeped in bitterness,   45
His politics tanned with elbow-grease.
To hear him fume and bitch, you'd guess
His guerrilla warfare's hopeless.

But talk about job satisfaction!
To take a tack from a tight-lipped smile,   50
Stick it like a thorn in an unworn sole,
To heft the hammer, and whack it!

When I step back out in the street
The city looks flimsy as a movie set.

Barton Sutter (b.1949)

QUESTIONS

1. Identify the rime scheme of the poem. What kinds of rimes does it use? What lines contain perfect rimes?
2. Contrast the language (diction and syntax) of this poem with that of "To Autumn" (p. 54) or "Ulysses" (p. 87). Is it less poetic?
3. What kinds of imagery does the poem employ? Is it less rich in imagery than the poems just named?
4. Identify and discuss the appropriateness of the metaphors and similes in lines 6, 10–12, 22, 24, 45, 46, 48. What links stanzas 3, 11, 12? What is a "counter industrial revolution"?
5. Explain the apparent contradiction between the cobbler's "bitterness" (45) and his "job satisfaction" (49). Why does the city look "flimsy as a movie set" to the narrator when he leaves the shop?

WINTER OCEAN

Many-maned scud-thumper, tub
of male whales, maker of worn wood, shrub-
ruster, sky-mocker, rave!
portly pusher of waves, wind-slave.

John Updike (b. 1932)

1. The fun of this poem lies chiefly in two features: in its invention of elaborate epithets (descriptive names) for something familiar (in Old English poetry, partially imitated here, these descriptive names were called *kennings*), and in its equally elaborate sound correspondences. How apt are the names? List or chart the sound correspondences. Are they also appropriate?
2. What figure of speech is most central to the poem?

PARTING, WITHOUT A SEQUEL

She has finished and sealed the letter
At last, which he so richly has deserved,
With characters venomous and hatefully curved,
And nothing could be better.

But even as she gave it   5
Saying to the blue-capped functioner of doom,
"Into his hands," she hoped the leering groom
Might somewhere lose and leave it.

Then all the blood
Forsook the face. She was too pale for tears,   10
Observing the ruin of her younger years.
She went and stood

Under her father's vaunting oak
Who kept his peace in wind and sun, and glistened
Stoical in the rain; to whom she listened   15
If he spoke.

And now the agitation of the rain
Rasped his sere leaves, and he talked low and gentle
Reproaching the wan daughter by the lintel;
Ceasing and beginning again.   20

Away went the messenger's bicycle,
His serpent's track went up the hill forever,
And all the time she stood there hot as fever
And cold as any icicle.

John Crowe Ransom (1888–1974)

QUESTIONS

1. Identify the figures of speech in lines 3 and 22 and discuss their effectiveness. Are there traces of dramatic irony in the poem? Where?

2. Is the oak literal or figurative? Neither? Both? Discuss the meanings of "vaunting" (13), "stoical" (15), "sere" (18), and "lintel" (19).
3. Do you find any trite language in the poem? Where? What does it tell us about the girl's action?
4. W. H. Auden has defined poetry as "the clear expression of mixed feelings." Discuss the applicability of the definition to this poem. Try it out on other poems.
5. A feminine rime that involves two syllables is known also as a DOUBLE RIME. Find examples in the poem of both perfect and approximate double rimes. A feminine rime that involves three syllables is a TRIPLE RIME. Find one example of a triple rime. Which lines employ masculine or SINGLE RIMES, either perfect or approximate?

SONG

The pints and the pistols, the pike-staves and pottles,
    The trooper's fierce shout and the toper's bold song;
O! theirs is such friendship that battles and bottles
    When going together can never go wrong.

The wine of the vintner, the blood of the Roundhead,   5
    The Cavalier taps them with equal delight;
And we are the boys for whom always abounded
    Good casks for the table, good casques for the fight.

Then thus do we drink to the flag and the flagon,
    The two stoutest allies the world ever saw;   10
For war without wine would so wearily drag on
    That none but a blockhead the bilbo would draw.

The can and the cannon sure never can bicker,
    Full quarts and free quarters shall still be our cry;
One hand draws the blade and the other the liquor,   15
    And grape is the best of all shot—when we're dry.

Drink sack and sack cities—whet swords and wet gullets,
    Nor blush, jolly boys, when we make it our boast
That friends as we are both to bowls and to bullets,
    We're not always fond of the charge of the host.   20

Who like not both swilling and killing are asses,
    For Bacchus was surely the brother of Mars;
So shrink not to charge to the muzzles your glasses
    And fire off a salvo for wine-cups and wars.

Attributed to *Winthrop Mackworth Praed* (*1802–1839*)

1. Vocabulary: *pottles* (1), *toper* (2), *casques* (8), *bilbo* (12).
2. In a drinking song we expect high spirits and jollity rather than profundity. How do the high spirits express themselves here in the very language itself? How many of the devices discussed in this chapter can you identify? How many puns do you count?

TRAVELING THROUGH THE DARK

Traveling through the dark I found a deer
dead on the edge of the Wilson River road.
It is usually best to roll them into the canyon:
that road is narrow; to swerve might make more dead.

By glow of the tail-light I stumbled back of the car   5
and stood by the heap, a doe, a recent killing;
she had stiffened already, almost cold.
I dragged her off; she was large in the belly.

My fingers touching her side brought me the reason—
her side was warm; her fawn lay there waiting,   10
alive, still, never to be born.
Beside that mountain road I hesitated.

The car aimed ahead its lowered parking lights;
under the hood purred the steady engine.
I stood in the glare of the warm exhaust turning red;   15
around our group I could hear the wilderness listen.

I thought hard for us all—my only swerving—,
then pushed her over the edge into the river.

William Stafford (b. 1914)

QUESTIONS

1. State precisely the speaker's dilemma. What kind of person is he? Does he make the right decision? Why does he call his hesitation "my only swerving" (17), and how does this connect with the word "swerve" in line 4?
2. What different kinds of imagery and of image contrasts give life to the poem? Do any of the images have symbolic overtones?
3. At first glance this poem may appear to be without end rime. Looking closer, do you find any correspondences between lines 2 and 4 in each stanza? between the final words of the concluding couplet? Can you find any line-end in the poem without some connection in sound to another line-end in its stanza?

NOTHING GOLD CAN STAY

Nature's first green is gold,
Her hardest hue to hold.
Her early leaf's a flower;
But only so an hour.
Then leaf subsides to leaf.
So Eden sank to grief,
So dawn goes down to day.
Nothing gold can stay.

Robert Frost (1874–1963)

QUESTIONS

1. Explain the paradoxes in lines 1 and 3.
2. Discuss the poem as a series of symbols. What are the symbolical meanings of "gold" in the final line of the poem?
3. Discuss the contributions of alliteration, assonance, consonance, rime, and other repetitions to the effectiveness of the poem.

AUTUMNUS

When the leaves in autumn wither,
    With a tawny tannèd face,
Warped and wrinkled-up together,
    The year's late beauty to disgrace:

There thy life's glass may'st thou find thee,
    Green now, gray now, gone anon;
    Leaving (worldling) of thine own,
Neither fruit, nor leaf behind thee.

Joshua Sylvester (1563–1618)

QUESTIONS

1. To whom is the poem addressed? What is the "glass" (5)?
2. Discuss the contribution of musical devices to the structure and meaning of the poem.

12. Rhythm and Meter

Our love of rhythm and meter is rooted even deeper in us than our love for musical repetition. It is related to the beat of our hearts, the pulse of our blood, the intake and outflow of air from our lungs. Everything that we do naturally and gracefully we do rhythmically. There is rhythm in the way we walk, the way we swim, the way we ride a horse, the way we swing a golf club or a baseball bat. So native is rhythm to us that we read it, when we can, into the mechanical world around us. Our clocks go tick-tick-tick-tick, but we hear them go tick-tock, tick-tock in an endless trochaic. The click of the railway wheels beneath us patterns itself into a tune in our heads. There is a strong appeal for us in language that is rhythmical.

The term RHYTHM refers to any wavelike recurrence of motion or sound. In speech it is the natural rise and fall of language. All language is to some degree rhythmical, for all language involves some kind of alternation between accented and unaccented syllables. Language varies considerably, however, in the degree to which it exhibits rhythm. In some forms of speech the rhythm is so unobtrusive or so unpatterned that we are scarcely, if at all, aware of it. In other forms of speech the rhythm is so pronounced that we may be tempted to tap our foot to it.

METER is the kind of rhythm we can tap our foot to. In language that is metrical the accents are so arranged as to occur at apparently equal intervals of time, and it is this interval we mark off with the tap of our foot. Metrical language is called VERSE. Nonmetrical language is PROSE.

Not all poetry is metrical, nor is all metrical language poetry. *Verse* and *poetry* are not synonymous terms, nor is a *versifier* necessarily a *poet.*

The study of meter is a fascinating but highly complex subject. It is by no means an absolute prerequisite to an enjoyment, even a rich enjoyment, of poetry. But a knowledge of its fundamentals does have certain values. It can make the beginning reader more aware of the rhythmical effects of poetry and of how poetry should be read. It can enable the more advanced reader to analyze how certain effects are achieved, to see how rhythm is adapted to thought, and to explain what makes one poem (in this respect) better than another. The beginning student ought to have at least an elementary knowledge of the subject. It is not so difficult as its terminology might suggest.

In every word of more than one syllable, one syllable is *accented* or *stressed,* that is, given more prominence in pronunciation than the rest.* We say to*day,* to*mor*row, *yes*terday, *dai*ly, inter*vene.* If words of even one syllable are arranged into a sentence, we give certain words, or syllables, more prominence in pronunciation than the rest. We say: "He *went* to the *store,*" or "*Jack* is *driv*ing his *car.*" There is nothing mysterious about this; it is the normal process of language. The only difference between prose and verse is that in prose these accents occur more or less haphazardly; in verse the poet has arranged them to occur at regular intervals.

The word *meter* comes from a word meaning "measure." To measure something we must have a unit of measurement. For measuring length we use the inch, the foot, and the yard; for measuring time we use the second, the minute, and the hour. For measuring verse we use the foot, the line, and (sometimes) the stanza.

The basic metrical unit, the FOOT, consists normally of one accented syllable plus one or two unaccented syllables, though occasionally there may be no unaccented syllables, and very rarely there may be three. For diagramming verse, various systems of visual symbols have been invented. In this book we shall use a short curved line to indicate an unaccented syllable, a short horizontal line to indicate an accented syllable, and a vertical bar to indicate the division between feet. The basic kinds of feet are thus as follows:

---

*Though the words *accent* and *stress* are generally used interchangeably, as here, a distinction is sometimes made between them in technical discussions. ACCENT, the relative prominence given a syllable in relation to its neighbors, is then said to result from one or more of four causes: *stress,* or force of utterance, producing loudness; *duration; pitch;* and *juncture,* the manner of transition between successive sounds. Of these, *stress,* in English verse, is most important.

Example	Name of foot	Name of meter*	
to-*day*	Iamb	Iambic	Duple meters
dai-ly	Trochee	Trochaic	
in-ter-*vene*	Anapest	Anapestic	Triple meters
yes-ter-day	Dactyl	Dactylic	
true-blue	Spondee	(Spondaic)	
day	Monosyllabic foot		

The secondary unit of measurement, the LINE, is measured by naming the number of feet in it. The following names are used:

Monometer	one foot	Pentameter	five feet
Dimeter	two feet	Hexameter	six feet
Trimeter	three feet	Heptameter	seven feet
Tetrameter	four feet	Octameter	eight feet

The third unit, the STANZA, consists of a group of lines whose metrical pattern is repeated throughout the poem. Since not all verse is written in stanzas, we shall save our discussion of this unit till a later chapter.

The process of measuring verse is referred to as SCANSION. To *scan* any specimen of verse, we do three things: (1) we identify the prevailing foot, (2) we name the number of feet in a line—if this length follows any regular pattern, and (3) we describe the stanza pattern—if there is one. We may try out our skill on the following poem.

VIRTUE

Sweet day, so cool, so calm, so bright,
The bridal of the earth and sky;
The dew shall weep thy fall to night,
For thou must die.

Sweet rose, whose hue, angry and brave,   5
Bids the rash gazer wipe his eye;

*In the spondee the accent is thought of as being distributed equally or almost equally over the two syllables and is sometimes referred to as a hovering accent. No whole poems are written in spondees or monosyllabic feet; hence there are only four basic meters: iambic, trochaic, anapestic, and dactylic. Iambic and trochaic are DUPLE METERS because they employ two-syllable feet; anapestic and dactylic are TRIPLE METERS because they employ three-syllable feet.

Thy root is ever in its grave,
    And thou must die.

Sweet spring, full of sweet days and roses,
    A box where sweets compacted lie;   10
My music shows ye have your closes,
    And all must die.

Only a sweet and virtuous soul,
    Like seasoned timber, never gives;
But though the whole world turn to coal,   15
    Then chiefly lives.

George Herbert (1593–1633)

QUESTIONS

1. Vocabulary: *bridal* (2), *brave* (5), *closes* (11).
2. How are the four stanzas interconnected? How do they build to a climax?
How does the fourth contrast with the first three?

The first step in scanning a poem is to read it normally, listening to
where the accents fall, and perhaps beating time with the hand. If we have
any doubt about how a line should be marked, we should skip it tempo-
rarily and go on to lines where we feel greater confidence, that is, to those
lines which seem most regular, with accents that fall unmistakably at
regular intervals. In "Virtue" lines 3, 10, and 14 clearly fall into this
category, as do also the short lines 4, 8, and 12. Lines 3, 10, and 14 may
be marked as follows:

The dew | shall weep | thy fall | to night, | 3

A box | where sweets | com- pact- | ed lie; | 10

Like sea- | soned tim- | ber, nev- | er gives. | 14

Lines 4, 8, and 12 are so nearly identical that we may let line 4 represent
all three:

For thou | must die. | 4

Surveying what we have done so far, we may with some confidence
say that the prevailing metrical foot of the poem is iambic; and we may
reasonably hypothesize that the second and third lines of each stanza are
tetrameter (four-foot) lines and the fourth line dimeter. What about the

first line? Line 1 contains eight syllables, and the last six are clearly iambic:

$$\text{Sweet day,} \mid \overset{\smile}{\text{so}} \; \overline{\text{cool,}} \mid \overset{\smile}{\text{so}} \; \overline{\text{calm,}} \mid \overset{\smile}{\text{so}} \; \overline{\text{bright.}} \mid \qquad 1$$

This too, then, is a tetrameter line, and the only question is whether to mark the first foot as another iamb or as a spondee. Many metrists, emphasizing the priority of pattern, would mark it as an iamb. Clearly, however, the word "Sweet" is more important and receives more emphasis in a sensitive reading than the three "so's" in the line. Other metrists, therefore, would give it equal emphasis with "day" and mark the first foot as a spondee. Neither marking can be called incorrect. It is a matter of the reader's personal judgment or of his metrical philosophy. Following my own preference, I mark it as a spondee, and mark the first foot in lines 5 and 9 correspondingly. Similar choices occur at several points in the poem (lines 11, 15, and 16). Many readers will quite legitimately perceive line 16 as parallel to lines 4, 8, and 12. Others, however, may argue that the word "Then"—emphasizing what happens to the virtuous soul when everything else has perished—has an importance that should be reflected in both the reading and the scansion and will therefore mark the first foot of this line as a spondee:

$$\overline{\text{Then}} \; \overline{\text{chief-}} \mid \overset{\smile}{\text{ly}} \; \overline{\text{lives.}} \mid \qquad 16$$

These readers will also see the third foot in line 15 as a spondee:

$$\overset{\smile}{\text{But}} \; \overline{\text{though}} \mid \overline{\text{the}} \; \overline{\text{whole}} \mid \overline{\text{world}} \; \overline{\text{turn}} \mid \overset{\smile}{\text{to}} \; \overline{\text{coal.}} \mid \qquad 15$$

Lines 2 and 7 introduce a different problem. Most readers, encountering these lines in a paragraph of prose, would read them thus:

$$\overset{\smile}{\text{The}} \; \overline{\text{bri-}} \; \overset{\smile}{\text{dal}} \; \overset{\smile}{\text{of}} \; \overset{\smile}{\text{the}} \; \overline{\text{earth}} \; \overset{\smile}{\text{and}} \; \overline{\text{sky,}} \qquad 2$$

$$\overset{\smile}{\text{Thy}} \; \overline{\text{root}} \; \overset{\smile}{\text{is}} \; \overline{\text{ev-}} \; \overset{\smile}{\text{er}} \; \overset{\smile}{\text{in}} \; \overset{\smile}{\text{its}} \; \overline{\text{grave.}} \qquad 7$$

But this reading leaves us with an anomalous situation. First, we have only three accents where our hypothetical pattern calls for four. Second, we have three unaccented syllables occurring together, a situation almost never encountered in verse of duple meter. From this situation we learn an important principle. Though normal reading of the sentences in a poem establishes its metrical pattern, the metrical pattern so established in turn influences the reading. A circular process is at work. In this poem the pressure of the pattern will cause most sensitive readers to stress the second of the three unaccented syllables slightly more than those on either side of it. In scansion we recognize this slight increase of stress by promoting the syllable to the status of an accented syllable. Thus we mark lines 2 and 7 respectively thus:

The brĭ- | dăl of | the eărth | ănd sky, | 2

Thy root ĭs ĕv- | ĕr ĭn | ĭts grave. | 7

Line 5 presents a situation about which there can be no dispute. The word "angry," though it occurs in a position where we would expect an iamb, *must* be accented on the first syllable, and thus must be marked as a trochee:

Sweet rose, | whŏse hue, | ăn- grў | ănd brave. | 5

There is little question also that the following line begins with a trochee in the first foot, followed by a spondee:

Bids thĕ | rash gaz- | ĕr wipe | hĭs eye. | 6

Similarly, the word "Only," beginning line 13, is accented on the first syllable, thus introducing a trochaic substitution in the first foot of that line. Line 13 presents also another problem. A modern reader perceives the word "virtuous" as a three-syllable word, but the poet (writing in the seventeenth century, when metrical requirements were stricter than they are today) would probably have meant the word to be pronounced as two syllables (*ver-tyus*). Following the tastes of my century, I mark it as three, thus introducing an anapest instead of the expected iamb in the last foot:

On- lў | ă sweet | ănd vir- | tŭ- oŭs soul. | 13

In doing this, however, I am consciously "modernizing"—altering the intention of the poet for the sake of a contemporary audience.

One problem remains. In the third stanza, lines 9 and 11 differ from the other lines of the poem in two respects: (a) they contain nine rather than eight syllables; (b) they end on unaccented syllables.

Sweet spring, | full ŏf | sweet days | ănd ros- | ĕs,   9

Mў mu- | sĭc shows | ye have | your clos- | ĕs.   11

Such left-over unaccented syllables are not counted in identifying and naming the meter. These lines are both tetrameter, and if we tap our foot while reading them, we shall tap it four times. Metrical verse will often have one and sometimes two left-over unaccented syllables. In iambic and anapestic verse they will come at the end of lines; in trochaic and dactylic at the beginning.

Our metrical analysis of "Virtue" is completed. Though (mainly for ease of discussion) we have skipped about eccentrically, we have indicated a scansion for all its lines. "Virtue" is written in iambic meter (meaning that most of its feet are iambs), and is composed of four-line stanzas, the first three lines tetrameter, and the final line dimeter. We are now ready to make a few generalizations about scansion.

1. Good readers will not ordinarily stop to scan a poem they are reading, and they certainly will not read a poem with the exaggerated emphasis on accented syllables that we sometimes give them in order to make the scansion more apparent. However, occasional scansion of a poem has value, as will become more apparent in the next chapter, which discusses the relation of sound and meter to sense. Just one example here. The structure of meaning in "Virtue" is unmistakable. It consists of three parallel stanzas concerning things that die, followed by a contrasting fourth stanza concerning the one thing that does not die. The first three stanzas all begin with the word "Sweet" preceding a noun, and the first metrical foot in these stanzas—whether we consider it iamb or spondee—is the same. The contrasting fourth stanza, however, begins with a trochee, thus departing both from the previous pattern and from the basic meter of the poem. This departure is significant, for the word "Only" is the hinge upon which the structure of the poem turns, and the metrical reversal gives it emphasis. Thus meter serves meaning.

2. Scansion is at best a gross way of describing the rhythmical quality of a poem. It depends on classifying all syllables into either accented or unaccented categories and on ignoring the sometimes considerable difference between degrees of accent. Whether we call a syllable accented or unaccented depends, moreover, on its degree of accent relative to the syllables on either side of it. In lines 2 and 7 of "Virtue," the accents on "of" and "in" are obviously much lighter than on the other accented syllables in the line. Unaccented syllables also vary in weight. In line 5 "whose" is clearly heavier than "-gry" and "and," and is arguably heavier even than the accented "of" and "in" of lines 2 and 7. The most ardent champion of spondees, moreover, would concede that the accentual weight is not really equivalent in "Sweet rose": the noun shoulders more of the burden. Scansion is thus incapable of dealing with the subtlest rhythmical effects in poetry. It is nevertheless a useful and serviceable tool. Any measurement device more refined or sensitive would be too complicated to be widely serviceable.

3. Scansion is not an altogether exact science. Within certain limits we may say that a certain scansion is right or wrong, but beyond these limits there is legitimate room for disagreement between qualified read-

ers. Line 11 of "Virtue" provides the best example. Some metrists—those
wanting scansion to reflect as closely as possible the underlying pat-
tern—would mark it as perfectly regular: a succession of four iambs.
Others—those wishing the scansion to reveal more nearly the nuances of
a sensitive reading—would find that three sensitive readers might read
this line in three different ways. One might stress "ye"; a second, "your";
and a third, both. The result is four possible scansions for this line:

$$\text{M\u{y} } \overline{\text{mu-}} \mid \text{s\u{i}c shows} \mid \overline{\text{ye}} \text{ have} \mid \text{y\u{o}ur } \overline{\text{close-}} \mid \text{\u{e}s,} \qquad 11$$

$$\text{M\u{y} } \overline{\text{mu-}} \mid \text{s\u{i}c shows} \mid \overline{\text{ye}} \text{ have} \mid \text{y\u{o}ur } \overline{\text{close-}} \mid \text{\u{e}s,} \qquad 11$$

$$\text{M\u{y} } \overline{\text{mu-}} \mid \text{s\u{i}c shows} \mid \text{y\u{e}} \overline{\text{have}} \mid \overline{\text{your}} \overline{\text{close-}} \mid \text{\u{e}s,} \qquad 11$$

$$\text{M\u{y} } \overline{\text{mu-}} \mid \text{s\u{i}c shows} \mid \overline{\text{ye}} \overline{\text{have}} \mid \overline{\text{your}} \overline{\text{close-}} \mid \text{\u{e}s.} \qquad 11$$

Notice that the divisions between feet have no meaning except to help
us identify the meter. They do not correspond to real divisions in the line;
indeed, they fall often in the middle of a word. We place them where we
do only to yield the most possible of a single kind of foot; in other words,
to reveal regularity. If line 14 is marked

$$\text{L\u{i}ke } \overline{\text{sea-}} \mid \text{son\u{e}d } \overline{\text{tim-}} \mid \text{b\u{e}r, } \overline{\text{nev-}} \mid \text{\u{e}r } \overline{\text{gives,}} \mid \qquad 14$$

it yields four regular iambs. If it were marked

$$\text{L\u{i}ke } \mid \overline{\text{sea-}} \text{ son\u{e}d} \mid \overline{\text{tim-}} \text{ b\u{e}r,} \mid \overline{\text{nev-}} \text{ \u{e}r} \mid \overline{\text{gives,}} \qquad 14$$

there would be an unaccented "left-over" syllable, three trochees, and a
monosyllabic foot. The basic pattern of the poem would be obscured.

4. Finally—and this is the most important generalization of all—
perfect regularity of meter is no criterion of merit. Beginning students
sometimes get the notion that it is. If the meter is smooth and perfectly
regular, they feel that the poet has handled his meter successfully and
deserves all credit for it. Actually there is nothing easier than for any
moderately talented versifier to make language go ta-*dum* ta-*dum* ta-*dum*.
But there are two reasons why this is not generally desirable. The first is
that, as we have said, all art consists essentially of repetition and variation.
If a meter alternates too regularly between light and heavy beats, the
result is to banish variation; the meter becomes mechanical and, for any
sensitive reader, monotonous. The second is that, once a basic meter has
been established, any deviations from it become highly significant and are
the means by which the poet can use meter to reinforce meaning. If a

meter is too perfectly regular, the probability is that the poet, instead of adapting rhythm to meaning, has simply forced his meaning into a metrical straitjacket.

Actually what gives the skillful use of meter its greatest effectiveness is that it consists, not of one rhythm, but of two. One of these is the *expected* rhythm. The other is the *heard* rhythm. Once we have determined the basic meter of a poem, say, iambic tetrameter, we have an expectation that this rhythm will continue. Thus a silent drumbeat is set up in our minds, and this drumbeat constitutes the expected rhythm. But the actual rhythm of the words—the heard rhythm—will sometimes confirm this expected rhythm and sometimes not. Thus the two rhythms are counterpointed, and the appeal of the verse is magnified just as when two melodies are counterpointed in music or as when we see two swallows flying together and around each other, following the same general course but with individual variations and making a much more eye-catching pattern than one swallow flying alone. If the heard rhythm conforms too closely to the expected rhythm, the meter becomes dull and uninteresting. If it departs too far from the expected rhythm, there ceases to be an expected rhythm. If the irregularity is too great, meter disappears and the result is prose rhythm or free verse.

There are several ways by which variation can be introduced into the poet's use of meter. The most obvious way is by the substitution of other kinds of feet for regular feet. In our scansion of line 9 of "Virtue," for instance, we found a spondee, a trochee, and another spondee substituted for the expected iambs in the first three feet (plus an unexpected unaccented syllable left over at the end of the line). A less obvious but equally important means of variation is through simple phrasing and variation of degrees of accent. Though we began our scansion of "Virtue" by marking lines 3, 10, and 14 as perfectly regular, there is actually a considerable difference among them. Line 3 is quite regular, for the phrasing corresponds with the metrical pattern, and the line can be read ta-*dum* ta-*dum* ta-*dum* ta-*dum*. Line 10 is less regular, for the three-syllable word "compacted" cuts across the division between two feet. We should read it ta-*dum* ta-*dum* ta-*dump*-ty *dum*. Line 14 is the least regular of the three, for here there is no correspondence between phrasing and metrical division. We should read this line ta-*dump*-ty *dump*-ty, *dump*-ty *dum*. Finally, variation can be introduced by grammatical and rhetorical pauses. The comma in line 14, by introducing a grammatical pause, provides an additional variation from its perfect regularity. Probably the most violently irregular line in the poem is line 5,

Sweet rose, | whose hue, | an- gry | and brave, | 5 for here the spondaic substitution in the first foot, and the unusual trochaic substitution in the middle of a line in the third foot, are set off and emphasized by grammatical pauses, and also (as we have noted) the unaccented "whose" is considerably heavier than the other two unaccented syllables in the line. It is worth noting that the violent irregularity of this line (only slightly diminished in the next) corresponds with, and reinforces, the most violent image in the poem. Again, meter serves meaning.

The uses of rhythm and meter are several. Like the musical repetitions of sound, the musical repetitions of accent can be pleasing for their own sake. In addition, rhythm works as an emotional stimulus and serves, when used skillfully, to heighten our attention and awareness to what is going on in a poem. Finally, by his choice of meter, and by his skillful use of variation within the metrical framework, the poet can adapt the sound of his verse to its content and thus make meter a powerful reinforcement of meaning. We should avoid, however, the notion that there is any mystical correspondence between certain meters and certain emotions. There are no "happy" meters and no "melancholy" ones. The poet's choice of meter is probably less important than how he handles it after he has chosen it. However, some meters are swifter than others, some slower; some are more lilting than others, some more dignified. The poet can choose a meter that is appropriate or one that is inappropriate to his content, and by his handling of it can increase the appropriateness or inappropriateness. If he chooses a swift, lilting meter for a serious and grave subject, the meter will probably act to keep the reader from feeling any really deep emotion. But if he chooses a more dignified meter, it will intensify the emotion. In all great poetry, meter works intimately with the other elements of the poem to produce the appropriate total effect.

We must not forget, of course, that poetry need not be metrical at all. Like alliteration and rime, like metaphor and irony, like even imagery, meter is simply one resource the poet may or may not use. His job is to employ his resources to the best advantage for the object he has in mind—the kind of experience he wishes to express. And on no other basis can we judge him.

SUPPLEMENTAL NOTE

Of the four standard meters, iambic is by far the commonest. Perhaps 80 percent of metered poetry in English is iambic. Anapestic meter (example: Praed's "Song," page 163, in anapestic tetrameter) is next most common. Trochaic meter (example: "Think'st thou to seduce me then," page 26, in trochaic heptameter) is relatively infrequent. Dactylic meter is so rare as to be almost a museum specimen ("Bedtime Story," page 292, in stanzas consisting of three tetrameter lines followed by a dimeter line, is the sole example in this book).

Because of the predominance of iambic and anapestic meters in English verse, and because most anapestic poems have a high percentage of iambic substitutions, Robert Frost has written that in our language there are virtually but two meters: "strict iambic and loose iambic."* This is, of course, an overstatement; but, like many overstatements, it contains a good deal of truth. "Strict iambic" is strictly duple meter: it admits no trisyllabic substitutions. Trochees, spondees, and, occasionally, monosyllabic feet may be substituted for the expected iambs, but not anapests or dactyls. The presence of a triple foot has such a conspicuous effect in speeding or loosening up a line that the introduction of a few of them quite alters the nature of the meter. Herbert's "Virtue" is written in "strict iambic" (most of its feet are iambic; and, with the dubious exception of "virtuous," it contains no trisyllabic feet). Praed's "Song" is anapestic (most of its feet are anapests). e. e. cummings's "what if a much of a which of a wind" (page 132) contains more iambic than anapestic feet, but *in effect* it sounds more anapestic than iambic, more like Praed's "Song" than like Herbert's "Virtue." It would be impossible to define what percentage of anapestic feet a poem must have before it ceases seeming iambic and begins seeming anapestic, but it would be considerably less than 50 percent and might be more like 25 percent. At any rate, a large number of poems fall into an area between "strict iambic" and "prevailingly anapestic," and they might be fittingly described as iambic-anapestic (what Frost called "loose iambic").

Finally, the importance of the final paragraph preceding this note must be underscored: *poetry need not be metrical at all.* Following the prodigious example of Walt Whitman in the nineteenth century, more and more twentieth-century poets have turned to the writing of *free verse*. FREE VERSE, by our definition, is not verse at all; that is, it is not metrical. It may be rimed or unrimed (most often unrimed). The only difference between free verse and rhythmical prose is that free verse introduces one additional rhythmical unit, the line. The arrangement into lines divides the material into rhythmical units, or cadences. Beyond its line arrangement there are no necessary differences between it and rhythmical prose. Possibly 50 percent of published contemporary poetry is written in free verse.

*"The Figure a Poem Makes," *Selected Prose of Robert Frost* (New York: Holt, 1966), pp. 17-18.

To add one further variation, a number of contemporary poets have begun writing "prose poems," or poems in prose (example: Russell Edson's "The Mouse Dinners," page 277). It is too early to determine whether this is a passing fashion or will be a lasting development.

EXERCISES

1. An important term which every student of poetry should know (and should be careful not to confuse with *free verse*) is *blank verse*. BLANK VERSE has a very specific meter: it is *iambic pentameter, unrimed*. It has a special name because it is the principal English meter, that is, the meter that has been used for a large proportion of the greatest English poetry, including the tragedies of Shakespeare and the epics of Milton. Iambic pentameter in English seems especially suitable for the serious treatment of serious themes. The natural movement of the English language tends to be iambic. Lines shorter than pentameter tend to be songlike, not suited to sustained treatment of serious material. Lines longer than pentameter tend to break up into shorter units, the hexameter line being read as two three-foot units, the heptameter line as a four-foot and a three-foot unit, and so on. Rime, while highly appropriate to most short poems, often proves a handicap for a long and lofty work. (The word *blank* implies that the end of the line is "blank," that is, bare of rime.) The above generalizations, of course, represent tendencies, not laws.

   Of the following poems, four are in blank verse, four are in free verse, and two are in other meters. Determine in which category each belongs.
   a. "Hyla Brook," page 24.
   b. "Mirror," page 30.
   c. "Being Herded Past the Prison's Honor Farm," page 43.
   d. "Ulysses," page 87.
   e. Excerpt from *Macbeth*, page 118.
   f. "in Just—," page 119.
   g. "Journey of the Magi," page 123.
   h. "The Telephone," page 146.
   i. "Grace to Be Said at the Supermarket," page 294.
   j. "Mending Wall," page 278.

2. Another useful distinction is that between end-stopped lines and run-on lines. An END-STOPPED LINE is one in which the end of the line corresponds with a natural speech pause; a RUN-ON LINE is one in which the sense of the line hurries on into the next line. (There are, of course, all degrees of end-stop and run-on. A line ending with a period or semicolon is heavily end-stopped. A line without punctuation at the end is normally considered a run-on line, but it is less forcibly run-on if it ends at a natural speech pause—as between subject and predicate—than if it ends, say, between an article and its noun, between an auxiliary and its verb, or between a preposition and its object.) The use of run-on lines is one way the poet can make use of grammatical or rhetorical pauses to vary his basic meter.
   a. Examine "Sound and Sense" (page 195) and "My Last Duchess" (page 112). Both are written in the same meter: iambic pentameter, rimed in couplets. Is their general rhythmical effect quite similar or markedly dif-

ferent? What accounts for the difference? Does the contrast support our statement that the poet's choice of meter is probably less important than the way he handles it?

b. Examine "The Hound" (page 57) and "The Dance" (page 202). Which is the more forcibly run-on in the majority of its lines? Describe the difference in effect.

* * *

SEAL LULLABY

Oh! hush thee, my baby, the night is behind us,
    And black are the waters that sparkled so green.
The moon, o'er the combers, looks downward to find us
    At rest in the hollows that rustle between.
Where billow meets billow, there soft be thy pillow;
    Ah, weary wee flipperling, curl at thy ease!
The storm shall not wake thee, nor shark overtake thee,
    Asleep in the arms of the slow-swinging seas.

Rudyard Kipling (1865–1936)

QUESTIONS

1. Identify speaker, audience, and situation.
2. What is a "flipperling" (6)? Answer without consulting a dictionary, and explain how you know.
3. Scan the poem and name its meter. Which lines have unaccented syllables left over at the end? Is this an incidental variation from the basic pattern of the poem (as in Herbert's "Virtue," lines 9 and 11), or is it part of the pattern? How does this feature strengthen one's sense of the basic meter?
4. In scanning "Virtue" we noted a circular process in which, while normal reading established the metrical pattern, the metrical pattern in turn influenced the reading, causing us in scansion to promote to accented status certain syllables which would have been unaccented in prose. With poems in triple meter this circular pattern operates in the opposite direction, causing us to demote some syllables that would be accented in prose. It happens twice in this poem. In line 7 the first syllable of "overtake" would normally receive a slight stress, but in the poem this stress is suppressed by the metrical pattern. What syllable in the last line is even more dramatically reduced in the scansion? Does the weight of this unstressed syllable nevertheless affect the sense and movement of the line? How?

"INTRODUCTION" TO *SONGS OF INNOCENCE*

Piping down the valleys wild,
Piping songs of pleasant glee,

On a cloud I saw a child,
And he laughing said to me:

"Pipe a song about a Lamb."   5
So I piped with merry cheer.
"Piper, pipe that song again."
So I piped; he wept to hear.

"Drop thy pipe, thy happy pipe;
Sing thy songs of happy cheer."   10
So I sung the same again
While he wept with joy to hear.

"Piper, sit thee down and write
In a book that all may read."
So he vanished from my sight,   15
And I plucked a hollow reed,

And I made a rural pen,
And I stained the water clear,
And I wrote my happy songs
Every child may joy to hear.   20

William Blake (1757–1827)

QUESTIONS

1. Poets have traditionally been thought of as inspired by one of the Muses (Greek female divinities whose duties were to nurture the arts). Blake's *Songs of Innocence*, a book of poems about childhood and the state of innocence, includes "The Chimney Sweeper" (page 101) and "The Lamb" (page 263). In this introductory poem to the book, what function is played by the child upon a cloud?
2. What is symbolized by "a Lamb" (5)?
3. What three stages of poetic composition are suggested in stanzas 1–2, 3, and 4–5 respectively?
4. What features of the poems in his book does Blake indicate in this "Introduction"? Name at least four.
5. Mark the stressed and unstressed syllables in lines 1–2 and 9–10. Do they establish the basic meter of the poem? If so, is that meter iambic or trochaic? Or could it be either? Some metrists have discarded the distinction between iambic and trochaic, and between anapestic and dactylic, as being artificial. The important distinction, they feel, is between duple and triple meters. Does this poem support their claim?

THE "JE NE SAIS QUOI"

Yes, I'm in love, I feel it now,
And Celia has undone me;

And yet I'll swear I can't tell how
    The pleasing plague stole on me.

'Tis not her face that love creates,   5
    For there no Graces revel;
'Tis not her shape, for there the Fates
    Have rather been uncivil.

'Tis not her air, for sure in that,
    There's nothing more than common;   10
And all her sense is only chat,
    Like any other woman.

Her voice, her touch, might give the alarm—
    'Tis both perhaps, or neither;
In short, 'tis that provoking charm   15
    Of Celia altogether.

William Whitehead (1715–1785)

QUESTIONS

1. *Je ne sais quoi* is a French expression meaning "I do not know what"—an indefinable something. Does the use of approximate rimes rather than perfect rimes in the even lines of this poem help to establish the quality of uncertainty which is the subject of the poem?
2. Find examples of OXYMORON (a compact paradox in which two successive words seemingly contradict each other) in the first and last stanzas. What broad paradox underlies the whole poem?
3. What is the reason for the capitalization and pluralization of "grace" and "fate" in the second stanza? What is the image here conveyed? Is "love" (5) the subject or object of the verb?
4. Describe the metrical pattern of the poem. What effect does the extra unaccented syllable in lines 2 and 4 of each stanza have on the tone of the poem? (The rimes in these lines are feminine, and the lines are said to have feminine endings.)

IF EVERYTHING HAPPENS
THAT CAN'T BE DONE

      if everything happens that can't be done
      (and anything's righter
      than books
      could plan)
      the stupidest teacher will almost guess   5

(with a run
skip
around we go yes)
there's nothing as something as one

one hasn't a why or because or although   10
(and buds know better
than books
don't grow)
one's anything old being everything new
(with a what   15
which
around we come who)
one's everyanything so

so world is a leaf so tree is a bough
(and birds sing sweeter   20
than books
tell how)
so here is away and so your is a my
(with a down
up   25
around again fly)
forever was never till now

now i love you and you love me
(and books are shuter
than books   30
can be)
and deep in the high that does nothing but fall
(with a shout
each
around we go all)   35
there's somebody calling who's we

we're anything brighter than even the sun
(we're everything greater
than books
might mean)   40
we're everyanything more than believe
(with a spin
leap
alive we're alive)
we're wonderful one times one   45

e. e. cummings (*1894–1962*)

1. Explain the last line. Of what very familiar idea is this poem a fresh treatment?
2. The poem is based on a contrast between heart and mind, or love and learning. Which does the poet prefer? What symbols does he use for each?
3. What is the tone of the poem?
4. Which lines of each stanza regularly rime with each other (either perfect or approximate rime)? How does the poet link the stanzas?
5. What is the basic metrical scheme of the poem? What does the meter contribute to the tone? What line (in the fourth stanza) most clearly states the subject and occasion of the poem? How does meter underline its significance?
6. Can you suggest any reason why the poet did not write lines 2–4 and 6–8 of each stanza as one line each? What metrical variations does the poet use in lines 6–8 of each stanza and with what effect?

OH WHO IS THAT YOUNG SINNER

Oh who is that young sinner with the handcuffs on his wrists?
And what has he been after that they groan and shake their fists?
And wherefore is he wearing such a conscience-stricken air?
Oh they're taking him to prison for the color of his hair.

'Tis a shame to human nature, such a head of hair as his;   5
In the good old time 'twas hanging for the color that it is;
Though hanging isn't bad enough and flaying would be fair
For the nameless and abominable color of his hair.

Oh a deal of pains he's taken and a pretty price he's paid
To hide his poll or dye it of a mentionable shade;   10
But they've pulled the beggar's hat off for the world to see and stare,
And they're taking him to justice for the color of his hair.

Now 'tis oakum for his fingers and the treadmill for his feet,
And the quarry-gang on Portland in the cold and in the heat,
And between his spells of labor in the time he has to spare   15
He can curse the God that made him for the color of his hair.

A. E. Housman (1859–1936)

1. Vocabulary: *poll* (10), *oakum* (13). Portland (14), an English peninsula, is the site of a famous criminal prison.
2. What kind of irony does the poem exhibit? Explain.
3. What symbolical meanings are suggested by "the color of his hair"?
4. This poem represents a kind of meter that we have not yet discussed. It *may* be scanned as iambic heptameter:

Oh who | is that | young sin-ner with | the hand-cuffs on | his wrists?|

But you will probably find yourself reading it as a four-beat line:

Oh who | is that young sin-ner with the hand-cuffs on his wrists?|

Although the meter is duple insofar as there is an alternation between unaccented and accented syllables, there is also an alternation in the degree of stress on the accented syllables: the first, third, fifth, and seventh stresses being heavier than the second, fourth, and sixth; the result is that the two-syllable feet tend to group themselves into larger units. We may scan it as follows, using a short line for a light accent, a longer one for a heavy accent:

Oh who | is that young sin-ner with the hand-cuffs on his wrists?|

And what | has he been af-ter that they groan | and shake their fists?|

And where-fore is he wear-ing such a con-science strick-en air?|

Oh they're tak-ing him to pris-on for the col-or of his hair.|

This kind of meter, in which there is an alternation between heavy and light stresses, is known as DIPODIC (two-footed) VERSE. The alternation may not be perfect throughout, but it will be frequent enough to establish a pattern in the reader's mind. Now scan the last three stanzas. For another example of dipodic verse, see "America for Me" (page 235).

DOWN BY THE SALLEY GARDENS

Down by the salley gardens my love and I did meet;
She passed the salley gardens with little snow-white feet.
She bid me take love easy, as the leaves grow on the tree;
But I, being young and foolish, with her would not agree.
In a field by the river my love and I did stand,
And on my leaning shoulder she laid her snow-white hand.
She bid me take life easy, as the grass grows on the weirs;
But I was young and foolish, and now am full of tears.

William Butler Yeats (1865–1939)

QUESTIONS

1. Vocabulary: *salley* (1), *weirs* (7).
2. This poem introduces an additional kind of metrical variation—the metrical pause or rest. Unlike grammatical and rhetorical pauses, the metrical pause affects scansion. If you beat out the rhythm of this poem with your hand, you will find that the fourth beat of each line (possibly excepting lines 3 and 7)

regularly falls *between* syllables.· A METRICAL PAUSE, then, is a pause that replaces an accented syllable. It is usually found in verse that has a pronounced lilt or swing. The first line of Yeats's poem may be scanned as follows (the metrical pause is represented with an *x*):

Down by | the sal- | ley gar-dens,ˣ | my love | and I | did meet. |

The third line might be scanned in several ways, as the following alternatives suggest:

She bid | me take | love eas- | y, as | the leaves | grow on | the tree, |

She bid | me take | love eas- | y,ˣ as the leaves | grow on | the tree. |

Scan the rest of the poem.

HAD I THE CHOICE

Had I the choice to tally greatest bards,
To limn their portraits, stately, beautiful, and emulate at will,
Homer with all his wars and warriors—Hector, Achilles, Ajax,
Or Shakespeare's woe-entangled Hamlet, Lear, Othello—Tennyson's
    fair ladies,
Meter or wit the best, or choice conceit to wield in perfect rhyme,
    delight of singers;
These, these, O sea, all these I'd gladly barter,
Would you the undulation of one wave, its trick to me transfer,
Or breathe one breath of yours upon my verse,
And leave its odor there.

Walt Whitman (1819–1892)

QUESTIONS

1. Vocabulary: *tally* (1), *limn* (2), *conceit* (5).
2. What poetic qualities does Whitman propose to barter in exchange for what? What qualities do the sea and its waves symbolize?
3. What kind of "verse" is this? Why does Whitman prefer it to "meter" and "perfect rhyme"?

THE AIM WAS SONG

Before man came to blow it right
    The wind once blew itself untaught,
And did its loudest day and night
    In any rough place where it caught.

Man came to tell it what was wrong: 5
    It hadn't found the place to blow;
It blew too hard—the aim was song.
    And listen—how it ought to go!

He took a little in his mouth,
    And held it long enough for north   10
To be converted into south,
    And then by measure blew it forth.

By measure. It was word and note,
    The wind the wind had meant to be—
A little through the lips and throat.   15
    The aim was song—the wind could see.

Robert Frost (1874–1963)

QUESTIONS

1. Frost invents a myth about the origin of poetry. What implications does it suggest about the relation of man to nature and of poetry to nature?
2. Contrast the thought and form of this poem with Whitman's.
3. Scan the poem and identify its meter. How does the poet give variety to a regular metrical pattern?

METRICAL FEET

Trochee | trips from | long to | short.

From long to long in solemn sort

Slow Spondee stalks; | strong foot! | yet ill able

Ever to | come up with | Dactyl trisyllable.

Iambics march | from short | to. long;—

With a leap | and a bound | the swift Anapests throng.

Samuel Taylor Coleridge (1772–1834)

QUESTION

If you have trouble remembering the metrical feet, memorize this.

13. Sound and Meaning

Rhythm and sound cooperate to produce what we call the music of poetry. This music, as we have pointed out, may serve two general functions: it may be enjoyable in itself; it may be used to reinforce meaning and intensify the communication.

Pure pleasure in sound and rhythm exists from a very early age in the human being—probably from the age the baby first starts cooing in its cradle, certainly from the age that children begin chanting nursery rimes and skipping rope. The appeal of the following verse, for instance, depends almost entirely on its "music":

Pease | por-ridge | hot, |

Pease | por-ridge | cold, |

Pease | por-ridge | in the | pot |

Nine | days | old. |

There is very little sense here; the attraction comes from the emphatic rhythm, the emphatic rimes (with a strong contrast between the short vowel and short final consonant of *hot-pot* and the long vowel and long final consonant combination of *cold-old*), and the heavy alliteration (exactly half the words begin with *p*). From nonsense rimes such as this, many of us graduate into a love of more meaningful poems whose appeal resides largely in the sound they make. Much of the pleasure that we find in poems like Vachel Lindsay's "The Congo" and Edgar Allan Poe's "The Bells" lies in their musical qualities.

The peculiar function of poetry as distinguished from music, however, is to convey not sounds but meaning or experience *through* sounds. In third- and fourth-rate poetry, sound and rhythm sometimes distract attention from sense. In first-rate poetry the sound exists, not for its own sake, not for mere decoration, but as a medium of meaning. Its function is to support the leading player, not to steal the scene.

There are numerous ways in which the poet may reinforce meaning through sound. Without claiming to exhaust them, perhaps we can include most of the chief means under four general headings.

First, the poet can choose words whose sound in some degree suggests their meaning. In its narrowest sense this is called onomatopoeia. ONO-MATOPOEIA, strictly defined, means the use of words which, at least supposedly, sound like what they mean, such as *hiss, snap,* and *bang.*

SONG: HARK, HARK!

> Hark, hark!
>   Bow-wow.
> The watch-dogs bark!
>   Bow-wow.
> Hark, hark! I hear
> The strain of strutting chanticleer
> Cry, "Cock-a-doodle-doo!"

William Shakespeare (1564-1616)

In this lyric, "bark," "bow-wow," and "cock-a-doodle-doo" are onomatopoetic words. In addition, Shakespeare has reinforced the onomatopoetic effect with the repeated use of "hark," which sounds like "bark." The usefulness of onomatopoeia, of course, is strictly limited, because it can be used only where the poet is describing sound, and most poems do not describe sound. And the use of pure onomatopoeia, as in the above example, is likely to be fairly trivial except as it forms an incidental part of a more complex poem. But by combining onomatopoeia with other devices that help convey meaning, the poet can achieve subtle and beautiful effects whose recognition is one of the keenest pleasures in reading poetry.

In addition to onomatopoetic words there is another group of words, sometimes called PHONETIC INTENSIVES, whose sound, by a process as yet obscure, to some degree suggests their meaning. An initial *fl-* sound, for instance, is often associated with the idea of moving light, as in *flame, flare, flash, flicker, flimmer.* An initial *gl-* also frequently accompanies the idea of light, usually unmoving, as in *glare, gleam, glint, glow, glisten*. An initial *sl-* often introduces words meaning "smoothly wet," as in *slippery, slick, slide, slime, slop, slosh, slobber, slushy*. An initial *st-* often suggests strength, as in *staunch, stalwart, stout, sturdy, stable, steady, stocky, stern, strong, stubborn, steel*. Short *-i-* often goes with the idea of smallness, as in *inch, imp, thin, slim, little, bit, chip, sliver, chink, slit, sip, whit, tittle, snip, wink, glint, glimmer, flicker, pigmy, midge, chick, kid, kitten, minikin, miniature*. Long *-o-* or *-oo-* may suggest melancholy or sorrow, as in *moan, groan, woe, mourn, forlorn, toll, doom, gloom, moody*. Medial and final *-are* sometimes goes with the idea of a big light or noise, as *flare, glare, stare, blare*. Medial *-att-* suggests some kind of particled movement, as in *spatter, scatter, shatter, chatter, rattle, prattle, clatter, batter*. Final *-er* and *-le* indicate repetition, as in *glitter, flutter, shimmer, whisper, jabber, chatter, clatter, sputter, flicker, twitter, mutter*, and *ripple, bubble, twinkle, sparkle, rattle, rumble, jingle*. None of these various sounds is invariably associated with the idea that it seems to suggest, and, in fact, a short *-i-* is found in *thick* as well as *thin*, in *big* as well as *little*. Language is a complex phenomenon. But there is enough association between these sounds and ideas to suggest some sort of intrinsic if obscure relationship, and a word like *flicker*, though not onomatopoetic, for it does not refer to sound, would seem somehow to suggest its sense, the *fl-* suggesting moving light, the *-i-* suggesting smallness, the *-ck* suggesting sudden cessation of movement (as in *crack, peck, pick, hack*, and *flick*), and the *-er* suggesting repetition. The above list of sound-idea correspondences is only a very partial one. A complete list, though it would involve only a small proportion of words in the language, would probably be a longer list than that of the more strictly onomatopoetic words, to which they are related.

SPLINTER

> The voice of the last cricket
> across the first frost
> is one kind of good-by.
> It is so thin a splinter of singing.

> *Carl Sandburg (1878–1967)*

QUESTIONS

1. Why is "so thin a splinter" a better choice of metaphor than *so small an atom* or *so meager a morsel?*
2. How does the poet intensify the effect of the two phonetic intensives in line 4?

A second way that the poet can reinforce meaning through sound is to choose sounds and group them so that the effect is smooth and pleasant sounding (*euphonious*) or rough and harsh sounding (*cacophonous*). The vowels are in general more pleasing than the consonants, for the vowels are musical tones, whereas the consonants are merely noises. A line with a high percentage of vowel sounds in proportion to consonant sounds will therefore tend to be more melodious than one in which the proportion is low. The vowels and consonants themselves differ considerably in quality. The "long" vowels, such as those in *fate, reed, rime, coat, food,* and *dune* are fuller and more resonant than the "short" vowels, as in *fat, red, rim, cot, foot,* and *dun.* Of the consonants, some are fairly mellifluous, such as the "liquids," *l, m, n,* and *r;* the soft *v* and *f* sounds; the semi-vowels *w* and *y;* and such combinations as *th* and *wh.* Others, such as the "plosives," *b, d, g, k, p,* and *t,* are harsher and sharper in their effect. These differences in sound are the poet's materials. However, he will not necessarily seek out the sounds that are pleasing and attempt to combine them in melodious combinations. Rather, he will use euphonious and cacophonous combinations as they are appropriate to his content. Consider, for instance, the following poem.

UPON JULIA'S VOICE

So smooth, so sweet, so silvery is thy voice,
As, could they hear, the Damned would make no noise,
But listen to thee (walking in thy chamber)
Melting melodious words to Lutes of Amber.

Robert Herrick (1591–1674)

QUESTION

Literally, an amber lute is as nonsensical as a silver voice. What connotations do "Amber" and "silvery" have that contribute to the meaning of this poem?

There are no strictly onomatopoetic words in this poem, and yet the sound seems marvelously adapted to the sense. Especially remarkable are the first and last lines, those most directly concerned with Julia's voice. In the first line the sounds that most strike the ear are the unvoiced *s*'s and the soft *v*'s, supported by *th:* "So smo*th,* so *s*weet, so *s*ilvery is *th*y *v*oice." In the fourth line the predominating sounds are the liquid consonants *m, l,* and *r,* supported by a *w:* "*M*e*l*ting *m*e*l*odious *w*ords to *L*utes of A*m*ber." The least euphonious line in the poem, on the other hand, is the second, where the subject is the tormented in hell, not Julia's voice. Here the prominent sounds are the *d*'s, supported by a voiced *s* (a voiced *s* buzzes, unlike the unvoiced *s*'s in line 1), and two *k* sounds: "A*s*, *c*oul*d* they hear, the *D*amne*d* would ma*k*e no noi*s*e." Throughout the poem there is a remarkable correspondence between the pleasant-sounding and the pleasant in idea, the unpleasant-sounding and the unpleasant in idea.

A third way in which a poet can reinforce meaning through sound is by controlling the speed and movement of the lines by the choice and use of meter, by the choice and arrangement of vowel and consonant sounds, and by the disposition of pauses. In meter the unaccented syllables go faster than the accented syllables; hence the triple meters are swifter than the duple. But the poet can vary the tempo of any meter by the use of substitute feet. Whenever two or more unaccented syllables come together, the effect will be to speed up the pace of the line; when two or more accented syllables come together, the effect will be to slow it down. This pace will also be affected by the vowel lengths and by whether the sounds are easily run together. The long vowels take longer to pronounce than the short ones. Some words are easily run together, while others demand that the position of the mouth be re-formed before the next word is uttered. It takes much longer, for instance, to say, "Watch dogs catch much meat" than to say, "My aunt is away," though the number of syllables is the same. And finally the poet can slow down the speed of a line through the introduction of grammatical and rhetorical pauses. Consider lines 54–56 from Tennyson's "Ulysses" (page 87):

The lights | be-gin | to twin-kle | from | the rocks; |

The long | day wanes; | the slow | moon climbs; | the deep | 55

Moans round | with man-ly voi-ces . . .

In these lines Tennyson wished the movement to be slow, in accordance with the slow waning of the long day and the slow climbing of the moon. His meter is iambic pentameter. This is not a swift meter, but in lines 55–56 he slows it down, (1) by introducing three spondaic feet, thus bringing three accented syllables together in three separate places; (2) by choosing for his accented syllables words that have long vowel sounds or dipthongs that the voice hangs on to: "long," "day," "wanes," "slow," "moon," "climbs," "deep," "moans," "round"; (3) by choosing words that are not easily run together (except for "day" and "slow," each of these words begins and ends with consonant sounds that demand varying degrees of readjustment of the mouth before pronunciation is continued); (4) by introducing two grammatical pauses, after "wanes" and "climbs," and a rhetorical pause after "deep." The result is an extremely effective use of the movement of the verse to accord with the movement suggested by the words.*

A fourth way for a poet to fit sound to sense is to control both sound and meter in such a way as to put emphasis on words that are important in meaning. He can do this by marking out such words by alliteration, assonance, consonance, or rime; by placing them before a pause; or by skillfully placing or displacing them in the metrical pattern. Look again at Shakespeare's "Spring" (page 10):

> When dai-sies pied | and vio-lets blue|
>   And la-dy-smocks | all sil-ver-white|
> And cuck-oo-buds | of yel-low hue|
>   Do paint | the mea-dows with | de-light,|
> The cuck-oo then, | on ev-ery tree,| 5
> Mocks mar-ried men; | for thus | sings he,|
>
>   "Cuckoo!
>
> Cuckoo, cuckoo!" O, word of fear,
>
> Unpleasing to a married ear!

The scansion is regular until the beginning of the sixth line: there we find a spondaic substitution in the first foot. In addition, the first three words in this line are heavily alliterated, all beginning with *m*. And further, each of these words ends in a consonant, thus preventing their being run together. The result is to throw heavy emphasis on these three words: to give them, one might almost say, a tone of solemnity, or mock-solemnity. Whether or not the solemnity is in the sound, the emphasis on these three words is appropriate, for it serves to signal the shift in tone that takes place at this point. The first five lines have contained nothing but delightful images; the concluding four introduce the note of irony.

Just as Shakespeare uses metrical irregularity, plus alliteration, to give emphasis to important words, Tennyson, in the concluding line of "Ulysses," uses marked regularity, plus skillful use of grammatical pause, to achieve the same effect:

> Though much | is ta-ken, much | a-bides; | and though|

---

*In addition, Tennyson uses one onomatopoetic word ("moans") and one phonetic intensive ("twinkle").

We are | not now | that strength | which in old | days|
Moved earth | and heav-en, that | which we are, | we are:|
One e-qual tem-per of he-ro-ic hearts,|
Made weak | by time | and fate, | but strong | in will|
To strive, | to seek, | to find, | and not | to yield.|

The blank verse rhythm throughout "Ulysses" is remarkably subtle and varied, but the last line is not only regular in its scansion but heavily regular, for a number of reasons. First, all the words are monosyllables: no words cross over the divisions between feet. Second, the unaccented syllables are all very small and unimportant words—four "to's" and one "and," whereas the accented syllables consist of four important verbs and a very important "not." Third, each of the verbs is followed by a grammatical pause pointed off by a mark of punctuation. The result is to cause a pronounced alternation between light and heavy syllables that brings the accent down on the four verbs and the "not" with sledgehammer blows. The line rings out like a challenge, which it is.

THE SPAN OF LIFE

The old dog barks backward without getting up.
I can remember when he was a pup.

Robert Frost (1874–1963)

QUESTIONS

1. Is the dog a dog only or also a symbol?
2. The first line presents a visual and auditory image; the second line makes a comment. But does the second line *call up images?* Does it suggest more than it says? Would the poem have been more or less effective if the second line had been, "He was frisky and lively when he was a pup"?

We may well conclude our discussion of the adaptation of sound to sense by analyzing this very brief poem. It consists of one riming anapestic tetrameter couplet. Its content is a contrast between the decrepitude of an old dog and his friskiness as a pup. The scansion is as follows:

The old | dog barks back-ward with-out | get-ting up.|
I | can re-mem-ber when he | was a pup.|

How is sound fitted to sense? In the first place, the triple meter chosen by the poet is a swift meter, but in the first line he has jammed it up in a remarkable way by substituting a kind of foot so rare that we do not even have a name for it. It might be called a triple spondee: at any rate it is a foot in which the accent is distributed over three syllables. This foot, following the accented syllable in the first foot, creates a situation where four accented syllables are pushed up together. In addition, each of these accented syllables begins and ends with a strong consonant sound or cluster of consonant sounds, so that they cannot be run together in pronunciation: the mouth must be re-formed between each syllable: "The *old dog barks backward.*" The result is to slow down the line drastically, to almost destroy its rhythmical quality, and to make it difficult to utter. Indeed, the line is as decrepit as the old dog who turns his head to greet his master but does not get up. When we get to the second line, however, the contrast is startling. The rhythm is swift and regular, the syllables end in vowels or liquid consonants and are easily run together, the whole line ripples fluently off the tongue. In addition, where the first line has a high proportion of explosive and cacophonous consonants—"The ol*d dog barks backward* without *getting up*"—the second line contains predominantly consonants which are smoother and more graceful—"I ca*n remember when he was* a pup." Thus the motion and the sound of the lines are remarkably in accord with the visual images they suggest. In addition, in the first line the poet has supported the onomatopoetic word *barks* with a near echo *back,* so that the sound reinforces the auditory image. If the poem does a great deal in just two lines, this skillful adaptation of sound to sense is one very important reason.

In analyzing verse for correspondence between sound and sense, we need to be very cautious not to make exaggerated claims. A great deal of nonsense has been written about the moods of certain meters and the effects of certain sounds, and it is easy to suggest correspondences that exist really only in our imaginations. Nevertheless, the first-rate poet has nearly always an instinctive tact about handling his sound so that it in some degree supports his meaning; the inferior poet is usually obtuse to these correspondences. One of the few absolute rules that can be applied to the judgment of poetry is that the form should be adequate to the content. This rule does not mean that there must always be a close and easily demonstrable correspondence. It does mean that there will be no glaring discrepancies. Poor poets, and even good poets in their third-rate work, sometimes go horribly wrong.

The two selections that introduce this chapter illustrate, first, the use of sound in verse almost purely for its own sake ("Pease porridge hot"), and, second, the use of sound in verse almost purely to *imitate* meaning ("Hark, hark! Bow-wow"), and they are, as significant poetry, perhaps the most trivial pieces in the whole book. But in between these extremes there is an abundant range of poetic possibilities where sound is pleasurable for itself without violating meaning and where sound to varying degrees corresponds with and corroborates meaning; and in this rich middle range, for the reader who can learn to perceive them, lie many of the greatest pleasures of reading poetry.

EXERCISE

In which of the following pairs of quotations is sound more successfully adapted to sense? As precisely as possible, explain why. (The poet named is in each case the author of the superior version.)

1. a. Go forth—and Virtue, ever in your sight
      Shall be your guide by day, your guard by night.
   b. Go forth—and Virtue, ever in your sight,
      Shall point your way by day, and keep you safe at night.

Charles Churchill

2. a. How charming is divine philosophy!
      Not harsh and rough as foolish men suppose
      But musical as is the lute of Phoebus.
   b. How charming is divine philosophy!
      Not harsh and crabbed as dull fools suppose
      But musical as is Apollo's lute.

Milton

3. a. All day the fleeing crows croak hoarsely over the snow.
   b. All day the out-cast crows croak hoarsely across the whiteness.

Elizabeth Coatsworth

4. a. Your talk attests how bells of singing gold
      Would sound at evening over silent water.
   b. Your low voice tells how bells of singing gold
      Would sound at twilight over silent water.

Edwin Arlington Robinson

5. a. A thousand streamlets flowing through the lawn,
      The moan of doves in gnarled ancient oaks,
      And quiet murmuring of countless bees.
   b. Myriads of rivulets hurrying through the lawn,
      The moan of doves in immemorial elms,
      And murmuring of innumerable bees.

Tennyson

6. a. It is the lark that sings so out of tune,
      Straining harsh discords and unpleasing sharps.

b. It is the lark that warbles out of tune
In harsh discordant tones with doleful flats.

Shakespeare

7. a. "Artillery" and "armaments" and "implements of war"
Are phrases too severe to please the gentle Muse.
b. Bombs, drums, guns, bastions, batteries, bayonets, bullets,—
Hard words, which stick in the soft Muses' gullets.

Byron

8. a. The hands of the sisters Death and Night incessantly softly wash
again, and ever again, this soiled world.
b. The hands of the soft twins Death and Night repeatedly wash
again, and ever again, this dirty world.

Whitman

9. a. The curfew sounds the knell of parting day,
The lowing cattle slowly cross the lea,
The plowman goes wearily plodding his homeward way,
Leaving the world to the darkening night and me.
b. The curfew tolls the knell of parting day,
The lowing herd wind slowly o'er the lea,
The plowman homeward plods his weary way,
And leaves the world to darkness and to me.

Thomas Gray

10. a. Let me chastise this odious, gilded bug,
This painted son of dirt, that smells and bites.
b. Yet let me flap this bug with gilded wings,
This painted child of dirt, that stinks and stings.

Pope

*   *   *

SOUND AND SENSE

True ease in writing comes from art, not chance,
As those move easiest who have learned to dance.
'Tis not enough no harshness gives offense,
The sound must seem an echo to the sense:
Soft is the strain when Zephyr gently blows,   5
And the smooth stream in smoother numbers flows;
But when loud surges lash the sounding shore,
The hoarse, rough verse should like the torrent roar;
When Ajax strives some rock's vast weight to throw,
The line too labors, and the words move slow;   10
Not so, when swift Camilla scours the plain,

Flies o'er the unbending corn, and skims along the main.
Hear how Timotheus' varied lays surprise,
And bid alternate passions fall and rise!

Alexander Pope (1688-1744)

QUESTIONS

1. Vocabulary: *numbers* (6), *lays* (13).
2. This excerpt is from a long poem (called *An Essay on Criticism*) on the arts of writing and judging poetry. Which line is the topic sentence of the passage?
3. There are four classical allusions: Zephyr (5) was god of the west wind; Ajax (9), a Greek warrior noted for his strength; Camilla (11), a legendary queen reputedly so fleet of foot that she could run over a field of grain without bending the blades or over the sea without wetting her feet; Timotheus (13), a famous Greek rhapsodic poet. Does the use of these allusions enable Pope to achieve greater economy?
4. Copy the passage and scan it. Then, considering both meter and sounds, show how Pope practices what he preaches. (Incidentally, on which syllable should "alternate" in line 14 be accented?)

I LIKE TO SEE IT LAP THE MILES

I like to see it lap the miles,
And lick the valleys up,
And stop to feed itself at tanks;
And then, prodigious, step

Around a pile of mountains,   5
And, supercilious, peer
In shanties by the sides of roads;
And then a quarry pare

To fit its ribs,
And crawl between,   10
Complaining all the while
In horrid, hooting stanza;
Then chase itself down hill

And neigh like Boanerges;
Then, punctual as a star,   15
Stop—docile and omnipotent—
At its own stable door.

Emily Dickinson (1830-1886)

QUESTIONS

1. Vocabulary: *prodigious* (4), *supercilious* (6), *Boanerges* (14).
2. What basic metaphor underlies the poem? Identify the literal and the metaphorical terms and explain how you were able to make both identifications.
3. What additional figures of speech do you find in lines 8, 12, 15, 16, and 17? Explain their appropriateness.
4. Point out examples of alliteration, assonance, and consonance. Does this poem have a rime scheme?
5. Considering such things as sounds and sound repetitions, grammatical pauses, run-on lines, monosyllabic and polysyllabic words, onomatopoeia, and meter, explain in detail how sound is fitted to sense in this poem.

WIND

This house has been far out at sea all night,
The woods crashing through darkness, the booming hills,
Winds stampeding the fields under the window
Floundering black astride and blinding wet

Till day rose; then under an orange sky   5
The hills had new places, and wind wielded
Blade-like, luminous black and emerald,
Flexing like the lens of a mad eye.

At noon I scaled along the house-side as far as
The coal-house door. I dared once to look up—   10
Through the brunt wind that dented the balls of my eyes
The tent of the hills drummed and strained its guyrope,

The fields quivering, the skyline a grimace,
At any second to bang and vanish with a flap:
The wind flung a magpie away and a black-   15
Back gull bent like an iron bar slowly. The house

Rang like some fine green goblet in the note
That any second would shatter it. Now deep
In chairs, in front of the great fire, we grip
Our hearts and cannot entertain book, thought,   20

Or each other. We watch the fire blazing,
And feel the roots of the house move, but sit on,
Seeing the window tremble to come in,
Hearing the stones cry out under the horizons.

Ted Hughes (b. 1930)

QUESTIONS

1. Explain the images, or metaphors, in lines 1, 3, 6, 7–8, 12–14, 15–16, 22. What kind of weather is the poem describing?
2. Discuss the adaptation of sound to sense.

HEAVEN-HAVEN

A Nun Takes the Veil

      I have desired to go
        Where springs not fail,
To fields where flies no sharp and sided hail
      And a few lilies blow.

      And I have asked to be
        Where no storms come,
Where the green swell is in the havens dumb,
      And out of the swing of the sea.

Gerard Manley Hopkins (1844–1889)

QUESTIONS

1. Vocabulary: *blow* (4).
2. Who is the speaker and what is the situation? Explain the metaphors that form the substance of the poem. What things are being compared?
3. Comment on the meaning of "springs" (2) and on the effectiveness of the poet's choice of "lilies" (4).
4. How do the sound repetitions of the title reinforce the meaning? Are there other instances in the poem where sound reinforces meaning?
5. Scan the poem. (The meter is basically iambic, but there is a great deal of variation.) How does the meter reinforce meaning, especially in the last line? What purpose is served by the displacement of "not" (2) from its normal order?

ANTHEM FOR DOOMED YOUTH

    What passing-bells for these who die as cattle?
    Only the monstrous anger of the guns.
    Only the stuttering rifles' rapid rattle
    Can patter out their hasty orisons.
    No mockeries now for them; no prayers nor bells,   5
    Nor any voice of mourning save the choirs,—
    The shrill, demented choirs of wailing shells;
    And bugles calling for them from sad shires.

What candles may be held to speed them all?
Not in the hands of boys, but in their eyes   10
Shall shine the holy glimmers of good-byes.
The pallor of girls' brows shall be their pall;
Their flowers the tenderness of patient minds,
And each slow dusk a drawing-down of blinds.

Wilfred Owen (1893–1918)

QUESTIONS

1. Vocabulary: *passing-bells* (1), *orisons* (4), *shires* (8), *pall* (12).
2. How do the octave and the sestet of this sonnet differ in (a) geographical
   setting, (b) subject matter, (c) kind of imagery used, and (d) tone? Who are the
   "boys" (10) and "girls" (12) referred to in the sestet? It was the custom during
   World War I to draw down the blinds in homes where a son had been
   lost (14).
3. What central metaphorical image runs throughout the poem? What secondary
   metaphors build up the central one?
4. Why are the "doomed youth" said to die "as cattle"? Why would prayers,
   bells, and so on, be "mockeries" for them (5)?
5. Show how sound is adapted to sense throughout the poem.

BOOT AND SADDLE

Boot, saddle, to horse, and away!
Rescue my castle before the hot day
Brightens to blue from its silvery gray.
    Chorus: *Boot, saddle, to horse, and away!*

Ride past the suburbs, asleep as you'd say;   5
Many's the friend there, will listen and pray,
"God's luck to gallants that strike up the lay—
    Chorus: *Boot, saddle, to horse, and away!*"

Forty miles off, like a roebuck at bay,
Flouts Castle Brancepeth the Roundheads' array;   10
Who laughs, "Good fellows ere this, by my fay,°   faith
    Chorus: *Boot, saddle, to horse, and away?*"

Who? My wife Gertrude; that, honest and gay,
Laughs when you talk of surrendering, "Nay!
I've better counselors; what counsel they?   15
    Chorus: *Boot, saddle, to horse, and away!*"

Robert Browning (1812–1889)

1. Vocabulary: *lay* (7).
2. The historical setting for this song is the English Civil War (1642–1649) between the Royalists (Cavaliers) and the Puritans (Roundheads). Who is the speaker? What is the situation? Who is imagined to be speaking in the three passages between quotation marks?
3. Comment on the choice of meter in relation to the subject, especially on the handling of the meter in the refrain.

NIGHT OF SPRING

Slow, horses, slow,
As through the wood we go—
We would count the stars in heaven,
Hear the grasses grow:

Watch the cloudlets few   5
Dappling the deep blue,
In our open palms outspread
Catch the blessèd dew.

Slow, horses, slow,
As through the wood we go—   10
We would see fair Dian rise
With her huntress bow:

We would hear the breeze
Ruffling the dim trees,
Hear its sweet love-ditty set   15
To endless harmonies.

Slow, horses, slow,
As through the wood we go—
All the beauty of the night
.We would learn and know!   20

Thomas Westwood (1814–1888)

QUESTIONS

1. Vocabulary: *Dian* (11).
2. Compare and contrast this poem with the preceding poem in subject and situation, and in adaptation of sound and meter to sense, especially in the refrain.
3. Find phonetic intensives in stanzas 2 and 4. How do the rimes function in stanza 4?

EIGHT O'CLOCK

He stood, and heard the steeple
　　Sprinkle the quarters on the morning town.
One, two, three, four, to market-place and people
　　It tossed them down.

Strapped, noosed, nighing his hour,
　　He stood and counted them and cursed his luck;
And then the clock collected in the tower
　　Its strength, and struck.

A. E. Housman (1859–1936)

QUESTIONS

1. Vocabulary: *quarters* (2).
2. Eight A.M. is the traditional hour in England for putting condemned men to death. Discuss the force of "morning" (2) and "struck" (8). Discuss the appropriateness of the image of the clock collecting its strength. Can you suggest any reason for the use of "nighing" (5) rather than *nearing?*
3. Scan the poem and note its musical devices. Comment on the adaptation of sound to sense.

ALL DAY I HEAR

All day I hear the noise of waters
　　Making moan,
Sad as the sea-bird is, when going
　　Forth alone,
He hears the winds cry to the waters'　　　　　　5
　　Monotone.

The grey winds, the cold winds are blowing
　　Where I go.
I hear the noise of many waters
　　Far below.　　　　　　　　　　　　　　10
All day, all night, I hear them flowing
　　To and fro.

James Joyce (1882–1941)

QUESTIONS

1. What is the central purpose of the poem? Is it primarily descriptive?
2. What kinds of imagery does the poem contain?

3. Discuss the adaptation of sound to meaning, commenting on the use of ono-
matopoeia, phonetic intensives, alliteration, consonance, rime, vowel quality,
stanzaic structure, the counterpointing of the rhythmically varied long lines
with the rhythmically regular short lines.

THE DANCE

In Breughel's great picture, The Kermess,
the dancers go round, they go round and
around, the squeal and the blare and the
tweedle of bagpipes, a bugle and fiddles
tipping their bellies (round as the thick-   5
sided glasses whose wash they impound)
their hips and their bellies off balance
to turn them. Kicking and rolling about
the Fair Grounds, swinging their butts, those
shanks must be sound to bear up under such   10
rollicking measures, prance as they dance
in Breughel's great picture, The Kermess.

William Carlos Williams (1883–1963)

QUESTION

Peter Breughel, the Elder, was a sixteenth-century Flemish painter of peasant
life. A *kermess* is an annual outdoor festival or fair. How do the form, the meter,
and the sounds of this poem reinforce its content?

TO FOOL, OR KNAVE

Thy praise or dispraise is to me alike:
One doth not stroke me, nor the other strike.

Ben Jonson (1573?–1637)

14. Pattern

rt, ultimately, is organization. It is a searching after order, after form. The primal artistic act was God's creation of the universe out of chaos, shaping the formless into form; and every artist since, on a lesser scale, has sought to imitate Him—by selection and arrangement to reduce the chaotic in experience to a meaningful and pleasing order. For this reason we evaluate a poem partially by the same criteria that an English instructor uses to evaluate a theme—by its unity, its coherence, and its proper placing of emphasis. In a well-constructed poem there is neither too little nor too much; every part of the poem belongs where it is and could be placed nowhere else; any interchanging of two stanzas, two lines, or even two words, would to some extent damage the poem and make it less effective. We come to feel, with a truly first-rate poem, that the choice and placement of every word is inevitable, that it could not be otherwise.

In addition to the internal ordering of materials—the arrangement of ideas, images, and thoughts, which we may refer to as the poem's STRUCTURE—the poet may impose some external pattern on his poem, may give it not only an inside logical order but an outside symmetry, or FORM. In doing so, he appeals to the human instinct for design, the instinct that has prompted men, at various times, to tattoo and paint their bodies, to decorate their swords and armor with beautiful and complex tracery, and to choose patterned fabrics for their clothing, carpets, curtains, and wallpapers. The poet appeals to our love of the shapely.

In general, there are three broad kinds of form into which the poet may cast his work: continuous form, stanzaic form, and fixed form.

In CONTINUOUS FORM, as illustrated by "Had I the Choice" (page

184), "Dover Beach" (page 258), "Ulysses" (page 87), and "My Last Duchess" (page 112), the element of formal design is slight. The lines follow each other without formal grouping, the only breaks being dictated by units of meaning, as paragraph breaks are in prose. Even here there are degrees of formal pattern. The free verse "Had I the Choice" has neither regular meter nor rime. "Dover Beach," on the other hand, is metrical; it has no regularity in length of line, but the meter is prevailingly iambic. "Ulysses" is regular in both meter and length of line; it is unrimed iambic pentameter, or blank verse. And to these regularities "My Last Duchess" adds regularity of rime, for it is written in riming iambic pentameter couplets. Thus, in increasing degrees, the authors of "Dover Beach," "Ulysses," and "My Last Duchess" have chosen a predetermined pattern in which to cast their work.

In STANZAIC FORM the poet writes in a series of STANZAS, that is, repeated units having the same number of lines, usually the same metrical pattern, and often an identical rime scheme. The poet may choose some traditional stanza pattern (for poetry, like colleges, is rich in tradition) or invent his own. The traditional stanza patterns (for example, terza rima, ballad meter, rime royal, Spenserian stanza) are many, and the student specializing in literature will wish to familiarize himself with some of them; the general student should know that they exist. Often the use of one of these traditional stanza forms constitutes a kind of literary allusion. The reader who is conscious of its traditional use or of its use by a previous great poet will be aware of subtleties in the communication that a less well-read reader may miss.

As with continuous form, there are degrees of formal pattern in stanzaic form. In "Being Herded Past the Prison's Honor Farm" (page 43) the stanzas are alike only in each having the same number of lines. In "Poem in October" (page 211) the stanzas are alike in length of line but are without a regular pattern of rime. In "Virtue" (page 168) a rime pattern is added to a metrical pattern. In Shakespeare's "Winter" (page 6) and "Spring" (page 10), a refrain is employed in addition to the patterns of meter and rime. The following poem illustrates additional elements of design:

THE GREEDY THE PEOPLE

the greedy the people
(as if as can yes)
they sell and they buy
and they die for because

though the bell in the steeple 5
says Why

the chary the wary
(as all as can each)
they don't and they do
and they turn to a which 10
though the moon in her glory
says Who

the busy the millions
(as you're as can i'm)
they flock and they flee 15
through a thunder of seem
though the stars in their silence
say Be

the cunning the craven
(as think as can feel) 20
they when and they how
and they live for until
though the sun in his heaven
says Now

the timid the tender 25
(as doubt as can trust)
they work and they pray
and they bow to a must
though the earth in her splendor
says May 30

e. e. cummings (1894–1962)

QUESTIONS

1. This poem is a constellation of interlocking patterns. To appreciate them fully, read it first in the normal fashion, one line after another; then read all the first lines of the stanzas, followed by the second lines, the third lines, and so on. Having done this, describe (a) the rime scheme; (b) the metrical design; (c) the sound pattern (How are the two main words in each of the first lines related?); (d) the syntactical pattern. Prepare a model of the poem in which the recurring words are written out, blanks are left for varying words, and recurring parts of speech are indicated in parentheses. The model for the third lines would be: *they* [*verb*] *and they* [*verb*]. Describe the pattern of meaning. How do the last two lines of each stanza relate to the first four? What blanks in your model are to be filled in by words related in meaning?
2. A trademark of e. e. cummings as a poet is his imaginative freedom with parts

of speech. For instance, in line 21 he uses conjunctions as verbs. What different parts of speech does he use as nouns in the fourth line of each stanza? Can you see meanings for these unusual nouns? Explain the contrast between the last words in the fourth and sixth lines of each stanza. What two meanings has the final word of the poem?

3. Sum up briefly the meaning of the poem.

A stanza form may be described by designating four things: the rime scheme (if there is one), the position of the refrain (if there is one), the prevailing metrical foot, and the number of feet in each line. Rime scheme is traditionally designated by using letters of the alphabet to indicate the riming lines, and x for unrimed lines. Refrain lines may be indicated by a capital letter, and the number of feet in the line by a numerical exponent after the letter. Thus the stanza pattern of Browning's "Meeting at Night" (page 47) is iambic tetrameter $abccba$ (or iambic $abccba^4$); that of cummings's "if everything happens that can't be done" (page 180) is anapestic $a^4x^2x^1a^1b^4x^1x^1b^2a^3$; that of Shakespeare's "Spring" (page 10) is iambic $ababCC^4X^1DD^4$.

A FIXED FORM is a traditional pattern that applies to a whole poem. In French poetry many fixed forms have been widely used: rondeaus, roundels, villanelles, triolets, sestinas, ballades, double ballades, and others. In English poetry, though most of the fixed forms have been experimented with, perhaps only two—the limerick and the sonnet—have really taken hold.

The LIMERICK, though really a subliterary form, will serve to illustrate the fixed form in general. Its pattern is anapestic $aa^3bb^2a^3$:

There was | a young la-dy of Ni-ger

Who smiled | as she rode | on a ti-ger;

They re-turned | from the ride

With the la-dy in-side,

And the smile | on the face | of the ti-ger.

Anonymous

The limerick form is used exclusively for humorous and nonsense verse, for which, with its swift catchy meter, short lines, and emphatic rimes, it is particularly suitable. By trying to recast these little jokes and bits of nonsense in a different meter and pattern or into prose, we may discover how much of their effect they owe particularly to the limerick form.

There is, of course, no magical or mysterious identity between certain forms and certain types of content, but there may be more or less correspondence. A form may be appropriate or inappropriate. The limerick form is inappropriate for the serious treatment of serious material.

The SONNET is less rigidly prescribed than the limerick. It must be fourteen lines in length, and it almost always is iambic pentameter, but in structure and rime scheme there may be considerable leeway. Most sonnets, however, conform more or less closely to one of two general models or types, the Italian and the English.

The ITALIAN or *Petrarchan* SONNET (so called because the Italian poet Petrarch practiced it so extensively) is divided usually between eight lines called the octave, using two rimes arranged *abbaabba,* and six lines called the sestet, using any arrangement of either two or three rimes: *cdcdcd* and *cdecde* are common patterns. Usually in the Italian sonnet, corresponding to the division between octave and sestet indicated by the rime scheme (and sometimes marked off in printing by a space), there is a division of thought. The octave presents a situation and the sestet a comment, or the octave an idea and the sestet an example, or the octave a question and the sestet an answer. Thus the form reflects the structure.

ON FIRST LOOKING INTO CHAPMAN'S HOMER

Much have I traveled in the realms of gold,
    And many goodly states and kingdoms seen;
    Round many western islands have I been
Which bards in fealty to Apollo hold.
Oft of one wide expanse had I been told   5
    That deep-browed Homer ruled as his demesne;
    Yet did I never breathe its pure serene
Till I heard Chapman speak out loud and bold:
Then felt I like some watcher of the skies
    When a new planet swims into his ken;   10
Or like stout Cortez when with eagle eyes
    He stared at the Pacific—and all his men
Looked at each other with a wild surmise—
    Silent, upon a peak in Darien.

John Keats (1795–1821)

QUESTIONS

1. Vocabulary: *fealty* (4), *Apollo* (4), *demesne* (6), *ken* (10). *Darien* (14) is an ancient name for the isthmus of Panama.

2. John Keats, at twenty-one, could not read Greek and was probably acquainted with Homer's *Iliad* and *Odyssey* only through the translations of Alexander Pope, which to him would have seemed prosy and stilted. Then one day he and a friend found a vigorous poetic translation by the Elizabethan poet George Chapman. Keats and his friend, enthralled, sat up late at night excitedly reading aloud to each other from Chapman's book. Toward morning Keats walked home and, before going to bed, wrote the above sonnet and sent it to his friend. What common ideas underlie the three major figures of speech in the poem?
3. What is the rime scheme? What division of thought corresponds to the division between octave and sestet?
4. Balboa, not Cortez, discovered the Pacific. How seriously does this mistake detract from the value of the poem?

The ENGLISH or *Shakespearean* SONNET (invented by the English poet Surrey and made famous by Shakespeare) is composed of three quatrains and a concluding couplet, riming *abab cdcd efef gg*. Again, there is often a correspondence between the units marked off by the rimes and the development of the thought. The three quatrains, for instance, may present three examples and the couplet a conclusion or (as in the following example) three metaphorical statements of one idea plus an application.

THAT TIME OF YEAR

That time of year thou mayst in me behold
When yellow leaves, or none, or few, do hang
Upon those boughs which shake against the cold,
Bare ruined choirs where late the sweet birds sang.
In me thou see'st the twilight of such day   5
As after sunset fadeth in the west,
Which by and by black night doth take away,
Death's second self, that seals up all in rest.
In me thou see'st the glowing of such fire,
That on the ashes of his youth doth lie   10
As the deathbed whereon it must expire,
Consumed with that which it was nourished by.
    This thou perceivest, which makes thy love more strong,
    To love that well which thou must leave ere long.

William Shakespeare (1564–1616)

QUESTIONS

1. What are the three major images introduced by the three quatrains? What do they have in common? Can you see any reason for presenting them in this particular order, or might they be rearranged without loss?

2. Each of the images is to some degree complicated rather than simple. For instance, what additional image is introduced by "bare ruined choirs" (4)? Explain its appropriateness.
3. What additional comparisons are introduced in the second and third quatrains? Explain line 12.
4. Whom does the speaker address? What assertion does he make in the concluding couplet, and with what degree of confidence? Paraphrase these lines so as to state their meaning as clearly as possible.

At first glance it may seem absurd that a poet should choose to confine himself in an arbitrary fourteen-line mold with prescribed meter and rime scheme. He does so partly from the desire to carry on a tradition, as all of us carry out certain traditions for their own sake, else why should we bring a tree indoors at Christmas time? But, in addition, the tradition of the sonnet has proved a useful one for, like the limerick, it seems effective for certain types of subject matter and treatment. Though this area cannot be as narrowly limited or as rigidly described as for the limerick, the sonnet is usually most effective when used for the serious treatment of love but has also been used for the discussion of death, religion, political situations, and related subjects. Again, there is no magical affinity between form and subject, or treatment, and excellent sonnets have been written outside these traditional areas. The sonnet tradition has also proved useful because it has provided a challenge to the poet. The inferior poet, of course, is often defeated by that challenge: he will use unnecessary words to fill out his meter or inappropriate words for the sake of his rime. The good poet is inspired by the challenge: it will call forth ideas and images that might not otherwise have come. He will subdue his form rather than be subdued by it; he will make it do his will. There is no doubt that the presence of a net makes good tennis players more precise in their shots than they otherwise would be. And finally, there is in all form the pleasure of form itself.

EXERCISES

1. "One Art" (page 262), "The Waking" (page 301), and "Do not go gentle into that good night" (page 308) are all examples of the French fixed form known as the *villanelle*. After reading the poems and studying their form, define the *villanelle*.
2. "Acquainted with the Night" (page 278) is written in the stanzaic form known as *terza rima* (most famous for its use by Dante in *The Divine Comedy*). Study its rime scheme and give a description of *terza rima*.
3. Reread the following sonnets; classify each (when possible) as primarily Italian or primarily English; then specify how closely each sticks to or how far it

departs from (in form and structure) the polarities represented by "On First Looking into Chapman's Homer" and "That time of year":

a. "When my love swears that she is made of truth," page 34.
b. "Spring," page 54.
c. "The Silken Tent," page 66.
d. "Redemption," page 84.
e. "Ozymandias," page 103.
f. "Batter my heart, three-personed God," page 106.
g. "On His Blindness," page 119.
h. "Leda and the Swan," page 122.
i. "Design," page 131.
j. "when serpents bargain for the right to squirm," page 133.
k. "The Caged Skylark," page 134.
l. "Since there's no help," page 143.
m. "God's Grandeur," page 157.
n. "Anthem for Doomed Youth," page 198.

*   *   *

A HANDFUL OF LIMERICKS*

I sat next the Duchess at tea.
It was just as I feared it would be:
　　Her rumblings abdominal
　　Were simply abominable,
And everyone thought it was me.

There was a young lady of Lynn
Who was so uncommonly thin
　　That when she essayed
　　To drink lemonade
She slipped through the straw and fell in.

A tutor who tooted the flute
Tried to tutor two tooters to toot.
　　Said the two to the tutor,
　　"Is it harder to toot or
To tutor two tooters to toot?"

There was a young maid who said, "Why
Can't I look in my ear with my eye?
　　If I put my mind to it,

---

*Most limericks are anonymous. If not written anonymously, they soon become so, unfortunately for the glory of their authors, because of repeated oral transmission and reprinting without accreditation.

I'm sure I can do it.
You never can tell till you try."

There was an old man of Peru
Who dreamt he was eating his shoe.
    He awoke in the night
    In a terrible fright,
And found it was perfectly true!

A decrepit old gas man named Peter,
While hunting around for the meter,
    Touched a leak with his light.
    He arose out of sight,
And, as anyone can see by reading this, he
    also destroyed the meter.

Well, it's partly the shape of the thing
That gives the old limerick wing;
    These accordion pleats
    Full of airy conceits
Take it up like a kite on a string.

POEM IN OCTOBER

It was my thirtieth year to heaven
Woke to my hearing from harbor and neighbor wood
    And the mussel pooled and the heron
        Priested shore
        The morning beckon   5
With water praying and call of seagull and rook
And the knock of sailing boats on the net webbed wall
        Myself to set foot
        That second
    In the still sleeping town and set forth.   10

My birthday began with the water-
Birds and the birds of the winged trees flying my name
    Above the farms and the white horses
        And I rose
        In rainy autumn   15
And walked abroad in a shower of all my days.
High tide and the heron dived when I took the road
        Over the border
        And the gates
    Of the town closed as the town awoke.   20

A springful of larks in a rolling
Cloud and the roadside bushes brimming with whistling
    Blackbirds and the sun of October
            Summery
        On the hill's shoulder,   25
Here were fond climates and sweet singers suddenly
Come in the morning where I wandered and listened
        To the rain wringing
            Wind blow cold
    In the woods faraway under me.   30

    Pale rain over the dwindling harbor
And over the sea wet church the size of a snail
    With its horns through mist and the castle
            Brown as owls
        But all the gardens   35
Of spring and summer were blooming in the tall tales
Beyond the border and under the lark full cloud.
        There could I marvel
            My birthday
    Away but the weather turned around.   40

    It turned away from the blithe country
And down the other air and the blue altered sky
    Streamed again a wonder of summer
            With apples
        Pears and red currants   45
And I saw in the turning so clearly a child's
Forgotten mornings when he walked with his mother
        Through the parables
            Of sun light
    And the legends of the green chapels   50

    And the twice told fields of infancy
That his tears burned my cheeks and his heart moved in mine.
    These were the woods the river and sea
            Where a boy
        In the listening   55
Summertime of the dead whispered the truth of his joy
To the trees and the stones and the fish in the tide.
        And the mystery
            Sang alive
    Still in the water and singingbirds.   60

    And there could I marvel my birthday
Away but the weather turned around. And the true
    Joy of the long dead child sang burning

In the sun.
It was my thirtieth   65
Year to heaven stood there then in the summer noon
Though the town below lay leaved with October blood.
   O may my heart's truth
      Still be sung
On this high hill in a year's turning.   70

Dylan Thomas (*1914–1953*)

QUESTIONS

1. The setting is a small fishing village on the coast of Wales. The poet's first name in Welsh means "water" (12). Trace the poet's walk in relation to the village, the weather, and the time of day.
2. "The weather turned around" is an expression indicating a change in the weather or the direction of the wind. In what psychological sense does the weather turn around during the poet's walk? Who is "the long dead child" (63), and what kind of child was he? With what wish does the poem close?
3. Explain "thirtieth year to heaven" (1), "horns" (33), "tall tales" (36), "green chapels" (50), "October blood" (67).
4. The elaborate stanza pattern in this poem is based not on the meter (which is very free) but on a syllable count. How many syllables are there in each line of the stanza? (In line 1 "thirtieth" may be counted as only two syllables.) Notice that the stanzas 1 and 3 consist of exactly one sentence each.
5. The poem makes a considerable use of approximate rime, though not according to a regular pattern. Point out examples.

TWO JAPANESE HAIKU

The lightning flashes!   A lightning gleam:
And slashing through the darkness,   into darkness travels
   A night-heron's screech.   a night heron's scream.

                                       Matsuo Bashō (*1644–1694*)

The falling flower   Fallen flowers rise
I saw drift back to the branch   back to the branch—I watch:
   Was a butterfly.   oh . . . butterflies!

                                       Moritake (*1452–1540*)

QUESTION

The *haiku*, a Japanese form, consists of three lines with five, seven, and five syllables respectively. The translators of the left-hand versions above (Earl Miner and Babette Deutsch respectively) preserve this syllable count; the translator of the right-hand versions (Harold G. Henderson) seeks to preserve the sense of formal structure by making the first and last lines rime. Moritake's haiku, as Miss Deutsch points out, "refers to the Buddhist proverb that the fallen flower never returns to the branch; the broken mirror never again reflects." From these two examples, what would you say are the characteristics of effective haiku?

WHEN I WAS ONE-AND-TWENTY

When I was one-and-twenty
    I heard a wise man say,
"Give crowns and pounds and guineas
    But not your heart away;
Give pearls away and rubies   5
    But keep your fancy free."
But I was one-and-twenty,
    No use to talk to me.

When I was one-and-twenty
    I heard him say again,   10
"The heart out of the bosom
    Was never given in vain;
'Tis paid with sighs a-plenty
    And sold for endless rue."
And I am two-and-twenty,   15
    And oh, 'tis true, 'tis true.

A. E. Housman (1859–1936)

QUESTIONS

1. Vocabulary: *fancy* (6), *rue* (14). Crowns, pounds, and guineas (3) are valuable English coins. The phrase "in vain" (12) here means "for nothing."
2. Describe (a) the metrical and rime pattern and (b) the thought structure of the two stanzas, as compared with each other. How do parallelism and contrast contribute to the poem's effectiveness? What central event is implied rather than stated?
3. Is the poem valuable primarily as an expression of wisdom or of truth of feeling?

PIAZZA PIECE

    —I am a gentleman in a dustcoat trying
To make you hear. Your ears are soft and small
And listen to an old man not at all,

They want the young men's whispering and sighing.
But see the roses on your trellis dying   5
And hear the spectral singing of the moon;
For I must have my lovely lady soon,
I am a gentleman in a dustcoat trying.

—I am a lady young in beauty waiting
Until my truelove comes, and then we kiss.   10
But what grey man among the vines is this
Whose words are dry and faint as in a dream?
Back from my trellis, Sir, before I scream!
I am a lady young in beauty waiting.

John Crowe Ransom (1888–1974)

QUESTIONS

1. What is the setting? Who is the "gentleman in a dustcoat" (a dustcoat was a light linen overcoat worn to protect the clothing of a traveler from dust)? What images and connotations suggest his identity? Do you think of any traditional subject of art and music of which this is a literary analogue?
2. What variations does this poem play on the traditional form and structure of the Italian sonnet? What is the effect in lines 8 and 14 of cutting off after the participle the thoughts expressed in lines 1–2 and 9–10 respectively?

FROM **ROMEO AND JULIET**

ROMEO If I profane with my unworthiest hand
   This holy shrine, the gentle sin is this;
   My lips, two blushing pilgrims, ready stand
   To smooth that rough touch with a tender kiss.
JULIET Good pilgrim, you do wrong your hand too much, 5
   Which mannerly devotion shows in this;
   For saints have hands that pilgrims' hands do touch,
   And palm to palm is holy palmers' kiss.
ROMEO Have not saints lips, and holy palmers too?
JULIET Ay, pilgrim, lips that they must use in prayer. 10
ROMEO O! then, dear saint, let lips do what hands do;
   They pray, Grant thou, lest faith turn to despair.
JULIET Saints do not move,° though grant for prayers' propose,
   sake.   instigate
ROMEO Then move not, while my prayers' effect I take.

William Shakespeare (1564–1616)

1. These fourteen lines have been lifted out of Act I, scene 5, of Shakespeare's play. They are the first words exchanged between Romeo and Juliet, who are meeting, for the first time, at a masquerade ball given by her father. Romeo is dressed as a pilgrim. Struck by Juliet's beauty, he has come up to greet her. What stage action accompanies this passage?
2. What is the basic metaphor employed? How does it affect the tone of the relationship between Romeo and Juliet?
3. What play on words do you find in lines 8 and 13–14? What two meanings has line 11?
4. By meter and rime scheme, these lines form a sonnet. Do you think this was coincidental or intentional on Shakespeare's part? Discuss.

THE MAGICIAN SUSPENDS THE CHILDREN

With this charm I keep the boy at six
and the girl fast at five
almost safe behind the four
walls of family. We three
are a feathery totem I tattoo   5
against time: I'll be one

again. Joy here is hard-won
but possible. Protector of six
found toads, son, you feel too
much, my Halloween mouse. Your five   10
finger exercises predict no three
quarter time gliding for

you. Symphonic storms are the fore-
cast, nothing unruffled for my wun-
derkind. Have two children: make three   15
journeys upstream. Son, at six
you run into angles where five
let you curve, let me hold onto

your fingers in drugstores. Too
intent on *them*, you're before   20
or behind me five
paces at least. Let no one
tie the sturdy boat of your six
years to me the grotesque, the three

headed mother. More than three   25
times you'll deny me. And my cockatoo,
my crested girl, how you cry to be six.

Age gathers on your fore-
head with that striving. Everyone
draws your lines and five   30

breaks out like a rash, five
crouches, pariah of the three
o'clock male rendezvous. Oh won-
derful girl, my impromptu
rainbow, believe it: you'll be four-   35
teen before you're six.

This is the one abracadabra I know to
keep us three, keep you five and six.
Grow now. Sing. Fly. Do what you're here for.

Carole Oles (b. 1939)

QUESTIONS

1. Vocabulary: *totem* (5), *tattoo* (5), *pariah* (32), *abracadabra* (37). "Wunderkind"
   (14–15) is a familiar German word meaning "child prodigy" (literally, "won-
   der child").
2. Who is the speaker in the poem? How old are her children? What would she
   like to do? How does this conflict with the wishes of her children? Does it
   conflict even with her own wish? Explain.
3. In what lines of the poem does the speaker address (a) herself, (b) her son,
   (c) her daughter, (d) both children? Does she do so in speech or in thought?
4. Who is the "Magician" of the title? What are "this charm" (1) and "the one
   abracadabra I know" (37)?
5. Explain the allusion in lines 25–26, and the paradox in lines 35–36.
6. In form this poem is a *sestina*, a fixed form consisting of six six-line stanzas, in
   which end-rime is replaced by a pattern of six recurrent end-words following
   a shifting but prescribed sequence in each stanza, plus a three-line *envoy*. The
   envoy must use the last three end-words of stanza six and must also include
   the remaining three end-words somewhere *within* its lines. The challenge to
   the poet is not only to fulfill a very demanding form gracefully, but also,
   while using the same end-words seven times, to avoid monotony. How does
   this poet meet the latter challenge? (For another example of a sestina, see page
   296.)

EDWARD

"Why dois° your brand° sae drap wi bluid,   does; sword
      Edward, Edward,
Why dois your brand sae drap wi bluid,
    And why sae sad gang° yee O?"   go
"O I hae killed my hauke sae guid,   5

                     Mither, mither,
          O I hae killed my hauke sae guid,
          And I had nae mair bot hee O.”

          “Your haukis bluid was nevir sae reid,
                     Edward, Edward,   10
          Your haukis bluid was nevir sae reid,
               My deir son I tell thee O.”
          “O I hae killed my reid-roan steid,
                     Mither, mither,
          O I hae killed my reid-roan steid,   15
               That erst° was sae fair and frie° O.”   formerly; spirited

          “Your steid was auld, and ye hae got mair,
                     Edward, Edward,
          Your steid was auld, and ye hae got mair,
               Sum other dule° ye drie° O.”   grief; suffer 20
          “O I hae killed my fadir deir,
                     Mither, mither,
          O I hae killed my fadir deir,
               Alas, and wae is mee O!”

          “And whatten penance wul ye drie for that,   25
                     Edward, Edward,
          And whatten penance wul ye drie for that?
               My deir son, now tell me O.”
          “Ile set my feit in yonder boat,
                     Mither, mither,   30
          Ile set my feit in yonder boat,
               And Ile fare ovir the sea O.”

          “And what wul ye doe wi your towirs and your ha,°   hall
                     Edward, Edward,
          And what wul ye doe wi your towirs and your ha,   35
               That were sae fair to see O?”
          “Ile let thame stand tul they doun fa,°   fall
                     Mither, mither,
          Ile let thame stand tul they doun fa,
               For here nevir mair maun° I bee O.”   must 40

          “And what wul ye leive to your bairns° and your wife,   children
                     Edward, Edward,
          And what wul ye leive to your bairns and your wife,
               Whan ye gang ovir the sea O?”   44

"The warldis° room, late them beg thrae° life,   world's; through
    Mither, mither,
The warldis room, late them beg thrae life,
    For thame nevir mair wul I see O."

"And what wul ye leive to your ain mither deir,
    Edward, Edward?   50
And what wul ye leive to your ain mither deir?
    My deir son, now tell me O."
"The curse of hell frae me sall ye beir,
    Mither, mither,
The curse of hell frae me sall ye beir,   55
    Sic° counseils ye gave to me O."   Such

Anonymous

QUESTIONS

1. What has Edward done and why? Where do the two climaxes of the poem come?
2. Tell as much as you can about Edward and his feelings toward what he has done. From what class of society is he? Why does he at first give false answers to his mother's questions? What reversal of feelings and loyalties has he undergone? Do his answers about his hawk and steed perhaps indicate his present feelings toward his father? How do you explain his behavior to his wife and children? What are his present feelings toward his mother?
3. Tell as much as you can about Edward's mother. Why does she ask what Edward has done—doesn't she already know? Is there any clue as to the motivation of her deed? How skillful is she in her questioning? What do we learn about her from her dismissal of Edward's steed as "auld" and only one of many (17)? From her asking Edward what penance *he* will do for his act (25)? From her reference to herself as Edward's "ain mither deir" (49)?
4. Structure and form are both important in this poem. Could any of the stanzas be interchanged without loss, or do they build up steadily to the two climaxes? What effect has the constant repetition of the two short refrains, "Edward, Edward" and "Mither, mither"? What is the effect of the final "O" at the end of each speech? Does the repetition of each question and answer simply waste words or does it add to the suspense and emotional intensity? (Try reading the poem omitting the third and seventh lines of each stanza. Is it improved or weakened?)
5. Much of what happened is implied, much is omitted. Does the poem gain anything in power from what is *not* told?

400-METER FREESTYLE

THE GUN full swing the swimmer catapults and cracks

s
i
x

feet   away   onto   that   perfect   glass   he   catches   at   5

a

n

d

throws behind him scoop after scoop cunningly moving

t   10
h
e

water back to move him forward. Thrift is his wonderful

s

e   15

c

ret; he has schooled out all extravagance. No muscle

r
i
p   20

ples without compensation wrist cock to heel snap to

h

i

s

mobile mouth that siphons in the air that nurtures   25

h
i
m

at   half   an   inch   above   sea   level   so   to   speak.

T   30

h

e

astonishing   whites   of   the   soles   of   his   feet   rise

a
n   35
d

salute us on the turns. He flips, converts, and is gone

a

l

l   40

in one. We watch him for signs. His arms are steady at

t
h
e

catch, his cadent feet tick in the stretch, they know   45
t
h
e
lesson well. Lungs know, too; he does not list for
                                              a   50
                                              i
                                              r
he drives along on little sips carefully expended
b
u   55
t
that plum red heart pumps hard cries hurt how soon
                                              i
                                              t
                                              s   60
near one more and makes its final surge TIME: 4:25:9

Maxine Kumin (b. 1925)

QUESTIONS

1. To what quality or qualities does this poem essentially pay tribute? What
   sentence in the poem most nearly expresses its theme?
2. Does the poem itself exhibit the qualities which it praises? Discuss.
3. How does the visual form of the poem reflect its content?

A CHRISTMAS TREE

Star
If you are
A love compassionate,
You will walk with us this year.
We face a glacial distance, who are here
Huddld
At your feet.

William Burford (b. 1927)

QUESTION

Why do you think the author misspelled "huddled" in line 6?

15. Bad Poetry and Good

he attempt to evaluate a poem should never be made before the poem is understood; and, unless one has developed the capacity to feel some poetry deeply, any judgments he makes will be worthless. A person who likes no wines can hardly be a judge of them. But the ability to make judgments, to discriminate between good and bad, great and good, good and half-good, is surely a primary object of all liberal education, and one's appreciation of poetry is incomplete unless it includes discrimination. Of the mass of verse that appears each year in print, as of all literature, most is "flat, stale, and unprofitable"; a very, very little is of any enduring value.

In judging a poem, as in judging any work of art, we need to ask three basic questions: (1) *What is its central purpose?* (2) *How fully has this purpose been accomplished?* (3) *How important is this purpose?* The first question we need to answer in order to understand the poem. The last two questions are those by which we evaluate it. The first of these measures the poem on a scale of perfection. The second measures it on a scale of significance. And, just as the area of a rectangle is determined by multiplying its measurements on two scales, breadth and height, so the greatness of a poem is determined by multiplying its measurements on two scales, perfection and significance. If the poem measures well on the first of these scales, we call it a good poem, at least of its kind. If it measures well on both scales, we call it a great poem.*

---

*As indicated in the footnote on page 21, some objection has been made to the use of the term "purpose" in literary criticism. For the two criteria suggested above may be substituted these two: (1) How thoroughly are the materials of the poem integrated or unified? (2) How many and how diverse are the materials that it integrates? Thus a poem becomes successful in proportion to the tightness of its organization—that is, according to the degree to which all its elements work together and require each other to produce the total effect—and it becomes great in proportion to its scope—that is, according to the amount and • diversity of the material it amalgamates into unity.

The measurement of a poem is a much more complex process, of course, than is the measurement of a rectangle. It cannot be done as exactly. Agreement on the measurements will never be complete. Yet over a period of time the judgments of qualified readers* tend to coalesce: there comes to be more agreement than disagreement. There is almost universal agreement, for instance, that Shakespeare is the greatest of English poets. Although there might be sharp disagreements among qualified readers as to whether Donne or Keats is the superior poet, or Wordsworth or Chaucer, or Shelley or Pope, there is almost universal agreement among them that each of these is superior to Kipling or Longfellow. And there is almost universal agreement that Kipling and Longfellow are superior to James Whitcomb Riley and Edgar Guest.

But your problem is to be able to discriminate, not between already established reputations, but between poems—poems you have not seen before and of which, perhaps, you do not even know the author. Here, of course, you will not always be right—even the most qualified readers occasionally go badly astray—but you should, we hope, be able to make broad distinctions with a higher average of success than you could when you began this book. And, unless you allow yourself to petrify, your ability to do this should improve throughout your college years and beyond.

For answering the first of our evaluative questions, *How fully has the poem's purpose been accomplished?* there are no easy yardsticks that we can apply. We cannot ask, Is the poem melodious? Does it have smooth meter? Does it use good grammar? Does it contain figures of speech? Are the rimes perfect? Excellent poems exist without any of these attributes. We can judge any element in a poem only as it contributes or fails to contribute to the achievement of the central purpose; and we can judge the total poem only as these elements work together to form an integrated whole. But we can at least attempt a few generalizations. In a perfect poem there are no excess words, no words that do not bear their full weight in contributing to the total meaning, and no words just to fill out the meter. Each word is the best word for expressing the total meaning: there are no inexact words forced by the rime scheme or the metrical pattern. The word order is the best order for expressing the author's total meaning; distortions or departures from normal order are for emphasis or some other meaningful purpose. The diction, the images, and the figures of speech are fresh, not trite (except, of course, when the poet uses trite language deliberately for purposes of irony). There are no clashes be-

---

*Throughout this discussion the term "qualified reader" is of utmost importance. By a qualified reader we mean briefly a person with considerable experience of literature and considerable experience of life: a person of intelligence, sensitivity, and knowledge.

tween the sound of the poem and its sense, or its form and its content; and in general the poet uses both sound and pattern in such a way as to support his meaning. The organization of the poem is the best possible organization: images and ideas are so effectively arranged that any rearrangement would be harmful to the poem. We will always remember, however, that a good poem may have flaws. We should never damn a poem for its flaws if these flaws are amply compensated for by positive excellence.

If a poem is to have true excellence, it must be in some sense a "new" poem; it must exact a fresh response from the qualified reader—make him respond in a new way. It will not be merely imitative of previous literature nor appeal to stock, preestablished ways of thinking and feeling that in some readers are automatically stimulated by words like *mother, baby, home, country, faith,* or *God,* as a coin put into a slot always gets an expected reaction.

And here, perhaps, may be discussed the kinds of poems that most frequently "fool" poor readers (and occasionally a few good ones) and achieve sometimes a tremendous popularity without winning the respect of most good readers. These poems are found pasted in great numbers in the scrapbooks of sweet old ladies and appear in anthologies entitled *Poems of Inspiration, Poems of Courage,* or *Heart-Throbs.* The people who write such poems and the people who like them are often the best of people, but they are not poets or lovers of poetry in any genuine sense. They are lovers of conventional ideas or sentiments or feelings, which they like to see expressed with the adornment of rime and meter, and which, when so expressed, they respond to in predictable ways.

Of the several varieties of inferior poetry, we shall concern ourselves with three: the sentimental, the rhetorical, and the purely didactic. All three are perhaps unduly dignified by the name of poetry. They might more aptly be described as verse.

SENTIMENTALITY is indulgence in emotion for its own sake, or expression of more emotion than an occasion warrants. A sentimental *person* is gushy, stirred to tears by trivial or inappropriate causes; he weeps at all weddings and all funerals; he is made ecstatic by manifestations of young love; he clips locks of hair, gilds baby shoes, and talks baby talk; he grows compassionate over hardened criminals when he hears of their being punished. His opposite is the callous or unfeeling person. The ideal is the person who responds sensitively on appropriate occasions and feels deeply on occasions that deserve deep feeling, but who has nevertheless a certain amount of emotional reserve, a certain command over his feelings. Sentimental *literature* is *"tear-jerking"* literature. It aims primarily at stimulating the emotions directly rather than at communicating experience truly and freshly; it depends on trite and well-tried formulas for exciting emotion; it revels in old oaken buckets, rocking chairs, mother love, and the pitter-patter of little feet; it oversimplifies; it is unfaithful to the full complexity of human experience. In our book the best example of sentimental verse is the first seven lines of the anonymous "Love" (page 151). If this verse had ended as it began, it would have been pure sentimentalism. The eighth line redeems it by making us realize that the writer is not serious and thus transfers the piece from the classification of sentimental verse to that of humorous verse. In fact, the writer is poking fun at sentimentality by showing that in its most maudlin form it is characteristic of drunks.

RHETORICAL poetry uses a language more glittering and high flown than its substance warrants. It offers a spurious vehemence of language—language without a corresponding reality of emotion or thought underneath. It is oratorical, overelegant, artificially eloquent. It is superficial and, again, often basically trite. It loves rolling phrases like "from the rocky coast of Maine to the sun-washed shores of California" and "our heroic dead" and "Old Glory." It deals in generalities. At its worst it is bombast. In this book an example is offered by the two lines quoted from the play-within-a-play in Shakespeare's *A Midsummer Night's Dream:*

> Whereat with blade, with bloody, blameful blade,
> He bravely broached his boiling bloody breast.

Another example may be found in the player's recitation in *Hamlet* (in Act II, scene 2):

> Out, out, thou strumpet Fortune! All you gods,
> In general synod take away her power,
> Break all the spokes and fellies from her wheel,
> And bowl the round nave down the hill of heaven
> As low as to the fiends!

DIDACTIC poetry has as a primary purpose to teach or preach. It is probable that all the very greatest poetry teaches in subtle ways, without being expressly didactic; and much expressly didactic poetry ranks high in poetic excellence: that is, it accomplishes its teaching without ceasing to be poetry. But when the didactic purpose supersedes the poetic purpose, when the poem communicates information or moral instruction only, then it ceases to be didactic poetry and becomes didactic verse. Such verse appeals to people who go to poetry primarily for noble thoughts or inspiring lessons and like them prettily expressed. It is recognizable often by its lack of any specific situation, the flatness of its diction, the poverty of its imagery and figurative language, its emphasis on moral platitudes, its lack of poetic freshness. It is either very trite or has little to distinguish it from informational prose except rime or meter. Bryant's "To a Waterfowl" (page 130) is an example of didactic *poetry*. The familiar couplet

> Early to bed and early to rise,
> Makes a man healthy, wealthy, and wise

is more aptly characterized as didactic *verse*.

Undoubtedly, so far in this chapter, we have spoken too categorically, have made our distinctions too sharp and definite. All poetic excellence is a matter of degree. There are no absolute lines between sentimentality and true emotion, artificial and genuine eloquence, didactic verse and didactic poetry. Though the difference between extreme examples is easy to recognize, subtler discriminations are harder to make. But a primary distinction between the educated person and the ignorant one is the ability to make informed judgments.

A final caution to students. In making judgments on literature, always be honest. Do not pretend to like what you really do not like. Do not be afraid to admit a liking for what you do like. A genuine enthusiasm for the second-rate is much better than false enthusiasm or no enthusiasm at all. Be neither hasty nor timorous in making your judgments. When you have attentively read a poem and thoroughly considered it, decide what you think. Do not hedge, equivocate, or try to find out others' opinions before forming your own. Having formed an opinion and expressed it, do not allow it to petrify. Compare your opinion *then* with the opinions of others; allow yourself to change it when convinced of its error: in this way you learn. Honesty, courage, and humility are the necessary moral foundations for all genuine literary judgment.

In the poems for comparison in this chapter, the distinction to be made is not always between black and white; it may be between varying degrees of poetic merit.

EXERCISE

Poetry is not so much a thing as a quality; it exists in varying degrees in different specimens of language. Though we cannot always say definitely, "This is poetry; that is not," we can often say, "This is more poetical than that." Rank the following passages from most poetical to least poetical or not poetical at all.

1. Why should we be in such desperate haste to succeed and in such desperate enterprises? If a man does not keep pace with his companions, perhaps it is

because he hears a different drummer. Let him step to the music which he hears, however measured or far away.

2. $(x - 12) (x - 2) = x^2 - 14x + 24.$

3. Thirty days hath September,
   April, June, and November.
   All the rest have thirty-one,
   Except February alone,
   To which we twenty-eight assign,
   Till leap year makes it twenty-nine.

4. "Meeting at Night" (page 47).

5. Thus, through the serene tranquilities of the tropical sea, among waves whose handclappings were suspended by exceeding rapture, Moby Dick moved on, still withholding from sight the full terrors of his submerged trunk, entirely hiding the wrenched hideousness of his jaw. But soon the fore part of him slowly rose from the water; for an instant his whole marbleized body formed a high arch, like Virginia's Natural Bridge, and warningly waving his bannered flukes in the air, the grand god revealed himself, sounded, and went out of sight. Hoveringly halting, and dipping on the wing, the white sea fowls longingly lingered over the agitated pool that he left.

6. Nature in the abstract is the aggregate of the powers and properties of all things. Nature means the sum of all phenomena, together with the causes which produce them; including not only all that happens, but all that is capable of happening; the unused capabilities of causes being as much a part of the idea of Nature, as those which take effect.

*   *   *

SAY NOT THE STRUGGLE NOUGHT AVAILETH

Say not the struggle nought availeth,
 The labor and the wounds are vain,
The enemy faints not, nor faileth,
 And as things have been they remain.

If hopes were dupes, fears may be liars;   5
 It may be, in yon smoke concealed,
Your comrades chase e'en now the fliers,
 And, but for you, possess the field.

For while the tired waves, vainly breaking,
 Seem here no painful inch to gain,   10
Far back, through creeks and inlets making,
 Comes silent, flooding in, the main.

And not by eastern windows only,
 When daylight comes, comes in the light,

In front, the sun climbs slow, how slowly,   15
But westward, look, the land is bright.

THE MAN WHO THINKS HE CAN

If you think you are beaten, you are;
   If you think you dare not, you don't.
If you'd like to win, but think you can't,
   It's almost a cinch you won't.
If you think you'll lose, you're lost,   5
   For out in the world we find
Success begins with a fellow's will;
   It's all in the state of mind.

If you think you're outclassed, you are;
   You've got to think high to rise.   10
You've got to be sure of yourself before
   You can ever win a prize.
Life's battles don't always go
   To the stronger or faster man;
But soon or late the man who wins   15
   Is the one who thinks he can.

QUESTION

Which of the above poems has more poetic merit? Discuss.

GOD'S WILL FOR YOU AND ME

Just to be tender, just to be true,
Just to be glad the whole day through,
Just to be merciful, just to be mild,
Just to be trustful as a child,
Just to be gentle and kind and sweet,   5
Just to be helpful with willing feet,
Just to be cheery when things go wrong,
Just to drive sadness away with a song,
Whether the hour is dark or bright,
Just to be loyal to God and right,   10
Just to believe that God knows best,
Just in his promises ever to rest—
Just to let love be our daily key,
That is God's will for you and me.

PIED BEAUTY

Glory be to God for dappled things—
　　For skies of couple-color as a brinded cow;
　　　　For rose-moles all in stipple upon trout that swim;
Fresh-firecoal chestnut-falls; finches' wings;
　　Landscape plotted and pieced—fold, fallow and plow;　　　5
　　And all trades, their gear and tackle and trim.

All things counter, original, spare, strange;
　　Whatever is fickle, freckled (who knows how?)
　　　　With swift, slow; sweet, sour; adazzle, dim;
He fathers-forth whose beauty is past change:　　　　　　10
　　　　Praise him.

QUESTION

Which is the superior poem? Explain in full.

PITCHER

His art is eccentricity, his aim
How not to hit the mark he seems to aim at,

His passion how to avoid the obvious,
His technique how to vary the avoidance.

The others throw to be comprehended. He　　　　　5
Throws to be a moment misunderstood.

Yet not too much. Not errant, arrant, wild,
But every seeming aberration willed.

Not to, yet still, still to communicate
Making the batter understand too late.　　　　　　10

THE OLD-FASHIONED PITCHER

How dear to my heart was the old-fashioned hurler
　　Who labored all day on the old village green.
He did not resemble the up-to-date twirler
　　Who pitches four innings and ducks from the scene.
The up-to-date twirler I'm not very strong for;　　　5
　　He has a queer habit of pulling up lame.
And that is the reason I hanker and long for
　　The pitcher who started and finished the game.

The old-fashioned pitcher,
The iron-armed pitcher, 10
The stout-hearted pitcher
Who finished the game.

QUESTION

Which poem is the more interesting and more meaningful? Why?

TO MY SON

Do you know that your soul is of my soul such part
That you seem to be fibre and cord of my heart?
None other can pain me as you, dear, can do;
None other can please me or praise me as you.

Remember the world will be quick with its blame 5
If shadow or stain ever darken your name;
"Like mother like son" is a saying so true,
The world will judge largely of "Mother" by you.

Be yours then the task, if task it shall be,
To force the proud world to do homage to me; 10
Be sure it will say when its verdict you've won,
"She reaped as she sowed, Lo! this is her son."

ON THE BEACH AT FONTANA

Wind whines and whines the shingle,
The crazy pierstakes groan;
A senile sea numbers each single
Slimesilvered stone.

From whining wind and colder 5
Gray sea I wrap him warm
And touch his trembling fineboned shoulder
And boyish arm.

Around us fear, descending
Darkness of fear above 10
And in my heart how deep unending
Ache of love!

QUESTIONS

1. Vocabulary: *shingle* (1).
2. Identify the speaker in each poem (the first was written by a woman, the second by a man). Which is the better poem, and why?

A POISON TREE

I was angry with my friend:
I told my wrath, my wrath did end.
I was angry with my foe:
I told it not, my wrath did grow.

And I watered it in fears,   5
Night and morning with my tears;
And I sunnèd it with smiles,
And with soft deceitful wiles.

And it grew both day and night
Till it bore an apple bright;   10
And my foe beheld it shine,
And he knew that it was mine,

And into my garden stole
When the night had veiled the pole:°   sky
In the morning glad I see   15
My foe outstretched beneath the tree.

THE MOST VITAL THING IN LIFE

When you feel like saying something
    That you know you will regret,
Or keenly feel an insult
    Not quite easy to forget,
That's the time to curb resentment   5
    And maintain a mental peace,
For when your mind is tranquil
    All your ill-thoughts simply cease.

It is easy to be angry
    When defrauded or defied,   10
To be peeved and disappointed
    If your wishes are denied;
But to win a worthwhile battle
    Over selfishness and spite,
You must learn to keep strict silence   15
    Though you know you're in the right.

So keep your mental balance
    When confronted by a foe,
Be it enemy in ambush
    Or some danger that you know.   20
If you are poised and tranquil

When all around is strife,
Be assured that you have mastered
The most vital thing in life.

QUESTION

Which poem has more poetic merit? Explain.

ON A DEAD CHILD

Man proposes, God in His time disposes,
    And so I wandered up to where you lay,
A little rose among the little roses,
    And no more dead than they.

It seemed your childish feet were tired of straying,   5
    You did not greet me from your flower-strewn bed,
Yet still I knew that you were only playing—
    Playing at being dead.

I might have thought that you were really sleeping,
    So quiet lay your eyelids to the sky,   10
So still your hair, but surely you were peeping;
    And so I did not cry.

God knows, and in His proper time disposes,
    And so I smiled and gently called your name,
Added my rose to your sweet heap of roses,   15
    And left you to your game.

BELLS FOR JOHN WHITESIDE'S DAUGHTER

There was such speed in her little body,
And such lightness in her footfall,
It is no wonder her brown study
Astonishes us all.

Her wars were bruited in our high window.   5
We looked among orchard trees and beyond
Where she took arms against her shadow,
Or harried unto the pond

The lazy geese, like a snow cloud
Dripping their snow on the green grass,   10

Tricking and stopping, sleepy and proud,
Who cried in goose, Alas,

For the tireless heart within the little
Lady with rod that made them rise
From their noon apple-dreams and scuttle   15
Goose-fashion under the skies!

But now go the bells, and we are ready,
In one house we are sternly stopped
To say we are vexed at her brown study,
Lying so primly propped.   20

QUESTIONS

1. Vocabulary: *brown study* (3, 19), *bruited* (5).
2. Which is the sentimental poem? Which is the honest one? Explain.

SOME KEEP THE SABBATH GOING TO CHURCH

Some keep the Sabbath going to church;
I keep it staying at home,
With a bobolink for a chorister,
And an orchard for a dome.

Some keep the Sabbath in surplice;   5
I just wear my wings,
And instead of tolling the bell for church,
Our little sexton sings.

God preaches,—a noted clergyman,—
And the sermon is never long;   10
So instead of getting to heaven at last,
I'm going all along!

MY CHURCH

My church has but one temple,
    Wide as the world is wide,
Set with a million stars,
    Where a million hearts abide.

My church has no creed to bar   5
    A single brother man

But says, "Come thou and worship"
   To every one who can.

My church has no roof nor walls,
   Nor floors save the beautiful sod—   10
For fear, I would seem to limit
   The love of the illimitable God.

QUESTION

Which is the better poem, and why?

BOY-MAN

England's lads are miniature men
To start with, grammar in their shiny hats,
And serious: in America who knows when
Manhood begins? Presidents dance and hug
And while the kind King waves and gravely chats   5
America wets on England's old green rug.

The boy-man roars. Worry alone will give
This one the verisimilitude of age.
Those white teeth are his own, for he must live
Longer, grow taller than the Texas race.   10
Fresh are his eyes, his darkening skin the gauge
Of bloods that freely mix beneath his face.

He knows the application of the book
But not who wrote it; shuts it like a shot.
Rather than read he thinks that he will look,   15
Rather than look he thinks that he will talk,
Rather than talk he thinks that he will not
Bother at all; would rather ride than walk.

His means of conversation is the joke,
Humor his language underneath which lies   20
The undecoded dialect of the folk.
Abroad he scorns the foreigner: what's old
Is worn, what's different bad, what's odd unwise.
He gives off heat and is enraged by cold.

Charming, becoming to the suits he wears,   25
The boy-man, younger than his eldest son,
Inherits the state; upon his silver hairs

Time like a panama hat sits at a tilt
And smiles. To him the world has just begun
And every city waiting to be built.   30

Mister, remove your shoulder from the wheel
And say this prayer, "Increase my vitamins,
Make my decisions of the finest steel,
Pour motor oil upon my troubled spawn,
Forgive the Europeans for their sins,   35
Establish them, that values may go on."

QUESTIONS

1. Vocabulary: *verisimilitude* (8), *spawn* (34).
2. What is the subject of the poem?
3. What is the tone—admiration? mockery? or both?
4. Explain fully the figures of speech in lines 2, 6, 26, 28–29, and their appropriateness. What kind of irony appears in the last stanza?

AMERICA FOR ME

'Tis fine to see the Old World, and travel up and down
Among the famous palaces and cities of renown,
To admire the crumbly castles and the statues of the kings—
But now I think I've had enough of antiquated things.

So it's home again, and home again, America for me!   5
My heart is turning home again, and there I long to be,
In the land of youth and freedom beyond the ocean bars,
Where the air is full of sunlight and the flag is full of stars.

Oh, London is a man's town, there's power in the air;
And Paris is a woman's town, with flowers in her hair;   10
And it's sweet to dream in Venice, and it's great to study Rome;
But when it comes to living there is no place like home.

I like the German fir-woods, in green battalions drilled;
I like the gardens of Versailles with flashing fountains filled;
But, oh, to take your hand, my dear, and ramble for a day   15
In the friendly western woodlands where Nature has her way!

I know that Europe's wonderful, yet something seems to lack:
The Past is too much with her, and the people looking back.
But the glory of the Present is to make the Future free—
We love our land for what she is and what she is to be.   20

Oh, it's home again, and home again, America for me!
I want a ship that's westward bound to plow the rolling sea,
To the blessèd Land of Room Enough beyond the ocean bars,
Where the air is full of sunlight and the flag is full of stars.

QUESTIONS

1. In what respects do the attitudes expressed in this poem fit the characterization made in "Boy-Man"?
2. "America for Me" and "Boy-Man" were both written by Americans. Which is more worthy of prolonged consideration? Why?

LITTLE BOY BLUE

The little toy dog is covered with dust,
　　But sturdy and staunch he stands;
And the little toy soldier is red with rust,
　　And his musket moulds in his hands.
Time was when the little toy dog was new,　　　　　5
　　And the soldier was passing fair;
And that was the time when our Little Boy Blue
　　Kissed them and put them there.

"Now, don't you go till I come," he said,
　　"And don't you make any noise!"　　　　　　　10
So, toddling off to his trundle-bed,
　　He dreamt of the pretty toys;
And, as he was dreaming, an angel song
　　Awakened our Little Boy Blue—
Oh! the years are many, the years are long,　　　15
　　But the little toy friends are True!

Ay, faithful to Little Boy Blue they stand
　　Each in the same old place—
Awaiting the touch of a little hand,
　　The smile of a little face;　　　　　　　　　　20
And they wonder, as waiting the long years through
　　In the dust of that little chair,
What has become of our Little Boy Blue,
　　Since he kissed them and put them there.

THE TOYS

My little Son, who looked from thoughtful eyes
And moved and spoke in quiet grown-up wise,
Having my law the seventh time disobeyed,

I struck him, and dismissed
With hard words and unkissed,   5
His Mother, who was patient, being dead.
Then, fearing lest his grief should hinder sleep,
I visited his bed,
But found him slumbering deep,
With darkened eyelids, and their lashes yet   10
From his late sobbing wet.
And I, with moan,
Kissing away his tears, left others of my own;
For, on a table drawn beside his head,
He had put, within his reach,   15
A box of counters and a red-veined stone,
A piece of glass abraded by the beach,
And six or seven shells,
A bottle with bluebells,
And two French copper coins, ranged there with careful art,   20
To comfort his sad heart.
So when that night I prayed
To God, I wept, and said:
Ah, when at last we lie with trancèd breath,
Not vexing Thee in death,   25
And thou rememberest of what toys
We made our joys,
How weakly understood
Thy great commanded good,
Then, fatherly not less   30
Than I whom Thou hast moulded from the clay,
Thou'lt leave Thy wrath, and say,
"I will be sorry for their childishness."

QUESTION

One of these poems has an obvious appeal for the beginning reader. The other is
likely to have more meaning for the mature reader. Try to explain in terms of
sentimentality and honesty.

16. Good Poetry and Great

If a poem has successfully met the test in the question, *How fully has it accomplished its purpose?* we are ready to subject it to our second question, *How important is its purpose?*

Great poetry must, of course, be good poetry. Noble intent alone cannot redeem a work that does not measure high on the scale of accomplishment; otherwise the sentimental and purely didactic verse of much of the last chapter would stand with the world's masterpieces. But once a work has been judged as successful on the scale of execution, its final standing will depend on its significance of purpose.

Suppose, for instance, we consider three poems in our text: the limerick "There was a young lady of Niger" (page 206), Emily Dickinson's poem "It sifts from leaden sieves" (page 59), and Shakespeare's sonnet "That time of year" (page 208). Each of these would probably be judged by competent critics as highly successful in accomplishing what it sets out to do. The limerick tells its little story without an unnecessary word, with no "wrong" word, with no distortion of normal sentence order forced by exigencies of meter or rime; the limerick form is ideally suited to the author's humorous purpose; and the manner in which the story is told, with its understatement, its neat shift in position of the lady and her smile, is economical and delicious. Yet we should hardly call this poetry at all: it does not really communicate experience, nor does it attempt to. It attempts merely to relate a brief anecdote humorously and effectively. On the other hand, Emily Dickinson's poem *is* poetry, and very good poetry. It appeals richly to our senses and to our imaginations, and it succeeds excellently in its purpose: to convey the appearance and the quality of falling and newly fallen snow as well as a sense of the magic and the mystery of nature. Yet, when we compare this excellent poem with Shakespeare's, we again see important differences. Although the first poem engages the senses and the imagination and may affect us with wonder and cause us to meditate on nature, it does not deeply engage the emotions or the intellect. It does not come as close to the core of human living and suffering as does Shakespeare's sonnet. In fact, it is concerned primarily with that staple of small talk, the weather. On the other hand, Shakespeare's sonnet is concerned with the universal human tragedy of growing old, with approaching death, and with love. Of these three selections, then, Shakespeare's is the greatest. It "says" more than Emily Dickinson's poem or the limerick; it communicates a richer experience; it successfully accomplishes a more significant purpose. The discriminating reader will get from it a deeper enjoyment, because he has been nourished as well as delighted.

Great poetry engages the whole person—senses, imagination, emotion, intellect; it does not touch him merely on one or two sides of his nature. Great poetry seeks not merely to entertain the reader, but to bring him—along with pure pleasure—fresh insights, or renewed insights, and important insights, into the nature of human experience. Great poetry, we might say, gives its reader a broader and deeper understanding of life, of his fellow men, and of himself, always with the qualification, of course, that the kind of insight literature gives is not necessarily the kind that can be summed up in a simple "lesson" or "moral." It is *knowledge—felt* knowledge, *new* knowledge—of the complexities of human nature and of the tragedies and sufferings, the excitements and joys, that characterize human experience.

Is Shakespeare's sonnet a *great* poem? It is, at least, a great *sonnet*. Greatness, like goodness, is relative. If we compare any of Shakespeare's sonnets with his greatest plays—*Macbeth, Othello, Hamlet, King Lear*—another big difference appears. What is undertaken and accomplished in these tragedies is enormously greater, more difficult, and more complex than could ever be undertaken or accomplished in a single sonnet. Greatness in literature, in fact, cannot be entirely dissociated from size. In literature, as in basketball and football, a good big man is better than a good little man. The greatness of a poem is in proportion to the range and depth and intensity of experience that it brings to us: its amount of life. Shakespeare's plays offer us a multiplicity of life and a depth of living that could never be compressed into the fourteen lines of a sonnet. They organize a greater complexity of life and experience into unity.

Yet, after all, we have provided no easy yardsticks or rule-of-thumb measures for literary judgment. There are no mechanical tests. The final measuring rod can be only the responsiveness, the maturity, the taste and discernment of the cultivated reader. Such taste and discernment are partly a native endowment, partly the product of maturity and experience, partly the achievement of conscious study, training, and intellectual effort. They cannot be achieved suddenly or quickly; they can never be achieved in perfection. The pull is a long and a hard one. But success, even relative success, brings enormous rewards in enrichment and command of life.

*   *   *

ODE TO A NIGHTINGALE

My heart aches, and a drowsy numbness pains
  My sense, as though of hemlock° I had drunk,   a poisonous
Or emptied some dull opiate to the drains   drink
  One minute past, and Lethe-wards had sunk:
'Tis not through envy of thy happy lot,   5
  But being too happy in thine happiness,—
    That thou, light-wingèd Dryad° of the trees,   wood nymph
      In some melodious plot
Of beechen green, and shadows numberless,
  Singest of summer in full-throated ease.   10

O, for a draught of vintage! that hath been
  Cooled a long age in the deep-delvèd earth,
Tasting of Flora° and the country green,   goddess of flowers
  Dance, and Provençal song, and sunburnt mirth!
O for a beaker full of the warm South,   15
  Full of the true, the blushful Hippocrene,
    With beaded bubbles winking at the brim,
      And purple-stainèd mouth;
That I might drink, and leave the world unseen,
  And with thee fade away into the forest dim: 20

Fade far away, dissolve, and quite forget
  What thou among the leaves hast never known,
The weariness, the fever, and the fret
  Here, where men sit and hear each other groan;
Where palsy shakes a few, sad, last gray hairs,   25
    Where youth grows pale, and specter-thin, and dies;
      Where but to think is to be full of sorrow
      And leaden-eyed despairs,

Where Beauty cannot keep her lustrous eyes,
    Or new Love pine at them beyond to-morrow.   30

Away! away! for I will fly to thee,
    Not charioted by Bacchus and his pards,
But on the viewless° wings of Poesy,   invisible
    Though the dull brain perplexes and retards:
Already with thee! tender is the night,   35
    And haply the Queen-Moon is on her throne,
        Clustered around by all her starry Fays;
            But here there is no light,
    Save what from heaven is with the breezes blown
        Through verdurous glooms and winding mossy ways.   40

I cannot see what flowers are at my feet,
    Nor what soft incense hangs upon the boughs,
But, in embalmèd° darkness, guess each sweet   perfumed
    Wherewith the seasonable month endows
The grass, the thicket, and the fruit-tree wild;   45
    White hawthorn, and the pastoral eglantine;
        Fast fading violets covered up in leaves;
            And mid-May's eldest child,
    The coming musk-rose, full of dewy wine,
        The murmurous haunt of flies on summer eves.   50

Darkling° I listen; and, for many a time   in darkness
    I have been half in love with easeful Death,
Called him soft names in many a musèd rhyme,
    To take into the air my quiet breath;
Now more than ever seems it rich to die,   55
    To cease upon the midnight with no pain,
        While thou art pouring forth thy soul abroad
            In such an ecstasy!
    Still wouldst thou sing, and I have ears in vain—
        To thy high requiem become a sod.   60

Thou wast not born for death, immortal Bird!
    No hungry generations tread thee down;
The voice I hear this passing night was heard
    In ancient days by emperor and clown:
Perhaps the self-same song that found a path   65
    Through the sad heart of Ruth, when, sick for home,
        She stood in tears amid the alien corn;
            The same that oft-times hath
    Charmed magic casements, opening on the foam
        Of perilous seas, in faery lands forlorn.   70

Forlorn! the very word is like a bell
  To toll me back from thee to my sole self!
Adieu! the fancy cannot cheat so well
  As she is famed to do, deceiving elf.
Adieu! adieu! thy plaintive anthem fades   75
  Past the near meadows, over the still stream,
    Up the hill-side; and now 'tis buried deep
      In the next valley-glades:
Was it a vision, or a waking dream?
  Fled is that music:—Do I wake or sleep?   80

John Keats (*1795–1821*)

QUESTIONS

1. Vocabulary: *vintage* (11), *haply* (36), *Fays* (37), *verdurous* (40), *musèd* (53), *requiem* (60), *clown* (64). *Lethe* (4) was the river of forgetfulness in the Greek underworld. *Provençal* (14) refers to Provence, a wine-growing region in southern France, famous in the Middle Ages for its troubadours. *Hippocrene* (16) in Greek mythology was the fountain of the Muses on Mt. Helicon. *Bacchus* (32), the god of wine, went about in a chariot drawn by leopards.

2. Why does the poet experience the sensations described in lines 1–4?

3. The poet expresses a desire to escape from his world into the world of the nightingale. What is unsatisfactory about *his* world? In what two ways especially do his world and the world of the nightingale contrast (stanzas 3, 6, 7)? How is the fancied process of leaving the actual world described (lines 19–21)?

4. What means of escape does the poet first consider? How is it described? Why does he reject it? What means does he choose instead (what constitutes the "viewless wings" of poesy)?

5. Discuss the imagery in stanzas 4 and 5. From what to what (in terms of place and time) has the poet been transported? Why cannot the poet see what flowers are at his feet? How does he identify them? Why does this beautiful scene make him think of death?

6. Dying under the conditions described in stanza 6 is made to seem very attractive. How do the last two lines of the stanza affect this attractiveness? Why has the poet often been "half in love" with death? Why has he been *only* "half in love" with it?

7. In what sense (or senses) is the nightingale "immortal"? How is this immortality illustrated in stanza 7? Of what has the nightingale (or its song) become a symbol? (There may be more than one answer.)

8. Why does the word "forlorn" break the poet's reverie? Are its meanings the same in stanza 8 as in stanza 7? How are the poet's return to the actual world and the distancing of the nightingale's song described? In what two ways is the imagination a "deceiving elf"? What is the difference between a "vision" and a "waking dream"? Are we meant to be able to answer the questions in the last two lines?

9. What final conclusions, if any, does the poem reach about the possibilities of escaping from the actual world to that of the nightingale? about the desirability of doing so?

THE DEATH OF THE HIRED MAN

Mary sat musing on the lamp-flame at the table
Waiting for Warren. When she heard his step,
She ran on tip-toe down the darkened passage
To meet him in the doorway with the news
And put him on his guard. "Silas is back."   5
She pushed him outward with her through the door
And shut it after her. "Be kind" she said.
She took the market things from Warren's arms
And set them on the porch, then drew him down
To sit beside her on the wooden steps.   10

"When was I ever anything but kind to him?
But I'll not have the fellow back," he said.
"I told him so last haying, didn't I?
If he left then, I said, that ended it.
What good is he? Who else will harbor him   15
At his age for the little he can do?
What help he is there's no depending on.
Off he goes always when I need him most.
He thinks he ought to earn a little pay,
Enough at least to buy tobacco with,   20
So he won't have to beg and be beholden.
'All right,' I say, 'I can't afford to pay
Any fixed wages, though I wish I could.'
'Someone else can.' 'Then someone else will have to.'
I shouldn't mind his bettering himself   25
If that was what it was. You can be certain,
When he begins like that, there's someone at him
Trying to coax him off with pocket-money—
In haying time, when any help is scarce.
In winter he comes back to us. I'm done."   30

"Sh! not so loud: he'll hear you," Mary said.

"I want him to: he'll have to soon or late."

"He's worn out. He's asleep beside the stove.
When I came up from Rowe's I found him here,
Huddled against the barn-door fast asleep,   35
A miserable sight, and frightening, too—

You needn't smile—I didn't recognize him—
I wasn't looking for him—and he's changed.
Wait till you see."

          "Where did you say he'd been?"

"He didn't say, I dragged him to the house,   40
And gave him tea and tried to make him smoke.
I tried to make him talk about his travels.
Nothing would do: he just kept nodding off."

"What did he say? Did he say anything?"

"But little."

          "Anything? Mary, confess   45
He said he'd come to ditch the meadow for me."

"Warren!"

          "But did he? I just want to know."

"Of course he did. What would you have him say?
Surely you wouldn't grudge the poor old man
Some humble way to save his self-respect.   50
He added, if you really care to know,
He meant to clear the upper pasture, too.
That sounds like something you have heard before?
Warren, I wish you could have heard the way
He jumbled everything. I stopped to look   55
Two or three times—he made me feel so queer—
To see if he was talking in his sleep.
He ran on Harold Wilson—you remember—
The boy you had in haying four years since.
He's finished school, and teaching in his college.   60
Silas declares you'll have to get him back.
He says they two will make a team for work:
Between them they will lay this farm as smooth!
The way he mixed that in with other things.
He thinks young Wilson a likely lad, though daft   65
On education—you know how they fought
All through July under the blazing sun,
Silas up on the cart to build the load,
Harold along beside to pitch it on."

"Yes, I took care to keep well out of earshot."   70

"Well, those days trouble Silas like a dream.
You wouldn't think they would. How some things linger!

Harold's young college boy's assurance piqued him.
After so many years he still keeps finding
Good arguments he sees he might have used.   75
I sympathize. I know just how it feels
To think of the right thing to say too late.
Harold's associated in his mind with Latin.
He asked me what I thought of Harold's saying
He studied Latin like the violin   80
Because he liked it—that an argument!
He said he couldn't make the boy believe
He could find water with a hazel prong—
Which showed how much good school had ever done him.
He wanted to go over that. But most of all   85
He thinks if he could have another chance
To teach him how to build a load of hay—"

"I know, that's Silas' one accomplishment.
He bundles every forkful in its place,
And tags and numbers it for future reference,   90
So he can find and easily dislodge it
In the unloading. Silas does that well.
He takes it out in bunches like big birds' nests.
You never see him standing on the hay
He's trying to lift, straining to lift himself."   95

"He thinks if he could teach him that, he'd be
Some good perhaps to someone in the world.
He hates to see a boy the fool of books.
Poor Silas, so concerned for other folk,
And nothing to look backward to with pride,   100
And nothing to look forward to with hope,
So now and never any different."

Part of a moon was falling down the west,
Dragging the whole sky with it to the hills.
Its light poured softly in her lap. She saw it   105
And spread her apron to it. She put out her hand
Among the harp-like morning-glory strings,
Taut with the dew from garden bed to eaves,
As if she played unheard some tenderness
That wrought on him beside her in the night.   110
"Warren," she said, "he has come home to die:
You needn't be afraid he'll leave you this time."

"Home," he mocked gently.

                    "Yes, what else but home?

It all depends on what you mean by home.
Of course he's nothing to us, any more   115
Than was the hound that came a stranger to us
Out of the woods, worn out upon the trail."

"Home is the place where, when you have to go there,
They have to take you in."

                                        "I should have called it
Something you somehow haven't to deserve."   120

Warren leaned out and took a step or two,
Picked up a little stick, and brought it back
And broke it in his hand and tossed it by.
"Silas has better claim on us you think
Than on his brother? Thirteen little miles   125
As the road winds would bring him to his door.
Silas has walked that far no doubt today.
Why doesn't he go there? His brother's rich,
A somebody—director in the bank."

"He never told us that."

                                "We know it though."   130

"I think his brother ought to help, of course.
I'll see to that if there is need. He ought of right
To take him in, and might be willing to—
He may be better than appearances.
But have some pity on Silas. Do you think   135
If he had any pride in claiming kin
Or anything he looked for from his brother,
He'd keep so still about him all this time?"

"I wonder what's between them."

                                        "I can tell you.
Silas is what he is—we wouldn't mind him—   140
But just the kind that kinsfolk can't abide.
He never did a thing so very bad.
He don't know why he isn't quite as good
As anybody. Worthless though he is,
He won't be made ashamed to please his brother."   145

"*I* can't think Si ever hurt anyone."

"No, but he hurt my heart the way he lay
And rolled his old head on that sharp-edged chair-back.
He wouldn't let me put him on the lounge.

You must go in and see what you can do.   150
I made the bed up for him there tonight.
You'll be surprised at him—how much he's broken.
His working days are done; I'm sure of it."

"I'd not be in a hurry to say that."

"I haven't been. Go, look, see for yourself.   155
But, Warren, please remember how it is:
He's come to help you ditch the meadow.
He has a plan. You mustn't laugh at him.
He may not speak of it, and then he may.
I'll sit and see if that small sailing cloud   160
Will hit or miss the moon."

                                    It hit the moon.
Then there were three there, making a dim row,
The moon, the little silver cloud, and she.

Warren returned—too soon, it seemed to her,
Slipped to her side, caught up her hand and waited.   165

"Warren?" she questioned.

                                "Dead," was all he answered.

                                    Robert Frost (1874-1963)

QUESTIONS

1. Vocabulary: *beholden* (21), *piqued* (73).
2. What kind of person is Silas? Characterize him as fully as possible, showing, especially, what is revealed about his character by his relationships with Harold Wilson, with his brother, and with Warren and Mary.
3. Characterize Warren and Mary. Are they basically unlike in their natures and attitudes, or not really too far apart? Can you suggest reasons why Warren should at first be less solicitous than Mary?
4. Define as precisely as possible the moral problem faced by Warren and Mary. How would Warren finally have answered it (if an answer had not been made unnecessary)? Give reasons for your answer.
5. Is the poem written in free verse or blank verse? How would you describe its rhythm and language?

THE LOVE SONG OF J. ALFRED PRUFROCK

> *S'io credesse che mia risposta fosse*
> *A persona che mai tornasse al mondo,*
> *Questa fiamma staria senza piu scosse.*

Ma perciocche giammai di questo fondo
Non torno vivo alcun, s'i'odo il vero,
Senza tema d'infamia ti rispondo.

Let us go then, you and I,
When the evening is spread out against the sky
Like a patient etherized upon a table;
Let us go, through certain half-deserted streets,
The muttering retreats   5
Of restless nights in one-night cheap hotels
And sawdust restaurants with oyster-shells:
Streets that follow like a tedious argument
Of insidious intent
To lead you to an overwhelming question . . .   10
Oh, do not ask, "What is it?"
Let us go and make our visit.

    In the room the women come and go
Talking of Michelangelo.

    The yellow fog that rubs its back upon the window-panes,   15
The yellow smoke that rubs its muzzle on the window-panes
Licked its tongue into the corners of the evening,
Lingered upon the pools that stand in drains,
Let fall upon its back the soot that falls from chimneys,
Slipped by the terrace, made a sudden leap,   20
And seeing that it was a soft October night,
Curled once about the house, and fell asleep.

    And indeed there will be time
For the yellow smoke that slides along the street,
Rubbing its back upon the window-panes;   25
There will be time, there will be time
To prepare a face to meet the faces that you meet;
There will be time to murder and create,
And time for all the works and days of hands
That lift and drop a question on your plate;   30
Time for you and time for me,
And time yet for a hundred indecisions,
And for a hundred visions and revisions,
Before the taking of a toast and tea.

    In the room the women come and go   35
Talking of Michelangelo.

    And indeed there will be time
To wonder, "Do I dare?" and "Do I dare?"

Time to turn back and descend the stair,
With a bald spot in the middle of my hair— 40
(They will say: "How his hair is growing thin!")
My morning coat, my collar mounting firmly to the chin,
My necktie rich and modest, but asserted by a simple pin—
(They will say: "But how his arms and legs are thin!")
Do I dare 45
Disturb the universe?
In a minute there is time
For decisions and revisions which a minute will reverse.

For I have known them all already, known them all:—
Have known the evenings, mornings, afternoons, 50
I have measured out my life with coffee spoons;
I know the voices dying with a dying fall
Beneath the music from a farther room.
So how should I presume?

And I have known the eyes already, known them all— 55
The eyes that fix you in a formulated phrase,
And when I am formulated, sprawling on a pin,
When I am pinned and wriggling on the wall,
Then how should I begin
To spit out all the butt-ends of my days and ways 60
And how should I presume?

And I have known the arms already, known them all—
Arms that are braceleted and white and bare
(But in the lamplight, downed with light brown hair!)
Is it perfume from a dress 65
That makes me so digress?
Arms that lie along a table, or wrap about a shawl.
And should I then presume?
And how should I begin?

*   *   *

Shall I say, I have gone at dusk through narrow streets 70
And watched the smoke that rises from the pipes
Of lonely men in shirt-sleeves, leaning out of windows? . . .

I should have been a pair of ragged claws
Scuttling across the floors of silent seas.

*   *   *

And the afternoon, the evening, sleeps so peacefully! 75
Smoothed by long fingers,
Asleep . . . tired . . . or it malingers,
Stretched on the floor, here beside you and me.
Should I, after tea and cakes and ices,
Have the strength to force the moment to its crisis? 80
But though I have wept and fasted, wept and prayed,
Though I have seen my head (grown slightly bald) brought in
    upon a platter,
I am no prophet—and here's no great matter;
I have seen the moment of my greatness flicker,
And I have seen the eternal Footman hold my coat, and snicker, 85
And in short, I was afraid.

And would it have been worth it, after all,
After the cups, the marmalade, the tea,
Among the porcelain, among some talk of you and me,
Would it have been worth while, 90
To have bitten off the matter with a smile,
To have squeezed the universe into a ball
To roll it toward some overwhelming question,
To say: "I am Lazarus, come from the dead,
Come back to tell you all, I shall tell you all"— 95
If one, settling a pillow by her head,
    Should say: "That is not what I meant at all.
    That is not it, at all."

And would it have been worth it, after all,
Would it have been worth while, 100
After the sunsets and the dooryards and the sprinkled streets,
After the novels, after the teacups, after the skirts that trail
    along the floor—
And this, and so much more?—
It is impossible to say just what I mean!
But as if a magic lantern threw the nerves in patterns on a screen: 105
Would it have been worth while
If one, settling a pillow or throwing off a shawl,
And turning toward the window, should say:
    "That is not it at all,
    That is not what I meant, at all." 110

                  *   *   *

No! I am not Prince Hamlet, nor was meant to be;
Am an attendant lord, one that will do

To swell a progress, start a scene or two,
Advise the prince; no doubt, an easy tool,
Deferential, glad to be of use,   115
Politic, cautious, and meticulous:
Full of high sentence, but a bit obtuse;
At times, indeed, almost ridiculous—
Almost, at times, the Fool.

    I grow old . . . I grow old . . .   120
I shall wear the bottoms of my trousers rolled.°   cuffed

    Shall I part my hair behind? Do I dare to eat a peach?
I shall wear white flannel trousers, and walk upon the beach.
I have heard the mermaids singing, each to each.

    I do not think that they will sing to me.   125

    I have seen them riding seaward on the waves
Combing the white hair of the waves blown back
When the wind blows the water white and black.

    We have lingered in the chambers of the sea
By sea-girls wreathed with seaweed red and brown   130
Till human voices wake us, and we drown.

T. S. Eliot (1888–1965)

QUESTIONS

1. Vocabulary: *insidious* (9), *Michelangelo* (14), *muzzle* (16), *malingers* (77), *progress* (113), *deferential* (115), *politic* (116), *meticulous* (116), *sentence* (117).
2. This poem may be for you the most difficult in the book, because it uses a "stream of consciousness" technique (that is, presents the apparently random thoughts going through a person's head within a certain time interval), in which the transitional links are psychological rather than logical, and also because it uses allusions you may be unfamiliar with. Even if you do not at first understand the poem in detail, you should be able to get from it a quite accurate picture of Prufrock's character and personality. What kind of person is he? (Answer this as fully as possible.) From what class of society is he? What one line especially well sums up the nature of his past life? A brief initial orientation may be helpful: Prufrock is apparently on his way, at the beginning of the poem, to a late afternoon tea, at which he wishes (or does he?) to make a declaration of love to some lady who will be present. The "you and I" of the first line are divided parts of Prufrock's own nature, for he is undergoing internal conflict. Does he or does he not make the declaration? Where does the climax of the poem come? If the first half of the poem (up to the climax) is devoted to Prufrock's effort to prepare himself psychologically to make the declaration (or to postpone such effort), what is the latter half (after the climax) devoted to?

3. There are a number of striking or unusual figures of speech in the poem. Most of them in some way reflect Prufrock's own nature or his desires or fears. From this point of view discuss lines 2-3; 15-22 and 75-78; 57-58; 73-74; and 124-31. What figure of speech is lines 73-74? In what respect is the title ironical?

4. The poem makes an extensive use of literary allusion. The Italian epigraph is a passage from Dante's *Inferno* in which a man in Hell tells a visitor that he would never tell his story if there were a chance that it would get back to living ears. In line 29 the phrase "works and days" is the title of a long poem—a description of agricultural life and a call to toil—by the early Greek poet Hesiod. Line 52 echoes the opening speech of Shakespeare's *Twelfth Night*. The prophet of lines 81-83 is John the Baptist, whose head was delivered to Salome by Herod as a reward for her dancing (Matthew 14:1-11, and Oscar Wilde's play *Salome*). Line 92 echoes the closing six lines of Marvell's "To His Coy Mistress" (page 70). Lazarus (94-95) may be either the beggar Lazarus (of Luke 16) who was not permitted to return from the dead to warn the brothers of a rich man about Hell or the Lazarus (of John 11) whom Christ raised from death or both. Lines 111-19 allude to a number of characters from Shakespeare's *Hamlet:* Hamlet himself, the chamberlain Polonius, and various minor characters including probably Rosencrantz, Guildenstern, and Osric. "Full of high sentence" (117) echoes Chaucer's description of the Clerk of Oxford in the Prologue to *The Canterbury Tales*. Relate as many of these allusions as you can to the character of Prufrock. How is Prufrock particularly like Hamlet, and how is he unlike him? Contrast Prufrock with the speaker in "To His Coy Mistress."

5. This poem and "The Death of the Hired Man" are dramatic in structure. Frost's poem (though it has a slight narrative element) is largely a dialogue between two characters who speak in their own voices; Eliot's is a highly allusive soliloquy, or interior monologue. In what ways do their dramatic structures facilitate what they have to say?

EXERCISES

In the following exercises, use both scales of poetic measurement—perfection and significance of accomplishment.

1. Considering such matters as economy and richness of poetic communication, inevitability of organization, and the complexity and maturity of the attitude or philosophy expressed, decide whether "Barter" (page 127) or "Stopping by Woods on a Snowy Evening" (page 128) is the superior poem.

2. Rank the following short poems and explain the reasons for your ranking:
   a. "In the Garden" (page 125), "The Death of the Ball Turret Gunner" (page 286), "Fog" (page 302).
   b. "The Coming of Wisdom with Time" (page 143), "The Turtle" (page 153), "Splinter" (page 188).
   c. "Little Jack Horner" (page 126), "Seal Lullaby" (page 178), "Heaven-Haven" (page 198).
   d. "There is no frigate like a book" (page 33), "Apparently with no surprise" (page 140), "Love" (page 151).

3. The following poems are all on seasons of the year. Rank them on a scale of poetic accomplishment: "Winter" (page 6), "Spring" (Shakespeare, page 10), "Spring" (Hopkins, page 54), "To Autumn" (page 54).
4. "The Man He Killed" (page 19) and "Naming of Parts" (page 40) both treat the subject of war. Which is the superior poem?
5. "A Valediction: Forbidding Mourning" (page 69), "The 'Je Ne Sais Quoi'" (page 179), and "if everything happens that can't be done" (page 180) all treat the subject of love. Evaluate and rank them.
6. Rank the following poems by Robert Browning in order of their excellence and defend your ranking: "Meeting at Night" and "Parting at Morning" (considered as one poem) (pages 47–48), "My Star" (page 77), "My Last Duchess" (page 112).
7. Bryant's "To a Waterfowl" and Frost's "Design" (pages 130–31) have a similar subject. Which is the greater poem? Why?
8. Herrick's "To the Virgins, to Make Much of Time" (page 82) and Marvell's "To His Coy Mistress" (page 70) are both *carpe diem* poems of acknowledged excellence. Which achieves the more complex unity?
9. The following poems are all in praise of a beloved. Evaluate and rank them: "A Silken Tent" (page 66), "A Red, Red Rose" (page 97), "My mistress' eyes are nothing like the sun" (page 305).
10. The following poems all explore discord or disenchantment in love. Evaluate and rank them: "When my love swears that she is made of truth" (page 34), "Living in Sin" (page 52), "The Mouse Dinners" (page 277).
11. Each of the following pairs is written by a single author. Pick the poem of each pair that you think represents the higher poetic accomplishment and explain why.
   a. "Bredon Hill" and "To an Athlete Dying Young" (pages 283–84).
   b. "There's been a death in the opposite house" (page 26) and "Because I could not stop for death" (page 271).
   c. "Departmental" (page 110) and "Mending Wall" (page 278).
   d. "The Coming of Wisdom with Time" (page 143) and "Down by the Salley Gardens" (page 183).
   e. "The Lamb" and "The Tiger" (pages 263–64).
   f. "All day I hear" (page 201) and "On the Beach at Fontana" (page 230).
   g. "Song" (page 272) and "The Sun Rising" (page 275).
   h. "Naming of Parts" and "Judging Distances" (pages 40–41).
   i. "Bereft" (page 58) and "Design" (page 131).
   j. "A Hummingbird" (page 63) and "Apparently with no surprise" (page 140).
   k. "Loveliest of trees" (page 73) and "When I was one-and-twenty" (page 214).
   l. "Heaven-Haven" (page 198) and "Pied Beauty" (page 229).
   m. "The Sick Rose" (page 86) and "Soft Snow" (page 94).
   n. "Richard Cory" (page 39) and "Mr. Flood's Party" (page 299).
   o. "Winter" (page 6) and "Spring" (page 10).
   p. "A Silken Tent" (page 66) and "The Aim Was Song" (page 184).
   q. "There is no frigate like a book" (page 33) and "My life closed twice before its close" (page 96).
   r. "Reveille" (page 85) and "Farewell to barn and stack and tree" (page 144).

part two

Poems for
Further Reading

BLACK AND WHITE

"Rhodesia, sweaty
flank of the world . . ."
i read as quietly
as they lay: "guerillas,"
it went on,   5
"put here as a lesson . . ."

they lay like a catch
in the plaza sun,
still damp, the eyes
not yet clouded,   10
the African heat
raising the bellies . . .

"it is the way
of our generals
to count what is theirs,   15
what is done
in their name,"
the secretary announced . . .

from their circle
photographers stare   20
and snap at the dead men,
at the keyboard of rifles
above their heads,
at the small town
that leads to   25
the jungle's edge—
they snap and freeze
it all, store it
in the silent world
of black and white . . .   30

Leonard Adame (b. 1947)

TO SATCH

Sometimes I feel like I will *never* stop
Just go on forever
Till one fine mornin'

BLACK AND WHITE.   This poem was first published in 1977 before Rhodesia, then ruled by
a white minority comprising about 3 percent of its population, became the present African
state of Zimbabwe, in which Blacks have a majority voice.

I'm gonna reach up and grab me a handfulla stars
Throw out my long lean leg
And whip three hot strikes burnin' down the heavens
And look over at God and say
How about that!

Samuel Allen (b. 1917)

THE LAST WAR

The first country to die was normal in the evening,
Ate a good but plain dinner, chatted with some friends
Over a glass, and went to bed soon after ten;
And in the morning was found disfigured and dead.
      That was a lucky one.   5

At breakfast the others heard about it, and kept
Their eyes on their plates. Who was guilty? No one knew,
But by lunch-time three more would never eat again.
The rest appealed for frankness, quietly cocked their guns,
      Declared "This can't go on."   10

They were right. Only the strongest turned up for tea:
The old ones with the big estates hadn't survived
The slobbering blindfold violence of the afternoon.
One killer or many? Was it a gang, or all-against-all?
      Somebody must have known.   15

But each of them sat there watching the others, until
Night came and found them anxious to get it over.
Then the lights went out. A few might have lived, even then;
Innocent, they thought (at first) it still mattered what
      You had or hadn't done.   20

They were wrong. One had been lenient with his servants;
Another ran an island brothel, but rarely left it;
The third owned a museum, the fourth a remarkable gun;
The name of the fifth was quite unknown, but in the end
      What was the difference? None.   25

Homicide, pacifist, crusader, cynic, gentile, jew
Staggered about moaning, shooting into the dark.

TO SATCH. "Satch" or "Satchelfoot" Paige, one of the great baseball pitchers of all time, had an extraordinarily prolonged career. After more than two brilliant decades of pitching in organized Negro baseball, he played in the major leagues after their integration. As late as 1953, when he was over forty-seven years old, he participated in over fifty-seven games as a relief pitcher.

Next day, to tidy up as usual, the sun came in
When they and their ammunition were all used up,
    And found himself alone.   30

Upset, he looked them over, to separate, if he could,
The assassins from the victims, but every face
Had taken on the flat anonymity of pain;
And soon they'll all smell alike, he thought, and felt sick,
    And went to bed at noon.   35

                               Kingsley Amis (b. 1922)

DOVER BEACH

The sea is calm tonight,
The tide is full, the moon lies fair
Upon the straits;—on the French coast the light
Gleams and is gone; the cliffs of England stand,
Glimmering and vast, out in the tranquil bay.   5
Come to the window, sweet is the night-air!
Only, from the long line of spray
Where the sea meets the moon-blanched land,
Listen! you hear the grating roar
Of pebbles which the waves draw back, and fling,   10
At their return, up the high strand,
Begin, and cease, and then again begin,
With tremulous cadence slow, and bring
The eternal note of sadness in.

Sophocles long ago   15
Heard it on the Aegean, and it brought
Into his mind the turbid ebb and flow
Of human misery; we
Find also in the sound a thought,
Hearing it by this distant northern sea.   20

The Sea of Faith
Was once, too, at the full, and round earth's shore
Lay like the folds of a bright girdle furled.
But now I only hear
Its melancholy, long, withdrawing roar,   25
Retreating, to the breath
Of the night-wind, down the vast edges drear
And naked shingles° of the world.   pebbled beaches

Ah, love, let us be true
To one another! for the world, which seems   30

To lie before us like a land of dreams,
So various, so beautiful, so new,
Hath really neither joy, nor love, nor light,
Nor certitude, nor peace, nor help for pain;
And we are here as on a darkling plain   35
Swept with confused alarms of struggle and flight,
Where ignorant armies clash by night.

Matthew Arnold (1822–1888)

LANDCRAB

A lie, that we come from water.
The truth is we were born
from stones, dragons, the sea's
teeth, as you testify,
with your crust and jagged scissors.   5

Hermit, hard socket
for a timid eye,
you're a soft gut scuttling
sideways, a blue skull,
round bone on the prowl.   10
Wolf of treeroots and gravelly holes,
a mouth on stilts,
the husk of a small demon.

Attack, voracious
eating, and flight: 15
it's a sound routine
for staying alive on edges.
Then there's the tide, and that dance
you do for the moon
on wet sand, claws raised   20
to fend off your mate,
your coupling a quick
dry clatter of rocks.
For mammals
with their lobes and bulbs,   25
scruples and warm milk,
you've nothing but contempt.

Here you are, a frozen scowl
targeted in flashlight,
then gone: a piece of what   30
we are, not all,

my stunted child, my momentary
face in the mirror,
my tiny nightmare.

Margaret Atwood (*b. 1939*)

MUSÉE DES BEAUX ARTS

About suffering they were never wrong,
The Old Masters: how well they understood
Its human position; how it takes place
While someone else is eating or opening a window or just
    walking dully along;
How, when the aged are reverently, passionately waiting   5
For the miraculous birth, there always must be
Children who did not specially want it to happen, skating
On a pond at the edge of the wood:
They never forgot
That even the dreadful martyrdom must run its course   10
Anyhow in a corner, some untidy spot
Where the dogs go on with their doggy life and the
    torturer's horse
Scratches its innocent behind on a tree.

In Brueghel's *Icarus,* for instance: how everything turns away
Quite leisurely from the disaster; the ploughman may   15
Have heard the splash, the forsaken cry,
But for him it was not an important failure; the sun shone
As it had to on the white legs disappearing into the green
Water; and the expensive delicate ship that must have seen
Something amazing, a boy falling out of the sky,   20
Had somewhere to get to and sailed calmly on.

W. H. Auden (*1907–1973*)

"O WHERE ARE YOU GOING?"

"O where are you going?" said reader to rider,
"That valley is fatal when furnaces burn,
Yonder's the midden whose odors will madden,
That gap is the grave where the tall return."

"O do you imagine," said fearer to farer,   5
"That dusk will delay on your path to the pass,
Your diligent looking discover the lacking
Your footsteps feel from granite to grass?"

"O what was that bird," said horror to hearer,
"Did you see that shape in the twisted trees?   10
Behind you swiftly the figure comes softly,
The spot on your skin is a shocking disease?"

"Out of this house"—said rider to reader,
"Yours never will"—said farer to fearer,
"They're looking for you"—said hearer to horror,   15
As he left them there, as he left them there.

W. H. Auden (1907–1973)

ON READING POEMS TO A
SENIOR CLASS AT SOUTH HIGH

Before
I opened my mouth
I noticed them sitting there
as orderly as frozen fish
in a package.   5

Slowly water began to fill the room
though I did not notice it
till it reached
my ears

and then I heard the sounds   10
of fish in an aquarium

and I knew that though I had
tried to drown them
with my words
that they had only opened up   15
like gills for them
and let me in.

Together we swam around the room
like thirty tails whacking words
till the bell rang   20
puncturing
a hole in the door

where we all leaked out

They went to another class
I suppose and I home   25

where Queen Elizabeth
my cat met me
and licked my fins
till they were hands again.

D. C. Berry (b. 1947)

TWENTY-THIRD FLIGHT

Lo as I pause in the alien vale of the airport
fearing ahead the official ambush
a voice languorous and strange as these winds of Oahu
calleth my name and I turn to be quoited in orchids
and amazed with a kiss perfumed and soft as the *lei*   5
Straight from a travel poster thou steppest
thy arms like mangoes for smoothness
o implausible shepherdess for this one aging sheep
and leadest me through the righteous paths of the Customs
in a mist of my own wild hopes   10
Yea though I walk through the valley of Immigration
I fear no evil   for thou art a vision beside me
and my name is correctly spelled
and I shall dwell in the Hawaiian Village Hotel
where thy kindred prepareth a table before me   15
Thou restorest my baggage   and by limousine leadest me
to where I may lie on coral sands by a stream-lined pool

Nay but thou stayest not?
Thou anointest not my naked head with oil?
O shepherdess of Flight Number Twenty-three only   20
thou hastenest away on thy long brown legs to enchant
thy fellow-members in Local Five of the Greeters' Union
or that favored professor of Commerce mayhap
who leadeth thee into higher courses in Hotel Management
O nubile goddess of the Kaiser Training Programme   25
is it possible that tonight my cup runneth not over
and that I shall sit in the still pastures of the lobby
whilst thou leadest another old ram in garlands past me,
and   bland as papaya   appearest not to remember me?
And that I shall lie by the waters of Waikiki   and want?   30

Honolulu 1958   *Earle Birney (b. 1904)*

ONE ART

The art of losing isn't hard to master;
so many things seem filled with the intent
to be lost that their loss is no disaster.

Lose something every day. Accept the fluster
of lost door keys, the hour badly spent.
The art of losing isn't hard to master.

Then practice losing farther, losing faster:
places, and names, and where it was you meant
to travel. None of these will bring disaster.

I lost my mother's watch. And look! my last, or
next-to-last, of three loved houses went.
The art of losing isn't hard to master.

I lost two cities, lovely ones. And, vaster,
some realms I owned, two rivers, a continent.
I miss them, but it wasn't a disaster.

—Even losing you (the joking voice, a gesture
I love) I shan't have lied. It's evident
the art of losing's not too hard to master
though it may look like (*Write* it!) like disaster.

Elizabeth Bishop (*1911–1979*)

THE LAMB

Little Lamb, who made thee?
Dost thou know who made thee?
Gave thee life and bid thee feed
By the stream and o'er the mead;
Gave thee clothing of delight,
Softest clothing wooly bright;
Gave thee such a tender voice,
Making all the vales rejoice!
Little Lamb, who made thee?
Dost thou know who made thee?

Little Lamb, I'll tell thee,
Little Lamb, I'll tell thee!
He is callèd by thy name,
For he calls himself a Lamb;
He is meek and he is mild,
He became a little child;
I a child and thou a lamb,
We are callèd by his name.
Little Lamb, God bless thee.
Little Lamb, God bless thee.

William Blake (*1757–1827*)

THE TIGER

Tiger! Tiger! burning bright
In the forests of the night,
What immortal hand or eye
Could frame thy fearful symmetry?

In what distant deeps or skies   5
Burnt the fire of thine eyes?
On what wings dare he aspire?
What the hand dare seize the fire?

And what shoulder, and what art,
Could twist the sinews of thy heart?   10
And when thy heart began to beat,
What dread hand forged thy dread feet?

What the hammer? what the chain?
In what furnace was thy brain?
What the anvil? what dread grasp   15
Dare its deadly terrors clasp?

When the stars threw down their spears,
And watered heaven with their tears,
Did he smile his work to see?
Did he who made the Lamb make thee?   20

Tiger! Tiger! burning bright
In the forests of the night,
What immortal hand or eye
Dare frame thy fearful symmetry?

William Blake (1757–1827)

THE GARDEN OF LOVE

I went to the Garden of Love,
And saw what I never had seen:
A Chapel was built in the midst,
Where I used to play on the green.

And the gates of this Chapel were shut,   5
And "Thou shalt not" writ over the door;
So I turned to the Garden of Love
That so many sweet flowers bore;

And I saw it was filled with graves,
And tomb-stones where flowers should be;   10

And Priests in black gowns were walking their rounds,
And binding with briars my joys and desires.

William Blake (1757-1827)

SOUTHERN COP

Let us forgive Ty Kendricks.
The place was Darktown. He was young.
His nerves were jittery. The day was hot.
The Negro ran out of the alley.
And so Ty shot.   5

Let us understand Ty Kendricks.
The Negro must have been dangerous,
Because he ran;
And here was a rookie with a chance
To prove himself a man.   10

Let us condone Ty Kendricks
If we cannot decorate.
When he found what the Negro was running for,
It was too late;
And all we can say for the Negro is   15
It was unfortunate.

Let us pity Ty Kendricks.
He has been through enough,
Standing there, his big gun smoking,
Rabbit-scared, alone,   20
Having to hear the wenches wail
And the dying Negro moan.

Sterling Brown (b. 1901)

THE SCIENTIST

"There's nothing mysterious about the skull."
He may have been suspicious of my request,
That being mainly a poet, I mainly guessed
There might be an esoteric chance to cull

Some succulent, unfamiliar word; that being   5
Mainly a woman, I now for his sake embraced
An object I held in fact in some distaste.
But he complied, his slender fingers freeing

(There must be a surgeon somewhere with stubby hands)
The latch that held a coil across "The suture   10
Between the parietals and occipital feature."
And gently, his flesh on the bone disturbed the bands

Which illustrated the way that "The mandible
Articulates with the temple next to the ear.
The nasal bone gives onto the maxilla here."   15
He laughed, "It's a bore, but it's not expendable;

"The features depend, if not for their shape, on the narrow
Cranium, formed of the commonest elements;
Weighing nine ounces, worth about fourteen cents;
Not even room for what you would call a marrow."   20

In words resembling these, he judged them dull;
The specimen, his detail, and my suggestion.
"The skin and the brain, of course, are another question,"
He said again, "but there's nothing to the skull."

And that must be so. The quick mind most demands a   25
Miracle in the covering or the core.
What lies between is shallow and functional fare:
My hand between this thought and the posturing stanza.

But his face belied us both. As he spoke his own
Eyes rhymed depth from the sockets of that example;   30
His jawline articulated with the temple
Over the words, and his fingers along the bone

Revealed his god in the praying of their plying.
So that, wonderfully, I justify his doubt:
Am moved, as woman to love, as poet to write,   35
By the mystery and the function of his denying.

Janet Burroway (b. 1936)

LISA

Under the great down-curving lilac branches,
a dome of coolness and a cave of bloom,
Lisa, vague-eyed, chin-propped, cross-legged, is sitting
within a leaf-walled room.

Beyond the curtaining green, her brothers wrangle,   5
cars pass, a huckster shouts, a bicycle bell
is brisk, is brief, dogs bark. She does not hear them.
She is netted in silence, she is lost in a spell.

She has chosen to come here, but she is not hiding,
nor in disgrace, nor sulky. She is alone
of her free will—alone and yet not lonely:
this quarter hour her own.

She could not tell you herself what she is thinking,
or what she makes of this kingdom she has found.
Presently she will go and join the others:
her voice will sound

with theirs. But now the candid light, come sifting
thro leaves, illuminates another view.
O leaf and light, that can divide thus cleanly
the world in two

and give the halves to a child, so to acquaint her
with the mind's need of quietude for growth,
yet interpose no barrier between them,
that she may move in both.

Constance Carrier (*b. 1908*)

GIFT

You tell me that silence
is nearer to peace than poems
but if for my gift
I brought you silence
(for I know silence)
you would say
This is not silence
this is another poem
and you would hand it back to me.

Leonard Cohen (*b. 1934*)

KUBLA KHAN

In Xanadu did Kubla Khan
A stately pleasure-dome decree:
Where Alph, the sacred river, ran
Through caverns measureless to man
    Down to a sunless sea.
So twice five miles of fertile ground
With walls and towers were girdled round:
And here were gardens bright with sinuous rills,

Where blossomed many an incense-bearing tree;
And here were forests ancient as the hills,   10
Enfolding sunny spots of greenery.

But oh! that deep romantic chasm which slanted
Down the green hill athwart a cedarn cover!
A savage place! as holy and enchanted
As e'er beneath a waning moon was haunted   15
By woman wailing for her demon-lover!
And from this chasm, with ceaseless turmoil seething,
As if this earth in fast thick pants were breathing,
A mighty fountain momently was forced:
Amid whose swift half-intermitted burst   20
Huge fragments vaulted like rebounding hail,
Or chaffy grain beneath the thresher's flail:
And 'mid these dancing rocks at once and ever
It flung up momently the sacred river.
Five miles meandering with a mazy motion   25
Through wood and dale the sacred river ran,
Then reached the caverns measureless to man,
And sank in tumult to a lifeless ocean:
And 'mid this tumult Kubla heard from far
Ancestral voices prophesying war!   30

    The shadow of the dome of pleasure
    Floated midway on the waves;
    Where was heard the mingled measure
    From the fountain and the caves.
It was a miracle of rare device,   35
A sunny pleasure-dome with caves of ice!

    A damsel with a dulcimer
    In a vision once I saw:
    It was an Abyssinian maid,
    And on her dulcimer she played,   40
    Singing of Mount Abora.
    Could I revive within me
    Her symphony and song,
To such a deep delight, 'twould win me,
That with music loud and long,   45
I would build that dome in air,
That sunny dome! those caves of ice!
And all who heard should see them there,
And all should cry, Beware! Beware!
His flashing eyes, his floating hair!   50
Weave a circle round him thrice,

And close your eyes with holy dread,
For he on honey-dew hath fed,
And drunk the milk of Paradise.

Samuel Taylor Coleridge (1772-1834)

THE LISTENERS

"Is there anybody there?" said the Traveler,
    Knocking on the moonlit door;
And his horse in the silence champed the grasses
    Of the forest's ferny floor:
And a bird flew up out of the turret,   5
    Above the Traveler's head:
And he smote upon the door again a second time;
    "Is there anybody there?" he said.
But no one descended to the Traveler;
    No head from the leaf-fringed sill   10
Leaned over and looked into his grey eyes,
    Where he stood perplexed and still.
But only a host of phantom listeners
    That dwelt in the lone house then
Stood listening in the quiet of the moonlight   15
    To that voice from the world of men:
Stood thronging the faint moonbeams on the dark stair,
    That goes down to the empty hall,
Hearkening in an air stirred and shaken
    By the lonely Traveler's call.   20
And he felt in his heart their strangeness,
    Their stillness answering his cry,
While his horse moved, cropping the dark turf,
    'Neath the starred and leafy sky;
For he suddenly smote on the door, even   25
    Louder, and lifted his head:—
"Tell them I came, and no one answered,
    That I kept my word," he said.
Never the least stir made the listeners,
    Though every word he spake   30
Fell echoing through the shadowiness of the still house
    From the one man left awake:
Ay, they heard his foot upon the stirrup,
    And the sound of iron on stone,
And how the silence surged softly backward,   35
    When the plunging hoofs were gone.

Walter de la Mare (1873-1956)

THE BEE

To the football coaches of Clemson College, 1942

One dot
Grainily shifting   we at roadside and
The smallest wings coming   along the rail fence out
Of the woods   one dot   of all that green. It now
Becomes flesh-crawling   then the quite still   5
Of stinging. I must live faster for my terrified
Small son   it is on him. Has come. Clings.

Old wingback, come
To life. If your knee action is high
Enough, the fat may fall in time   God damn   10
You, Dickey, *dig*   this is your last time to cut
And run   but you must give it everything you have
Left, for screaming near your screaming child is the sheer
Murder of California traffic: some bee hangs driving

Your child   15
Blindly onto the highway. Get there however
Is still possible. Long live what I badly did
At Clemson   and all of my clumsiest drives
For the ball   all of my trying to turn
The corner downfield   and my spindling explosions   20
Through the five-hole over tackle. O backfield

Coach Shag Norton,
Tell me as you never yet have told me
To get the lead out   scream whatever will get
The slow-motion of middle age off me   I cannot   25
Make it this way   I will have to leave
My feet   they are gone   I have him where
He lives   and down we go singing with screams into

The dirt,
Son-screams of fathers   screams of dead coaches turning   30
To approval   and from between us the bee rises screaming
With flight   grainily shifting   riding the rail fence
Back into the woods   traffic blasting past us
Unchanged, nothing heard through the air-
conditioning glass   we lying at roadside full   35

Of the forearm prints
Of roadrocks   strawberries on our elbows as from
Scrimmage with the varsity   now we can get

Up   stand   turn away from the highway   look straight
Into trees. See, there is nothing coming out   no   40
Smallest wing   no shift of a flight-grain   nothing
Nothing. Let us go in, son, and listen

For some tobacco-
mumbling voice in the branches   to say "That's
a little better,"   to our lives still hanging   45
By a hair. There is nothing to stop us   we can go
Deep   deeper   into elms, and listen to traffic die
Roaring, like a football crowd from which we have
Vanished. Dead coaches live in the air, son   live

In the ear   50
Like fathers, and *urge*   and *urge.* They want you better
Than you are. When needed, they rise and curse you   they scream
When something must be saved. Here, under this tree,
We can sit down. You can sleep, and I can try
To give back what I have earned by keeping us   55
Alive, and safe from bees: the smile of some kind

Of savior—
Of touchdowns, of fumbles, battles,
Lives. Let me sit here with you, son
As on the bench, while the first string takes back   60
Over, far away   and say with my silentest tongue, with the man-
creating bruises of my arms   with a live leaf a quick
Dead hand on my shoulder, "Coach Norton, I am your boy."

James Dickey (*b. 1923*)

BECAUSE I COULD NOT STOP FOR DEATH

Because I could not stop for Death,
He kindly stopped for me;
The carriage held but just ourselves
And Immortality.

We slowly drove; he knew no haste,   5
And I had put away
My labor and my leisure too,
For his civility.

We passed the school, where children strove,
At recess, in the ring,   10
We passed the fields of gazing grain,
We passed the setting sun,

Or rather, he passed us;
The dews drew quivering and chill;
For only gossamer, my gown;   15
My tippet, only tulle.

We paused before a house that seemed
A swelling of the ground;
The roof was scarcely visible.
The cornice, in the ground.   20

Since then, 'tis centuries, and yet
Feels shorter than the day
I first surmised the horses' heads
Were toward eternity.

Emily Dickinson (1830–1886)

I TASTE A LIQUOR NEVER BREWED

I taste a liquor never brewed,
From tankards scooped in pearl;
Not all the vats upon the Rhine
Yield such an alcohol!

Inebriate of air am I,   5
And debauchee of dew,
Reeling, through endless summer days,
From inns of molten blue.

When landlords turn the drunken bee
Out of the foxglove's door,   10
When butterflies renounce their drams,
I shall but drink the more!

Till seraphs swing their snowy hats,
And saints to windows run,
To see the little tippler   15
Leaning against the sun!

Emily Dickinson (1830–1886)

SONG: GO AND CATCH A FALLING STAR

Go and catch a falling star,
    Get with child a mandrake root,
Tell me where all past years are,

SONG. 2. *mandrake:* supposed to resemble a human being because of its forked root.

Or who cleft the devil's foot,
Teach me to hear mermaids singing,   5
    Or to keep off envy's stinging,
        And find
        What wind
Serves to advance an honest mind.

If thou be'st born to strange sights,   10
    Things invisible to see,
Ride ten thousand days and nights,
    Till age snow white hairs on thee,
Thou, when thou return'st, wilt tell me
    All strange wonders that befell thee,   15
        And swear
        No where
Lives a woman true and fair.

If thou find'st one, let me know;
    Such a pilgrimage were sweet.   20
Yet do not; I would not go,
    Though at next door we might meet.
Though she were true when you met her,
    And last till you write your letter,
        Yet she   *women are false* 25
        Will be
False, ere I come, to two or three.

John Donne (1572–1631)

THE FLEA

Mark but this flea, and mark in this
How little that which thou deny'st me is;
It sucked me first, and now sucks thee,
And in this flea our two bloods mingled be;
Thou know'st that this cannot be said   5
A sin, nor shame, nor loss of maidenhead;
    Yet this enjoys before it woo,
    And pampered swells with one blood made of two,
    And this, alas, is more than we would do.   *wants to make love*

Oh stay, three lives in one flea spare,   10
Where we almost, yea more than married are.
This flea is you and I, and this
Our marriage bed, and marriage temple is;
Though parents grudge, and you, we are met

And cloistered in these living walls of jet.   15
Though use° make you apt to kill me,   habit
Let not to that, self-murder added be,
And sacrilege, three sins in killing three.

Cruel and sudden, hast thou since
Purpled thy nail in blood of innocence?   20
Wherein could this flea guilty be,
Except in that drop which it sucked from thee?
Yet thou triumph'st and say'st that thou
Find'st not thyself, nor me the weaker now.
    'Tis true. Then learn how false fears be: 25
    Just so much honor, when thou yield'st to me,
    Will waste, as this flea's death took life from thee.

John Donne (1572–1631)

THE GOOD-MORROW

I wonder, by my troth, what thou and I
Did till we loved? were we not weaned till then,
But sucked on country pleasures childishly?
Or snorted we in the seven sleepers' den?
'Twas so; but this, all pleasures fancies be.   5
If ever any beauty I did see,
Which I desired, and got, 'twas but a dream of thee.

And now good-morrow to our waking souls,
Which watch not one another out of fear;
For love all love of other sights controls,   10
And makes one little room an everywhere.
Let sea-discoverers to new worlds have gone;
Let maps to other,° worlds on worlds have shown;   others
Let us possess one world; each hath one, and is one.

My face in thine eye, thine in mine appears,   15
And true plain hearts do in the faces rest;
Where can we find two better hemispheres
Without sharp north, without declining west?
Whatever dies was not mixed equally;
If our two loves be one, or thou and I   20
Love so alike that none can slacken, none can die.

John Donne (1572–1631)

THE GOOD-MORROW.   4. *seven sleepers' den:* a cave where, according to Christian legend, seven youths escaped persecution and slept for two centuries.

THE SUN RISING

Busy old fool, unruly Sun,
　　Why dost thou thus
Through windows and through curtains call on us?
Must to thy motions lovers' seasons run?
　　　Saucy pedantic wretch, go chide 　　　　5
　　　Late schoolboys and sour prentices,
　　Go tell court-huntsmen that the king will ride,
　　Call country ants to harvest offices;
Love, all alike, no season knows, nor clime,
Nor hours, days, months, which are the rags of time. 　10

　　Thy beams so reverend and strong
　　　Why shouldst thou think?
I could eclipse and cloud them with a wink,
But that I would not lose her sight so long;
　　　If her eyes have not blinded thine, 　　　15
　　　Look, and tomorrow late tell me,
　　Whether both th' Indias of spice and mine
　　Be where thou left'st them, or lie here with me.
Ask for those kings whom thou saw'st yesterday,
And thou shalt hear, "All here in one bed lay." 　　20

　　She's all states, and all princes I;
　　　Nothing else is.
Princes do but play us; compared to this,
All honor's mimic, all wealth alchemy.
　　　Thou, Sun, art half as happy as we, 　　　25
　　　In that the world's contracted thus;
　　Thine age asks ease, and since thy duties be
　　To warm the world, that's done in warming us.
Shine here to us, and thou art everywhere;
This bed thy center is, these walls thy sphere. 　　30

John Donne (1572–1631)

VERGISSMEINNICHT

Three weeks gone and the combatants gone,
returning over the nightmare ground
we found the place again, and found
the soldier sprawling in the sun.

VERGISSMEINNICHT. The German title means "Forget me not." The author, an English poet,
fought with a tank battalion in World War II and was killed in the invasion of Normandy.

The frowning barrel of his gun   5
overshadowing. As we came on
that day, he hit my tank with one
like the entry of a demon.

Look. Here in the gunpit spoil
the dishonored picture of his girl   10
who has put: *Steffi.*° *Vergissmeinnicht*   a girl's name
in a copybook gothic script.

We see him almost with content
abased, and seeming to have paid
and mocked at by his own equipment   15
that's hard and good when he's decayed.

But she would weep to see to-day
how on his skin the swart flies move;
the dust upon the paper eye
and the burst stomach like a cave.   20

For here the lover and killer are mingled
who had one body and one heart.
And death who had the soldier singled
has done the lover mortal hurt.

Keith Douglas (1920–1944)

THE DEBT

This is the debt I pay
Just for one riotous day,
Years of regret and grief,
Sorrow without relief.

Pay it I will to the end—   5
Until the grave, my friend,
Gives me a true release—
Gives me the clasp of peace.

Slight was the thing I bought,
Small was the debt I thought,   10
Poor was the loan at best—
God but the interest!

Paul Laurence Dunbar (1872–1906)

AWARD

A Gold Watch to the FBI
Man who has followed
me for 25 years.

Well, old spy
looks like I
led you down some pretty blind alleys,
took you on several trips to Mexico,
fishing in the high Sierras,   5
jazz at the Philharmonic.
You've watched me all your life,
I've clothed your wife,
put your two sons through college.
what good has it done?   10
the sun keeps rising every morning.
ever see me buy an Assistant President?
or close a school?
or lend money to Trujillo?
ever catch me rigging airplane prices?   15
I bought some after-hours whiskey in L. A.
but the Chief got his pay.
I ain't killed no Koreans
or fourteen-year-old boys in Mississippi.
neither did I bomb Guatemala,   20
or lend guns to shoot Algerians.
I admit I took a Negro child
to a white rest room in Texas,
but she was my daughter, only three,
who had to pee.   25

Ray Durem (1915–1963)

THE MOUSE DINNERS

A woman was cooking a mouse for her husband's dinner, roasting it with a blueberry in its mouth.

He'll use a dentist's pick and a surgeon's scalpel to get the meat off, bending over the tiny roastling with a jeweler's loupe in his eye . . . Twenty years of this . . .

AWARD. 14. *Trujillo:* Dictator of the Dominican Republic, 1930–1961.

After dinner he'll make a long gassy belch as he pats his stomach, saying, it's the best mouse he's ever had, and (as he always reminds her) one less vermin in this world.

Then she'll say, you say that every night, like last night, the curried mouse, the night before, the garlic and butter mouse, sauteed in its own fur. Oh, and then there was the mouse pie. Or was it my mouse-in-the-trap, the mouse I baked in its own trap for variety? My mouse tartare? Or was it mouse poached in menstrual blood at the full of the moon, the best you'd ever had?—Hypocrite!

Hypocrite? No no, I never liked mouse. I thought you liked mouse, so I liked mouse so you'd like me, cried the husband.

You mouse! cried his wife.

Ah yes, he is a mouse; but it came so slowly he hadn't noticed . . . Perhaps it was the twenty years of mouse, eaten to please a wife, who he thought liked mice, has worked the metamorphosis. But now he sees she never liked mouse, and sees this only now that he has himself become a mouse . . .

Russell Edson (b. 1935)

ACQUAINTED WITH THE NIGHT

I have been one acquainted with the night.
I have walked out in rain—and back in rain.
I have outwalked the furthest city light.

I have looked down the saddest city lane.
I have passed by the watchman on his beat   5
And dropped my eyes, unwilling to explain.

I have stood still and stopped the sound of feet
When far away an interrupted cry
Came over houses from another street,

But not to call me back or say good-by;   10
And further still at an unearthly height
One luminary clock against the sky

Proclaimed the time was neither wrong nor right.
I have been one acquainted with the night.

Robert Frost (1874–1963)

MENDING WALL

Something there is that doesn't love a wall,
That sends the frozen-ground-swell under it

And spills the upper boulders in the sun,
And makes gaps even two can pass abreast.
The work of hunters is another thing: 5
I have come after them and made repair
Where they have left not one stone on a stone,
But they would have the rabbit out of hiding,
To please the yelping dogs. The gaps I mean,
No one has seen them made or heard them made,   10
But at spring mending-time we find them there.
I let my neighbor know beyond the hill;
And on a day we meet to walk the line
And set the wall between us once again.
We keep the wall between us as we go.   15
To each the boulders that have fallen to each.
And some are loaves and some so nearly balls
We have to use a spell to make them balance:
"Stay where you are until our backs are turned!"
We wear our fingers rough with handling them.   20
Oh, just another kind of outdoor game,
One on a side. It comes to little more:
There where it is we do not need the wall:
He is all pine and I am apple orchard.
My apple trees will never get across   25
And eat the cones under his pines, I tell him.
He only says, "Good fences make good neighbors."
Spring is the mischief in me, and I wonder
If I could put a notion in his head:
"*Why* do they make good neighbors? Isn't it   30
Where there are cows? But here there are no cows.
Before I built a wall I'd ask to know
What I was walling in or walling out,
And to whom I was like to give offense.
Something there is that doesn't love a wall,   35
That wants it down." I could say "Elves" to him,
But it's not elves exactly, and I'd rather
He said it for himself. I see him there,
Bringing a stone grasped firmly by the top
In each hand, like an old-stone savage armed.   40
He moves in darkness as it seems to me,
Not of woods only and the shade of trees.
He will not go behind his father's saying,
And he likes having thought of it so well
He says again, "Good fences make good neighbors."   45

Robert Frost (1874–1963)

CHANNEL FIRING

That night your great guns, unawares,
Shook all our coffins as we lay,
And broke the chancel window-squares,
We thought it was the Judgment-day

And sat upright. While drearisome   5
Arose the howl of wakened hounds:
The mouse let fall the altar-crumb,
The worms drew back into the mounds,

The glebe cow drooled. Till God called, "No;
It's gunnery practice out at sea   10
Just as before you went below;
The world is as it used to be:

"All nations striving strong to make
Red war yet redder. Mad as hatters
They do no more for Christès sake   15
Than you who are helpless in such matters.

"That this is not the judgment-hour
For some of them's a blessed thing,
For if it were they'd have to scour
Hell's floor for so much threatening. . . .   20

"Ha, ha. It will be warmer when
I blow the trumpet (if indeed
I ever do; for you are men,
and rest eternal sorely need)."

So down we lay again. "I wonder,   25
Will the world ever saner be,"
Said one, "than when He sent us under
In our indifferent century!"

And many a skeleton shook his head.
"Instead of preaching forty year,"   30
My neighbor Parson Thirdly said,
"I wish I had stuck to pipes and beer."

CHANNEL FIRING. 35–36. *Stourton Tower:* memorial at the spot where Alfred the Great
resisted the invading Danes in 879; *Camelot:* legendary capital of Arthur's kingdom; *Stone-
henge:* mysterious circle of huge stones erected in Wiltshire by very early inhabitants of
Britain. The three references move backward in time through the historic, the legendary,
and the prehistoric.

Again the guns disturbed the hour,
Roaring their readiness to avenge,
As far inland as Stourton Tower,   35
And Camelot, and starlit Stonehenge.

April 1914.

Thomas Hardy (1840–1928)

THE DARKLING THRUSH

I leant upon a coppice gate
    When Frost was specter-gray,
And Winter's dregs made desolate
    The weakening eye of day.
The tangled bine-stems scored the sky   5
    Like strings of broken lyres,
And all mankind that haunted nigh
    Had sought their household fires.

The land's sharp features seemed to be
    The Century's corpse outleant,   10
His crypt the cloudy canopy,
    The wind his death-lament.
The ancient pulse of germ and birth
    Was shrunken hard and dry,
And every spirit upon earth   15
    Seemed fervorless as I.

At once a voice arose among
    The bleak twigs overhead
In a full-hearted evensong
    Of joy illimited;   20
An aged thrush, frail, gaunt, and small,
    In blast-beruffled plume,
Had chosen thus to fling his soul
    Upon the growing gloom.

So little cause for carolings   25
    Of such ecstatic sound
Was written on terrestrial things
    Afar or nigh around,
That I could think there trembled through
    His happy good-night air   30

Some blessed Hope, whereof he knew
And I was unaware.

December 1900.

Thomas Hardy (1840–1928)

"MORE LIGHT! MORE LIGHT!"

Composed in the Tower before his execution
These moving verses, and being brought at that time
Painfully to the stake, submitted, declaring thus:
"I implore my God to witness that I have made no crime."

Nor was he forsaken of courage, but the death was horrible,   5
The sack of gunpowder failing to ignite.
His legs were blistered sticks on which the black sap
Bubbled and burst as he howled for the Kindly Light.

And that was but one, and by no means one of the worst;
Permitted at least his pitiful dignity;   10
And such as were by made prayers in the name of Christ,
That shall judge all men, for his soul's tranquility.

We move now to outside a German wood.
Three men are there commanded to dig a hole
In which the two Jews are ordered to lie down   15
And be buried alive by the third, who is a Pole.

Not light from the shrine at Weimar beyond the hill
Nor light from heaven appeared. But he did refuse.
A Lüger settled back deeply in its glove.
He was ordered to change places with the Jews.   20

Much casual death had drained away their souls.
The thick dirt mounted toward the quivering chin.

"MORE LIGHT! MORE LIGHT!" Title: These words are sometimes said to have been the last uttered by Goethe (1749–1832), the great German poet and scientist, before his death. 1. *Tower:* the Tower of London, for centuries a place of imprisonment for high-ranking offenders against the English Crown. The account in stanzas 1–3 is composite, but based largely on the death of Bishop Nicholas Ridley, burned at Oxford in 1553. 6. *gunpowder:* used to ignite the faggots and thus make the death occur more quickly. 8. *Kindly Light:* "Lead, Kindly Light" are the opening words of a famous hymn ("The Pillar of Cloud") by Cardinal Newman (1801–1890). 13. *German wood:* Stanzas 4–8 give an accurate account of an incident that occurred at Buchenwald in 1944. 17. *Weimar:* the intellectual center of Germany during the late eighteenth and early nineteenth centuries; Goethe died there. It is near Buchenwald.

When only the head was exposed the order came
To dig him out again and to get back in.

No light, no light in the blue Polish eye.   25
When he finished a riding boot packed down the earth.
The Lüger hovered lightly in its glove.
He was shot in the belly and in three hours bled to death.

No prayers or incense rose up in those hours
Which grew to be years, and every day came mute   30
Ghosts from the ovens, sifting through crisp air,
And settled upon his eyes in a black soot.

Anthony Hecht (b. 1923)

BREDON HILL

In summertime on Bredon
    The bells they sound so clear;
Round both the shires they ring them
    In steeples far and near,
    A happy noise to hear.   5

Here of a Sunday morning
    My love and I would lie,
And see the colored counties,
    And hear the larks so high
    About us in the sky.   10

The bells would ring to call her
    In valleys miles away:
"Come all to church, good people;
    Good people, come and pray."
    But here my love would stay.   15

And I would turn and answer
    Among the springing thyme,
"Oh, peal upon our wedding,
    And we will hear the chime,
    And come to church in time."   20

But when the snows at Christmas
    On Bredon top were strown,
My love rose up so early
    And stole out unbeknown
    And went to church alone.   25

They tolled the one bell only,
   Groom there was none to see,
The mourners followed after,
   And so to church went she,
   And would not wait for me.   30

The bells they sound on Bredon,
   And still the steeples hum.
"Come all to church, good people,"—
   Oh, noisy bells, be dumb;
   I hear you, I will come.   35

A. E. Housman (1859–1936)

TO AN ATHLETE DYING YOUNG

The time you won your town the race
We chaired you through the market-place;
Man and boy stood cheering by,
And home we brought you shoulder-high.

To-day, the road all runners come,   5
Shoulder-high, we bring you home,
And set you at your threshold down,
Townsman of a stiller town.

Smart lad, to slip betimes away
From fields where glory does not stay   10
And early though the laurel grows
It withers quicker than the rose.

Eyes the shady night has shut
Cannot see the record cut,
And silence sounds no worse than cheers   15
After earth has stopped the ears:

Now you will not swell the rout
Of lads that wore their honors out,
Runners whom renown outran
And the name died before the man.   20

So set, before its echoes fade,
The fleet foot on the sill of shade,
And hold to the low lintel up
The still-defended challenge-cup.

And round that early-laureled head   25
Will flock to gaze the strengthless dead,
And find unwithered on its curls
The garland briefer than a girl's.

A. E. Housman (1859–1936)

PIKE

Pike, three inches long, perfect
Pike in all parts, green tigering the gold.
Killers from the egg: the malevolent aged grin.
They dance on the surface among the flies.

Or move, stunned by their own grandeur   5
Over a bed of emerald, silhouette
Of submarine delicacy and horror.
A hundred feet long in their world.

In ponds, under the heat-struck lily pads—
Gloom of their stillness: 10
Logged on last year's black leaves, watching upwards.
Or hung in an amber cavern of weeds

The jaws' hooked clamp and fangs
Not to be changed at this date;
A life subdued to its instrument;   15
The gills kneading quietly, and the pectorals.

Three we kept behind glass,
Jungled in weed: three inches, four,
And four and a half: fed fry to them—
Suddenly there were two. Finally one.   20

With a sag belly and the grin it was born with.
And indeed they spare nobody.
Two, six pounds each, over two feet long,
High and dry and dead in the willow-herb—

One jammed past its gills down the other's gullet: 25
The outside eye stared: as a vice locks—
The same iron in this eye
Though its film shrank in death.

A pond I fished, fifty yards across,
Whose lilies and muscular tench   30

Had outlasted every visible stone
Of the monastery that planted them—

Stilled legendary depth:
It was as deep as England. It held
Pike too immense to stir, so immense and old   35
That past nightfall I dared not cast

But silently cast and fished
With the hair frozen on my head
For what might move, for what eye might move.
The still splashes on the dark pond,   40

Owls hushing the floating woods
Frail on my ear against the dream
Darkness beneath night's darkness had freed,
That rose slowly towards me, watching.

Ted Hughes (b. 1930)

THE DEATH OF THE BALL TURRET GUNNER

From my mother's sleep I fell into the State,
And I hunched in its belly till my wet fur froze.
Six miles from earth, loosed from its dream of life,
I woke to black flak and the nightmare fighters.
When I died they washed me out of the turret with a hose.

Randall Jarrell (1914–1965)

PATHEDY OF MANNERS

At twenty she was brilliant and adored,
Phi Beta Kappa, sought for every dance;
Captured symbolic logic and the glance
Of men whose interest was their sole reward.

She learned the cultured jargon of those bred   5
To antique crystal and authentic pearls,
Scorned Wagner, praised the Degas dancing girls,
And when she might have thought, conversed instead.

PATHEDY OF MANNERS. *Pathedy:* a coined word formed from the Greek root *path-* (as in *pathetic, pathology*) plus the suffix *-edy* (as in *tragedy, comedy*).

She hung up her diploma, went abroad,
Saw catalogues of domes and tapestry,   10
Rejected an impoverished marquis,
And learned to tell real Wedgwood from a fraud.

Back home her breeding led her to espouse
A bright young man whose pearl cufflinks were real.
They had an ideal marriage, and ideal   15
But lonely children in an ideal house.

I saw her yesterday at forty-three
Her children gone, her husband one year dead,
Toying with plots to kill time and re-wed
Illusions of lost opportunity.   20

But afraid to wonder what she might have known
With all that wealth and mind had offered her,
She shuns conviction, choosing to infer
Tenets of every mind except her own.

A hundred people call, though not one friend,   25
To parry a hundred doubts with nimble talk.
Her meanings lost in manners, she will walk
Alone in brilliant circles to the end.

Ellen Kay (b. 1931)

LA BELLE DAME SANS MERCI
A BALLAD

O, what can ail thee, knight-at-arms,
    Alone and palely loitering?
The sedge has withered from the lake,
    And no birds sing.

O, what can ail thee, knight-at-arms,   5
    So haggard and so woe-begone?
The squirrel's granary is full,
    And the harvest's done.

I see a lily on thy brow,
    With anguish moist and fever dew;   10

LA BELLE DAME SANS MERCI. The title means "The beautiful woman without mercy."

And on thy cheeks a fading rose
    Fast withereth too.

I met a lady in the meads,
    Full beautiful—a faery's child
Her hair was long, her foot was light,   15
    And her eyes were wild.

I made a garland for her head,
    And bracelets too, and fragrant zone;
She looked at me as she did love,
    And made sweet moan.   20

I set her on my pacing steed,
    And nothing else saw all day long;
For sidelong would she bend, and sing
    A faery's song.

She found me roots of relish sweet,   25
    And honey wild, and manna dew,
And sure in language strange she said—
    "I love thee true."

She took me to her elfin grot,
    And there she wept and sighed full sore,   30
And there I shut her wild wild eyes
    With kisses four.

And there she lullèd me asleep
    And there I dreamed—Ah! woe betide!
The latest dream I ever dreamed   35
    On the cold hill side.

I saw pale kings and princes too,
    Pale warriors, death-pale were they all;
They cried—"La Belle Dame sans Merci
    Hath thee in thrall!"   40

I saw their starved lips in the gloam
    With horrid warning gapèd wide,
And I awoke and found me here
    On the cold hill's side.

And this is why I sojourn here   45
    Alone and palely loitering,
Though the sedge has withered from the lake,
    And no birds sing.

John Keats (1795–1821)

ODE ON A GRECIAN URN

Thou still unravished bride of quietness,
    Thou foster-child of silence and slow time,
Sylvan historian, who canst thus express
    A flowery tale more sweetly than our rhyme:
What leaf-fringed legend haunts about thy shape   5
    Of deities or mortals, or of both,
        In Tempe or the dales of Arcady?
    What men or gods are these? What maidens loth?
What mad pursuit? What struggle to escape?
        What pipes and timbrels? What wild ecstasy?   10

Heard melodies are sweet, but those unheard
    Are sweeter; therefore, ye soft pipes, play on;
Not to the sensual ear, but, more endeared,
    Pipe to the spirit ditties of no tone:
Fair youth, beneath the trees, thou canst not leave   15
    Thy song, nor ever can those trees be bare;
        Bold Lover, never, never canst thou kiss,
Though winning near the goal—yet, do not grieve;
        She cannot fade, though thou hast not thy bliss,
    For ever wilt thou love, and she be fair!   20

Ah, happy, happy boughs! that cannot shed
    Your leaves, nor ever bid the Spring adieu;
And, happy melodist, unwearièd,
    For ever piping songs for ever new;
More happy love! more happy, happy love!   25
    For ever warm and still to be enjoyed,
        For ever panting and for ever young;
All breathing human passion far above,
    That leaves a heart high-sorrowful and cloyed,
        A burning forehead, and a parching tongue.   30

Who are these coming to the sacrifice?
    To what green altar, O mysterious priest,
Lead'st thou that heifer lowing at the skies,
    And all her silken flanks with garlands drest?
What little town by river or sea shore,   35

ODE ON A GRECIAN URN. 49–50. In the 1820 edition of Keats's poems the words "Beauty is truth, truth beauty" were enclosed in quotation marks, and the poem is often reprinted that way. It is now generally agreed, however, on the basis of examination of contemporary transcripts of Keats's poem, that Keats intended the entire last two lines of the poem to be spoken by the Urn.

Or mountain-built with peaceful citadel,
    Is emptied of its folk, this pious morn?
And, little town, thy streets for evermore
    Will silent be; and not a soul to tell
      Why thou art desolate, can e'er return.   40

O Attic shape! Fair attitude! with brede
    Of marble men and maidens overwrought,
With forest branches and the trodden weed;
    Thou, silent form, dost tease us out of thought
As doth eternity: Cold Pastoral!   45
    When old age shall this generation waste,
      Thou shalt remain, in midst of other woe
Than ours, a friend to man, to whom thou say'st,
Beauty is truth, truth beauty,—that is all
      Ye know on earth, and all ye need to know.   50

John Keats (1795–1821)

FOR THE SISTERS OF THE HOTEL DIEU

In pairs,
as if to illustrate their sisterhood,
the sisters pace the hospital garden walks.
In their robes black and white immaculate hoods
they are like birds,   5
the safe domestic fowl of the House of God.

O biblic birds,
who fluttered to me in my childhood illnesses
—me little, afraid, ill, not of your race,—
the cool wing for my fever, the hovering solace,   10
the sense of angels—
be thanked, O plumage of paradise, be praised.

A. M. Klein (1909–1972)

MR. EDWARDS AND THE SPIDER

I saw the spiders marching through the air,
Swimming from tree to tree that mildewed day
    In latter August when the hay
    Came creaking to the barn. But where

FOR THE SISTERS OF THE HOTEL DIEU.   9. *not of your race:* The poet was born in Montreal to
immigrant Jewish parents.

The wind is westerly,   5
Where gnarled November makes the spiders fly
Into the apparitions of the sky,
They purpose nothing but their ease and die
Urgently beating east to sunrise and the sea;

What are we in the hands of the great God?   10
It was in vain you set up thorn and briar
    In battle array against the fire
    And treason crackling in your blood;
        For the wild thorns grow tame
And will do nothing to oppose the flame;   15
Your lacerations tell the losing game
You play against a sickness past your cure.
How will the hands be strong? How will the heart endure?

A very little thing, a little worm,
Or hourglass-blazoned spider, it is said,   20
    Can kill a tiger. Will the dead
    Hold up his mirror and affirm
        To the four winds the smell
And flash of his authority? It's well
If God who holds you to the pit of hell,   25
Much as one holds a spider, will destroy,
Baffle and dissipate your soul. As a small boy

On Windsor Marsh, I saw the spider die
When thrown into the bowels of fierce fire:
    There's no long struggle, no desire   30
    To get up on its feet and fly—
        It stretches out its feet
And dies. This is the sinner's last retreat;
Yes, and no strength exerted on the heat
Then sinews the abolished will, when sick   35
And full of burning, it will whistle on a brick.

But who can plumb the sinking of that soul?
Josiah Hawley, picture yourself cast
    Into a brick-kiln where the blast
    Fans your quick vitals to a coal—   40

MR. EDWARDS AND THE SPIDER.   Title: Jonathan Edwards, Puritan preacher and theologian
(1703–1758), as a boy of eleven wrote an essay describing how spiders are borne on the
wind, at the end of a strand of web, toward the sea, where they die. The images in the poem
are taken from this essay and from his famous sermons "Sinners in the Hands of an Angry
God" and "The Future Punishment of the Wicked."   38. *Joseph* (or *Josiah*) *Hawley:* leader
of the faction that got Edwards dismissed from his pastorate in Northhampton, Mass.

If measured by a glass
How long would it seem burning! Let there pass
A minute, ten, ten trillion; but the blaze
Is infinite, eternal: this is death,
To die and know it. This is the Black Widow, death.   45

Robert Lowell (*1917–1977*)

BEDTIME STORY

Long long ago when the world was a wild place
Planted with bushes and peopled by apes, our
Mission Brigade was at work in the jungle.
    Hard by the Congo

Once, when a foraging detail was active   5
Scouting for green-fly, it came on a grey man, the
Last living man, in the branch of a baobab
    Stalking a monkey.

Earlier men had disposed of, for pleasure,
Creatures whose names we scarcely remember—   10
Zebra, rhinoceros, elephants, wart-hog,
    Lion, rats, deer. But

After the wars had extinguished the cities
Only the wild ones were left, half-naked
Near the Equator: and here was the last one,   15
    Starved for a monkey.

By then the Mission Brigade had encountered
Hundreds of such men: and their procedure,
History tells us, was only to feed them:
    Find them and feed them;   20

Those were the orders. And this was the last one.
Nobody knew that he was, but he was. Mud
Caked on his flat grey flanks. He was crouched, half-
    Armed with a shaved spear

Glinting beneath broad leaves. When their jaws cut   25
Swathes through the bark and he saw fine teeth shine,
Round eyes roll round and forked arms waver
    Huge as the rough trunks

Over his head, he was frightened. Our workers
Marched through the Congo before he was born, but   30

This was the first time perhaps that he'd seen one.
    Staring in hot still

Silence, he crouched there: then jumped. With a long swing
Down from his branch, he had angled his spear too
Quickly, before they could hold him, and hurled it   35
    Hard at the soldier

Leading the detail. How could he know Queen's
Orders were only to help him? The soldier
Winced when the tipped spear pricked him. Unsheathing his
    Sting was a reflex.   40

Later the Queen was informed. There were no more
Men. An impetuous soldier had killed off,
Purely by chance, the penultimate primate.
    When she was certain,

Squadrons of workers were fanned through the Congo   45
Detailed to bring back the man's picked bones to be
Sealed in the archives in amber. I'm quite sure
    Nobody found them

After the most industrious search, though.
Where had the bones gone? Over the earth, dear,   50
Ground by the teeth of the termites, blown by the
    Wind, like the dodo's.

George MacBeth (b. 1932)

NEVERTHELESS

      you've seen a strawberry
             that's had a struggle; yet
             was, where the fragments met,

      a hedgehog or a star-
             fish for the multitude   5
             of seeds. What better food

      than apple seeds—the fruit
             within the fruit—locked in
             like counter-curved twin

NEVERTHELESS. 12. *kok-saghyz:* a perennial dandelion native to south central U.S.S.R., cultivated for its fleshy roots, which contain a high rubber content. 15. *prickly-pear:* a flat-jointed cactus with edible fruit. 19. *mandrakes:* The root of the carrot sometimes is forked, resembling the root of the mandrake plant, the subject of superstition because it may look like a human being.

hazelnuts? Frost that kills   10
    the little rubber-plant-
    leaves of *kok-saghyz*-stalks, can't

harm the roots; they still grow
    in frozen ground. Once where
    there was a prickly-pear-   15

leaf clinging to barbed wire,
    a root shot down to grow
    in earth two feet below;

as carrots form mandrakes
    or a ram's-horn root some-   20
    times. Victory won't come

to me unless I go
    to it; a grape tendril
    ties a knot in knots till

knotted thirty times—so   25
    the bound twig that's under-
    gone and over-gone, can't stir.

The weak overcomes its
    menace, the strong over-
    comes itself. What is there   30

like fortitude! What sap
    went through that little thread
    to make the cherry red!

Marianne Moore (1887–1972)

GRACE TO BE SAID AT THE SUPERMARKET

That God of ours, the Great Geometer,
Does something for us here, where He hath put
(if you want to put it that way) things in shape,
Compressing the little lambs in orderly cubes,
Making the roast a decent cylinder,   5
Fairing the tin ellipsoid of a ham,
Getting the luncheon meat anonymous
In squares and oblongs with the edges bevelled
Or rounded (streamlined, maybe, for greater speed).

Praise Him, He hath conferred aesthetic distance   10
Upon our appetites, and on the bloody

Mess of our birthright, our unseemly need,
Imposed significant form. Through Him the brutes
Enter the pure Euclidean kingdom of number,
Free of their bulging and blood-swollen lives   15
They come to us holy, in cellophane
Transparencies, in the mystical body,

That we may look unflinchingly on death
As the greatest good, like a philosopher should.

Howard Nemerov (b. 1920)

THE TRURO BEAR

There's a bear in the Truro woods.
People have seen it—three or four,
or two, or one. I think
of the thickness of the serious woods
around the dark bowls of the Truro ponds;   5
I think of the blueberry fields, the blackberry tangles,
the cranberry bogs. And the sky
with its new moon, its familiar star-trails,
burns down like a brand-new heaven,
while everywhere I look on the scratchy hillsides   10
shadows seem to grow shoulders. Surely
a beast might be clever, be lucky, move quietly
through the woods for years, learning to stay away
from roads and houses. Common sense mutters:
it can't be true, it must be somebody's   15
runaway dog. But the seed
has been planted, and when has happiness ever
required much evidence to begin
its leaf-green breathing?

Mary Oliver (b. 1935)

THE LANDLADY

Through sepia air the boarders come and go,
impersonal as trains. Pass silently
the craving silence swallowing her speech;
click doors like shutters on her camera eye.

Because of her their lives become exact: 5
their entrances and exits are designed;

phone calls are cryptic. Oh, her ticklish ears
advance and fall back stunned.

Nothing is unprepared. They hold the walls
about them as they weep or laugh. Each face   10
is dialed to zero publicly. She peers
stippled with curious flesh;

pads on the patient landing like a pulse,
unlocks their keyholes with the wire of sight,
searches their rooms for clues when they are out,   15
pricks when they come home late.

Wonders when they are quiet, jumps when they move,
dreams that they dope or drink, trembles to know
the traffic of their brains, jaywalks their street
in clumsy shoes.   20

Yet knows them better than their closest friends:
their cupboards and the secrets of their drawers,
their books, their private mail, their photographs
are theirs and hers.

Knows when they wash, how frequently their clothes   25
go to the cleaners, what they like to eat,
their curvature of health, but even so
is not content.

And like a lover must know all, all, all.
Prays she may catch them unprepared at last   30
and palm the dreadful riddle of their skulls—
hoping the worst.

P. K. Page (b. 1917)

SESTINA: ALTAFORTE

LOQUITUR: *En* Bertrans de Born. Dante Alighieri put this man in hell for that
he was a stirrer up of strife. Eccovi! Judge ye! Have I dug him up again? The
scene is at his castle, Altaforte. "Papiols" is his jongleur. "The Leopard," the
device of Richard Coeur de Lion.

SESTINA: ALTAFORTE.   The speaker (*Loquitur*) is Sir (*En*) Bertran de Born, a twelfth-century
French nobleman and troubadour, whom the great Italian poet Dante pictures in hell in the
Inferno, first part of his *Divine Comedy. Eccovi!:* Here you are! *jongleur:* singer. *Richard
Coeur de Lion:* Duke of Aquitaine, later Richard I, king of England; Bertran's enemy.

Damn it all! all this our South stinks peace.
You whoreson dog, Papiols, come! Let's to music!
I have no life save when the swords clash.
But ah! when I see the standards gold, vair, purple, opposing
And the broad fields beneath them turn crimson,   5
Then howl I my heart nigh mad with rejoicing.

In hot summer have I great rejoicing
When the tempests kill the earth's foul peace,
And the lightnings from black heav'n flash crimson,
And the fierce thunders roar me their music   10
And the winds shriek through the clouds mad, opposing,
And through all the riven skies God's swords clash.

Hell grant soon we hear again the swords clash!
And the shrill neighs of destriers° in battle rejoicing,   war horses
Spiked breast to spiked breast opposing!   15
Better one hour's stour° than a year's peace   battle
With fat boards, bawds, wine and frail music!
Bah! there's no wine like the blood's crimson!

And I love to see the sun rise blood-crimson.
And I watch his spears through the dark clash   20
And it fills all my heart with rejoicing
And pries wide my mouth with fast music
When I see him so scorn and defy peace,
His lone might 'gainst all darkness opposing.

The man who fears war and squats opposing   25
My words for stour, hath no blood of crimson
But is fit only to rot in womanish peace
Far from where worth's won and the swords clash
For the death of such sluts I go rejoicing;
Yea, I fill all the air with my music.   30

Papiols, Papiols, to the music!
There's no sound like to swords swords opposing,
No cry like the battle's rejoicing
When our elbows and swords drip the crimson
And our charges 'gainst "The Leopard's" rush clash.   35
May God damn for ever all who cry "Peace!"

And let the music of the swords make them crimson!
Hell grant soon we hear again the swords clash!
Hell blot black for alway the thought "Peace!"

Ezra Pound (1885–1972)

AFTER THE KILLING

"We will kill,"
said the blood-thirster,
"and after the killing
there will be peace."

But after the killing   5
their sons
killed his sons,
and his sons
killed their sons,
and their sons   10
killed his sons

until

at last

a blood-thirster said,
"We will kill.   15
And after the killing
there will be   peace."

Dudley Randall (b. 1914)

THE MILL

The miller's wife had waited long,
   The tea was cold, the fire was dead;
And there might yet be nothing wrong
   In how he went and what he said:
"There are no millers any more,"   5
   Was all that she had heard him say;
And he had lingered at the door
   So long that it seemed yesterday.

Sick with a fear that had no form
   She knew that she was there at last;   10
And in the mill there was a warm
   And mealy fragrance of the past.
What else there was would only seem
   To say again what he had meant;
And what was hanging from a beam   15
   Would not have heeded where she went.

And if she thought it followed her,
   She may have reasoned in the dark

That one way of the few there were
    Would hide her and would leave no mark: 20
Black water, smooth above the weir
    Like starry velvet in the night,
Though ruffled once, would soon appear
    The same as ever to the sight.

Edwin Arlington Robinson (1869–1935)

MR. FLOOD'S PARTY

Old Eben Flood, climbing alone one night
Over the hill between the town below
And the forsaken upland hermitage
That held as much as he should ever know
On earth again of home, paused warily.   5
The road was his with not a native near;
And Eben, having leisure, said aloud,
For no man else in Tilbury Town to hear:

"Well, Mr. Flood, we have the harvest moon
Again, and we may not have many more;   10
The bird is on the wing, the poet says,
And you and I have said it here before.
Drink to the bird." He raised up to the light
The jug that he had gone so far to fill,
And answered huskily: "Well, Mr. Flood,   15
Since you propose it, I believe I will."

Alone, as if enduring to the end
A valiant armor of scarred hopes outworn,
He stood there in the middle of the road
Like Roland's ghost winding a silent horn.   20
Below him, in the town among the trees,
Where friends of other days had honored him,
A phantom salutation of the dead
Rang thinly till old Eben's eyes were dim.

Then, as a mother lays her sleeping child   25
Down tenderly, fearing it may awake,
He set the jug down slowly at his feet

MR. FLOOD'S PARTY. 11. *bird:* Mr. Flood is quoting from *The Rubáiyát of Omar Khayyám,*
"The bird of Time . . . is on the wing." 20. *Roland:* hero of the French epic poem *The
Song of Roland.* He died fighting a rearguard action for Charlemagne against the Moors in
Spain; before his death he sounded a call for help on his famous horn, but the king's army
arrived too late.

With trembling care, knowing that most things break;
And only when assured that on firm earth
It stood, as the uncertain lives of men   30
Assuredly did not, he paced away,
And with his hand extended paused again:

"Well, Mr. Flood, we have not met like this
In a long time; and many a change has come
To both of us, I fear, since last it was   35
We had a drop together. Welcome home!"
Convivially returning with himself,
Again he raised the jug up to the light;
And with an acquiescent quaver said:
"Well, Mr. Flood, if you insist, I might.   40

"Only a very little, Mr. Flood—
For auld lang syne. No more, sir; that will do."
So, for the time, apparently it did,
And Eben evidently thought so too;
For soon amid the silver loneliness   45
Of night he lifted up his voice and sang,
Secure, with only two moons listening,
Until the whole harmonious landscape rang—

"For auld lang syne." The weary throat gave out,
The last word wavered, and the song was done.   50
He raised again the jug regretfully
And shook his head, and was again alone.
There was not much that was ahead of him,
And there was nothing in the town below—
Where strangers would have shut the many doors   55
That many friends had opened long ago.

Edwin Arlington Robinson (1869–1935)

I KNEW A WOMAN

I knew a woman, lovely in her bones,
When small birds sighed, she would sigh back at them;
Ah, when she moved, she moved more ways than one:
The shapes a bright container can contain!
Of her choice virtues only gods should speak,   5
Or English poets who grew up on Greek
(I'd have them sing in chorus, cheek to cheek).

How well her wishes went! She stroked my chin,
She taught me Turn, and Counter-turn, and Stand;

She taught me Touch, that undulant white skin;   10
I nibbled meekly from her proffered hand;
She was the sickle; I, poor I, the rake,
Coming behind her for her pretty sake
(But what prodigious mowing we did make).

Love likes a gander, and adores a goose: 15
Her full lips pursed, the errant note to seize;
She played it quick, she played it light and loose;
My eyes, they dazzled at her flowing knees;
Her several parts could keep a pure repose,
Or one hip quiver with a mobile nose   20
(She moved in circles, and those circles moved).

Let seed be grass, and grass turn into hay:
I'm martyr to a motion not my own;
What's freedom for? To know eternity.
I swear she cast a shadow white as stone.   25
But who would count eternity in days?
These old bones live to learn her wanton ways:
(I measure time by how a body sways).

Theodore Roethke (*1908–1963*)

THE WAKING

I wake to sleep, and take my waking slow.
I feel my fate in what I cannot fear.
I learn by going where I have to go.

We think by feeling. What is there to know?
I hear my being dance from ear to ear.   5
I wake to sleep, and take my waking slow.

Of those so close beside me, which are you?
God bless the Ground! I shall walk softly there,
And learn by going where I have to go.

Light takes the Tree; but who can tell us how?   10
The lowly worm climbs up a winding stair;
I wake to sleep, and take my waking slow.

Great Nature has another thing to do
To you and me; so take the lively air,
And, lovely, learn by going where to go.   15

This shaking keeps me steady. I should know.
What falls away is always. And is near.

I wake to sleep, and take my waking slow.
I learn by going where I have to go.

Theodore Roethke (1908–1963)

SONG

When I am dead, my dearest,
    Sing no sad songs for me;
Plant thou no roses at my head,
    Nor shady cypress tree;
Be the green grass above me   5
    With showers and dewdrops wet;
And if thou wilt, remember,
    And if thou wilt, forget.

I shall not see the shadows,
    I shall not feel the rain;   10
I shall not hear the nightingale
    Sing on, as if in pain;
And dreaming through the twilight
    That doth not rise nor set,
Haply I may remember,   15
    And haply may forget.

Christina Rossetti (1830–1894)

FOG

The fog comes
on little cat feet.

It sits looking
over harbor and city
on silent haunches.
and then moves on.

Carl Sandburg (1878–1967)

PAIN FOR A DAUGHTER

Blind with love, my daughter
has cried nightly for horses,
those long-necked marchers and churners
that she has mastered, any and all,
reigning them in like a circus hand—   5

the excitable muscles and the ripe neck—
tending, this summer, a pony and a foal.
She who is too squeamish to pull
a thorn from the dog's paw
watched her pony blossom with distemper,   10
the underside of the jaw swelling
like an enormous grape.
Gritting her teeth with love,
she drained the boil and scoured it
with hydrogen peroxide until pus   15
ran like milk on the barn floor.

Blind with loss all winter,
in dungarees, a ski jacket, and a hard hat,
she visits the neighbors' stable,
our acreage not zoned for barns,   20
they who own the flaming horses
and the swan-whipped thoroughbred
that she tugs at and cajoles,
thinking it will burn like a furnace
under her small-hipped English seat.   25

Blind with pain, she limps home.
The thoroughbred has stood on her foot.
He rested there like a building.
He grew into her foot until they were one.
The marks of the horseshoe printed   30
into her flesh, the tips of her toes
ripped off like pieces of leather,
three toenails swirled like shells
and left to float in blood in her riding boot.

Blind with fear, she sits on the toilet,   35
her foot balanced over the washbasin,
her father, hydrogen peroxide in hand,
performing the rites of the cleansing.
She bites on a towel, sucked in breath,
sucked in and arched against the pain,   40
her eyes glancing off me where
I stand at the door, eyes locked
on the ceiling, eyes of a stranger,
and then she cries . . .
Oh, my God, help me!   45
Where a child would have cried *Mama!*
Where a child would have believed *Mama!*
She bit the towel and called on God,

and I saw her life stretch out . . .
I saw her torn in childbirth,   50
and I saw her, at that moment,
in her own death, and I knew that she
knew.

Anne Sexton (*1928-1974*)

FEAR NO MORE

Fear no more the heat o' the sun,
   Nor the furious winter's rages;
Thou thy worldly task hast done,
   Home art gone, and ta'en thy wages.
Golden lads and girls all must,   5
As chimney-sweepers, come to dust.

Fear no more the frown o' the great;
   Thou art past the tyrant's stroke;
Care no more to clothe and eat;
   To thee the reed is as the oak.   10
The scepter, learning, physic,° must   art of healing
All follow this, and come to dust.

Fear no more the lightning-flash,
   Nor the all-dreaded thunder-stone;°   thunderbolt
Fear not slander, censure rash;   15
   Thou hast finished joy and moan.
All lovers young, all lovers must
Consign to thee,° and come to dust.   yield to your condition

William Shakespeare (*1564-1616*)

LET ME NOT TO THE MARRIAGE
OF TRUE MINDS

Let me not to the marriage of true minds
Admit impediments. Love is not love
Which alters when it alteration finds,
Or bends with the remover to remove.
O no! it is an ever-fixèd mark   5
That looks on tempests and is never shaken;
It is the star to every wandering bark,
Whose worth's unknown, although his height be taken.
Love's not Time's fool, though rosy lips and cheeks
Within his bending sickle's compass come;   10

Love alters not with his brief hours and weeks,
But bears it out even to the edge of doom.
    If this be error and upon me proved,
    I never writ, nor no man ever loved.

William Shakespeare (1564–1616)

MY MISTRESS EYES ARE NOTHING
LIKE THE SUN

My mistress' eyes are nothing like the sun;
Coral is far more red than her lips' red:
If snow be white, why then her breasts are dun;
If hairs be wires, black wires grow on her head.   4
I have seen roses damasked,° red and white,   of different colors
But no such roses see I in her cheeks;
And in some perfumes is there more delight
Than in the breath that from my mistress reeks.°   exhales
I love to hear her speak, yet well I know
That music hath a far more pleasing sound: 10
I grant I never saw a goddess go,—
My mistress, when she walks, treads on the ground.
    And yet, by heaven, I think my love as rare
    As any she belied with false compare.

William Shakespeare (1564–1616)

TELEPHONE CONVERSATION

The price seemed reasonable, location
Indifferent. The landlady swore she lived
Off premises. Nothing remained
But self-confession. "Madam," I warned,
"I hate a wasted journey—I am African."   5
Silence. Silenced transmission of
Pressurized good-breeding. Voice, when it came,
Lipstick-coated, long gold-rolled
Cigarette-holder tipped. Caught I was, foully.
"HOW DARK?" . . . I had not misheard . . . "ARE YOU LIGHT   10

TELEPHONE CONVERSATION. 11–14. Public telephones in England once required the pushing
of buttons to make connections and deposit coins. Telephone booths, mailboxes (called
pillar boxes), and buses are painted red. 19. *plain chocolate:* dark chocolate.

OR VERY DARK?" Button B. Button A. Stench
Of rancid breath of public hide-and-speak.
Red booth. Red pillar box. Red double-tiered
Omnibus squelching tar. It *was* real! Shamed
By ill-mannered silence, surrender   15
Pushed dumbfounded to beg simplification.
Considerate she was, varying the emphasis—
"ARE YOU DARK? OR VERY LIGHT?" Revelation came.
"You mean—like plain or milk chocolate?"
Her assent was clinical, crushing in its light   20
Impersonality. Rapidly, wave-length adjusted,
I chose. "West African sepia"—and as afterthought,
"Down in my passport." Silence for spectroscopic
Flight of fancy, till truthfulness clanged her accent
Hard on the mouthpiece. "WHAT'S THAT?" conceding   25
"DON'T KNOW WHAT THAT IS." "Like brunette."
"THAT'S DARK, ISN'T IT?" "Not altogether.
Facially, I am brunette, but madam, you should see
The rest of me. Palm of my hand, soles of my feet
Are a peroxide blonde. Friction, caused—   30
Foolishly madam—by sitting down, has turned
My bottom raven black—One moment, madam!—sensing
Her receiver rearing on the thunderclap
About my ears—"Madam," I pleaded, "wouldn't you rather
See for yourself?"   35

Wole Soyinka (b. 1935)

THE SNOW MAN

One must have a mind of winter
To regard the frost and the boughs
Of the pine-trees crusted with snow;

And have been cold a long time
To behold the junipers shagged with ice,   5
The spruces rough in the distant glitter

Of the January sun; and not to think
Of any misery in the sound of the wind,
In the sound of a few leaves,

Which is the sound of the land   10
Full of the same wind
That is blowing in the same bare place

For the listener, who listens in the snow,
And, nothing himself, beholds
Nothing that is not there and the nothing that is.   15

Wallace Stevens (1879–1955)

LION

In the bend of your mouth soft murder
   in the flints of your eyes
   the sun-stained openings of caves
Your nostrils breathe the ordained air
   of chosen loneliness   5

Magnificently maned as the lustrous pampas
   your head heavy with heraldic curls
   wears a regal frown between the brows

The wide bundle of your chest
   your loose-skinned belly frilled with fur   10
   you carry easily sinuously pacing on suede paws

Between tight thighs
   under the thick root of your tufted tail
   situated like a full-stoned fruit beneath a bough
   the quiver of your never-used malehood is slung   15

You pace in dung on cement
   the bars flick past your eyeballs
   fixed beyond the awestruck stares of children
Watching you they remember their fathers
   the frightening hairs in their fathers' ears   20

Young girls remember lovers too timid and white
   and I remember how I played lion with my brothers
   under the round yellow-grained table
   the shadow our cave in the lamplight

Your beauty burns the brain   25
   though your paws slue on foul cement
   the fetor of captivity you do right to ignore
   the bars too an illusion

Your heroic paranoia plants you in the Indian jungle
   pacing by the cool water-hole as dawn streaks the sky   30
   and the foretaste of the all-day hunt

is sweet as yearling's blood
in the corners of your lips

May Swenson (b. *1919*)

A DESCRIPTION OF THE MORNING

Now hardly here and there a hackney-coach
Appearing, showed the ruddy morn's approach.
Now Betty from her master's bed had flown,
And softly stole to discompose her own.
The slip-shod 'prentice from his master's door   5
Had pared the dirt, and sprinkled round the floor.
Now Moll had whirled her mop with dextrous airs,
Prepared to scrub the entry and the stairs.
The youth with broomy stumps began to trace
The kennel's edge, where wheels had worn the place.   10
The small-coal man was heard with cadence deep,
Till drowned in shriller notes of chimney-sweep.
Duns at his lordship's gate began to meet;
And Brickdust Moll had screamed through half the street.
The turnkey now his flock returning sees,   15
Duly let out a-nights to steal for fees.
The watchful bailiffs take their silent stands;
And schoolboys lag with satchels in their hands.

Jonathan Swift (*1667–1745*)

DO NOT GO GENTLE INTO THAT GOOD NIGHT

Do not go gentle into that good night,
Old age should burn and rave at close of day;
Rage, rage against the dying of the light.

Though wise men at their end know dark is right,
Because their words had forked no lightning they   5
Do not go gentle into that good night.

Good men, the last wave by, crying how bright
Their frail deeds might have danced in a green bay,
Rage, rage against the dying of the light.

A DESCRIPTION OF THE MORNING.   9. *youth:* he is apparently searching for salvage.
10. *kennel:* gutter.   14. *Brickdust:* red-complexioned.

Wild men who caught and sang the sun in flight,   10
And learn, too late, they grieved it on its way
Do not go gentle into that good night.

Grave men, near death, who see with blinding sight
Blind eyes could blaze like meteors and be gay,
Rage, rage against the dying of the light.   15

And you, my father, there on the sad height,
Curse, bless, me now with your fierce tears, I pray.
Do not go gentle into that good night.
Rage, rage against the dying of the light.

Dylan Thomas (*1914–1953*)

FERN HILL

Now as I was young and easy under the apple boughs
About the lilting house and happy as the grass was green,
    The night above the dingle starry,
      Time let me hail and climb
    Golden in the heydays of his eyes,   5
And honored among wagons I was prince of the apple towns
And once below a time I lordly had the trees and leaves
      Trail with daisies and barley
    Down the rivers of the windfall light.

And as I was green and carefree, famous among the barns   10
About the happy yard and singing as the farm was home,
    In the sun that is young once only,
      Time let me play and be
    Golden in the mercy of his means,
And green and golden I was huntsman and herdsman, the calves   15
Sang to my horn, the foxes on the hills barked clear and cold,
      And the sabbath rang slowly
    In the pebbles of the holy streams.

All the sun long it was running, it was lovely, the hay
Fields high as the house, the tunes from the chimneys, it was air   20
    And playing, lovely and watery
      And fire green as grass.
    And nightly under the simple stars
As I rode to sleep the owls were bearing the farm away,
All the moon long I heard, blessed among stables, the nightjars   25
    Flying with the ricks, and the horses
      Flashing into the dark.

And then to awake, and the farm, like a wanderer white
With the dew, come back, the cock on his shoulder: it was all
    Shining, it was Adam and maiden,   30
        The sky gathered again
    And the sun grew round that very day.
So it must have been after the birth of the simple light
In the first, spinning place, the spellbound horses walking warm
    Out of the whinnying green stable   35
        On to the fields of praise.

And honored among foxes and pheasants by the gay house
Under the new made clouds and happy as the heart was long,
    In the sun born over and over,
        I ran my heedless ways,   40
    My wishes raced through the house high hay
And nothing I cared, at my sky blue trades, that time allows
In all his tuneful turning so few and such morning songs
    Before the children green and golden
        Follow him out of grace,   45

Nothing I cared, in the lamb white days, that time would take me
Up to the swallow thronged loft by the shadow of my hand,
    In the moon that is always rising,
        Nor that riding to sleep
I should hear him fly with the high fields   50
And wake to the farm forever fled from the childless land.
Oh as I was young and easy in the mercy of his means,
        Time held me green and dying
    Though I sang in my chains like the sea.

Dylan Thomas (1914–1953)

THE OWL

    Downhill I came, hungry, and yet not starved;
    Cold, yet had heat within me that was proof
    Against the North wind; tired, yet so that rest
    Had seemed the sweetest thing under a roof.

    Then at the inn I had food, fire, and rest,   5
    Knowing how hungry, cold, and tired was I.
    All of the night was quite barred out except
    An owl's cry, a most melancholy cry

    Shaken out long and clear upon the hill,
    No merry note, nor cause of merriment,   10

But one telling me plain what I escaped
And others could not, that night, as in I went.

And salted was my food, and my repose,
Salted and sobered, too, by the bird's voice
Speaking for all who lay under the stars,   15
Soldiers and poor, unable to rejoice.

Edward Thomas (1878–1917)

THE VIRGINS

Down the dead streets of sun-stoned Frederiksted,
the first free port to die for tourism,
strolling at funeral pace, I am reminded
of life not lost to the American dream;
but my small-islander's simplicities   5
can't better our new empire's civilized
exchange of cameras, watches, perfumes, brandies
for the good life, so cheaply underpriced
that only the crime rate is on the rise
in streets blighted with sun, stone arches   10
and plazas blown dry by the hysteria
of rumor. A condominium drowns
in vacancy; its bargains are dusted,
but only a jeweled housefly drones
over the bargains. The roulettes spin   15
rustily to the wind—the vigorous trade
that every morning would begin afresh
by revving up green water round the pierhead
heading for where the banks of silver thresh.

Derek Walcott (b. 1930)

BOY WANDERING IN SIMMS' VALLEY

Through brush and love-vine, well blooded by blackberry thorn
Long dry past prime, all under the molten light
Of late summer, and past the last rock-slide at ridge-top and stubborn,
Raw cedar, I clambered, breath short and spit white

THE VIRGINS. 1. *Frederiksted*: chief port of St. Croix, largest of the American Virgin Islands, is a free port where goods can be bought without payment of customs duties and therefore at bargain prices. The economy of St. Croix, once based on sugar cane, is now chiefly dependent on tourism. Like the other American Virgin Islands, it has suffered from uncontrolled growth, building booms, unevenly distributed prosperity, destruction of natural beauty, and pollution. 5. *my . . . simplicities:* The poet is a native of St. Lucia in the West Indies. 16. *trade:* cf. trade wind.

From lung-depth. Then down the lone valley, called Simms' Valley still,   5
Where Simms, for long years, had nursed a sick wife till she died.
Then turned out his spindly stock to forage at will,
And took down his .12 gauge, and simply lay down by her side.

No kin they had, and nobody came just to jaw.
It was two years before some straggling hunter sat down   10
On the porch-edge to rest, then started to prowl. He saw
What he saw, saw no reason to linger, but high-tailed to town.

A dirt-farmer needs a good wife to keep a place trim,
So the place must have gone to wrack with his old lady sick.
And when I came there, years later, old furrows were dim,   15
And dimmer in fields where grew maples and such, two-span thick.

So for years the farm had contracted: now barn down, and all
The yard gone part of the wilderness, and only
The house to mark human hope, and that ready to fall.
No buyer at tax-sale. It waited, forgotten and lonely.   20

I stood in the bedroom upstairs, in lowering sun,
And saw sheets hang spiderweb-rotten, and blankets a mass
Of what weather and leaves from the broken window had done,
Not to mention the rats, and thought what had there come to pass.

But lower was sinking the sun. I shook myself,   25
And flung a last glance around, then suddenly
Saw the old enameled bedpan, high on a shelf.
I stood still again, as the last sun fell on me,

And stood wondering what life is, and love, and what they may be.

Robert Penn Warren (b. *1905*)

A NOISELESS PATIENT SPIDER

A noiseless patient spider,
I marked where on a little promontory it stood isolated,
Marked how to explore the vacant vast surrounding,
It launched forth filament, filament, filament, out of itself,
Ever unreeling them, ever tirelessly speeding them.   5

And you O my soul where you stand,
Surrounded, detached, in measureless oceans of space,
Ceaselessly musing, venturing, throwing, seeking the spheres to connect them,
Till the bridge you will need be formed, till the ductile anchor hold,
Till the gossamer thread you fling catch somewhere, O my soul.   10

Walt Whitman (*1819–1892*)

THERE WAS A CHILD WENT FORTH

There was a child went forth every day,
And the first object he looked upon, that object he became,
And that object became part of him for the day or a
    certain part of the day,
Or for many years or stretching cycles of years.

The early lilacs became part of this child,   5
And grass and white and red morning-glories, and white and red
    clover, and the song of the phoebe-bird,
And the Third-month lambs and the sow's pink-faint litter, and the
    mare's foal and the cow's calf,
And the noisy brood of the barnyard or by the mire of the
    pond-side,
And the fish suspending themselves so curiously below there,
    and the beautiful curious liquid,
And the water-plants with their graceful flat heads, all became
    part of him.   10

The field-sprouts of Fourth-month and Fifth-month became
    part of him,
Winter-grain sprouts and those of the light-yellow corn, and the
    esculent roots of the garden,
And the apple-trees covered with blossoms and the fruit afterward,
    and wood-berries, and the commonest weeds by the road,
And the old drunkard staggering home from the outhouse of the
    tavern whence he had lately risen,
And the schoolmistress that passed on her way to the school,   15
And the friendly boys that passed, and the quarrelsome boys,
And the tidy and fresh-cheeked girls, and the barefoot negro boy
    and girl,
And all the changes of city and country wherever he went.

His own parents, he that had fathered him and she that had conceived
    him in her womb and birthed him,
They gave this child more of themselves than that,   20
They gave him afterward every day, they became part of him.

The mother at home quietly placing the dishes on the supper-table,
The mother with mild words, clean her cap and gown, a wholesome
    odor falling off her person and clothes as she walks by,
The father, strong, self-sufficient, manly, mean, angered, unjust,
The blow, the quick loud word, the tight bargain, the crafty lure,   25
The family usages, the language, the company, the furniture,
    the yearning and swelling heart,
Affection that will not be gainsayed, the sense of what is real,
    the thought if after all it should prove unreal,

The doubts of day-time and the doubts of night-time, the curious
    whether and how,
Whether that which appears so is so, or is it all flashes and specks?
Men and women crowding fast in the streets, if they are not
    flashes and specks what are they?   30
The streets themselves and the façades of houses, and goods
    in the windows,
Vehicles, teams, the heavy-planked wharves, the huge crossing
    at the ferries,
The village on the highland seen from afar at sunset, the river between,
Shadows, aureola and mist, the light falling on roofs and gables
    of white or brown two miles off,
The schooner near by sleepily dropping down the tide, the little boat
    slack-towed astern,   35
The hurrying tumbling waves, quick-broken crests, slapping,
The strata of colored clouds, the long bar of maroon-tint away
    solitary by itself, the spread of purity it lies motionless in,
The horizon's edge, the flying sea-crow, the fragrance of salt marsh
    and shore mud,
These became part of that child who went forth every day, and who
    now goes, and will always go forth every day.

Walt Whitman (1819–1892)

WHEN I HEARD THE LEARN'D ASTRONOMER

When I heard the learn'd astronomer,
When the proofs, the figures, were ranged in columns before me,
When I was shown the charts and diagrams, to add, divide,
    and measure them,
When I sitting heard the astronomer where he lectured with much
    applause in the lecture-room,
How soon unaccountable I became tired and sick,
Till rising and gliding out I wandered off by myself,
In the mystical moist night-air, and from time to time,
Looked up in perfect silence at the stars.

Walt Whitman (1819–1892)

THE MILL

    The spoiling daylight inched along the bar-top,
    Orange and cloudy, slowly igniting lint,
    And then that glow was gone, and still your voice,
    Serene with failure and with the ease of dying,
    Rose from the shades that more and more became you.   5

Turning among its images, your mind
Produced the names of streets, the exact look
Of lilacs, 1903, in Cincinnati,
—Random, as if your testament were made,
The round sums all bestowed, and now you spent   10
Your pocket change, so as to be rid of it.
Or was it that you half-hoped to surprise
Your dead life's sound and sovereign anecdote?
What I remember best is the wrecked mill
You stumbled on in Tennessee; or was it   15
Somewhere down in Brazil? It slips my mind
Already. But there it was in a still valley
Far from the towns. No road or path came near it.
If there had been a clearing now it was gone,
And all you found amidst the choke of green   20
Was three walls standing, hurdled by great vines
And thatched by height on height of hushing leaves.
But still the mill-wheel turned! its crazy buckets
Creaking and lumbering out of the clogged race
And sounding, as you said, as if you'd found   25
Time all alone and talking to himself
In his eternal rattle.
                    How should I guess
Where they are gone to, now that you are gone,
Those fading streets and those most fragile lilacs,
Those fragmentary views, those times of day?   30
All that I can be sure of is the mill-wheel.
It turns and turns in my mind, over and over.

Richard Wilbur (*b. 1921*)

THE RED WHEELBARROW

so much depends
upon

a red wheel
barrow

glazed with rain
water

beside the white
chickens.

William Carlos Williams (*1883–1963*)

THE SOLITARY REAPER

Behold her, single in the field,
Yon solitary Highland lass!
Reaping and singing by herself;
Stop here, or gently pass!
Alone she cuts and binds the grain,   5
And sings a melancholy strain;
O listen! for the vale profound
Is overflowing with the sound.

No nightingale did ever chaunt
More welcome notes to weary bands   10
Of travelers in some shady haunt
Among Arabian sands.
A voice so thrilling ne'er was heard
In springtime from the cuckoo-bird,
Breaking the silence of the seas   15
Among the farthest Hebrides.

Will no one tell me what she sings?—
Perhaps the plaintive numbers° flow   measures
For old, unhappy, far-off things,
And battles long ago.   20
Or is it some more humble lay,°   song
Familiar matter of today?
Some natural sorrow, loss, or pain,
That has been, and may be again?

Whate'er the theme, the maiden sang   25
As if her song could have no ending;
I saw her singing at her work,
And o'er the sickle bending—
I listened, motionless and still;
And, as I mounted up the hill,   30
The music in my heart I bore
Long after it was heard no more.

William Wordsworth (1770–1850)

THE WORLD IS TOO MUCH WITH US

The world is too much with us; late and soon,
Getting and spending, we lay waste our powers:
Little we see in Nature that is ours;

THE SOLITARY REAPER. 2. *Highland:* Scottish upland. The girl is singing in the Highland language, a form of Gaelic, quite different from English. 16. *Hebrides:* islands off the northwest tip of Scotland.

We have given our hearts away, a sordid boon!
This Sea that bares her bosom to the moon;   5
The winds that will be howling at all hours,
And are up-gathered now like sleeping flowers;
For this, for everything, we are out of tune;
It moves us not.—Great God! I'd rather be
A Pagan suckled in a creed outworn;   10
So might I, standing on this pleasant lea,
Have glimpses that would make me less forlorn;
Have sight of Proteus rising from the sea;
Or hear old Triton blow his wreathèd horn.

William Wordsworth (1770–1850)

SAILING TO BYZANTIUM

That is no country for old men. The young
In one another's arms, birds in the trees
—Those dying generations—at their song,
The salmon-falls, the mackerel-crowded seas,
Fish, flesh, or fowl, commend all summer long   5
Whatever is begotten, born, and dies.
Caught in that sensual music all neglect
Monuments of unaging intellect.

An aged man is but a paltry thing,
A tattered coat upon a stick, unless   10
Soul clap its hands and sing, and louder sing
For every tatter in its mortal dress,
Nor is there singing school but studying
Monuments of its own magnificence;
And therefore I have sailed the seas and come   15
To the holy city of Byzantium.

O sages standing in God's holy fire
As in the gold mosaic of a wall,
Come from the holy fire, perne in a gyre,°   spin in spiraling or
And be the singing-masters of my soul.   cone-shaped flight
Consume my heart away; sick with desire   21
And fastened to a dying animal
It knows not what it is; and gather me
Into the artifice of eternity.

SAILING TO BYZANTIUM. *Byzantium:* Ancient eastern capital of the Roman Empire; here symbolically a holy city of the imagination. 1. *That:* Ireland, or the ordinary sensual world. 27–31. *such . . . Byzantium:* The Byzantine Emperor Theophilus had made for himself mechanical golden birds which sang upon the branches of a golden tree.

Once out of nature I shall never take 25
My bodily form from any natural thing,
But such a form as Grecian goldsmiths make
Of hammered gold and gold enameling
To keep a drowsy Emperor awake;
Or set upon a golden bough to sing 30
To lords and ladies of Byzantium
Of what is past, or passing, or to come.

William Butler Yeats (1865-1939)

THE SECOND COMING

Turning and turning in the widening gyre°   spiral
The falcon cannot hear the falconer;
Things fall apart; the center cannot hold;
Mere anarchy is loosed upon the world,
The blood-dimmed tide is loosed, and everywhere 5
The ceremony of innocence is drowned;
The best lack all conviction, while the worst
Are full of passionate intensity.

Surely some revelation is at hand;
Surely the Second Coming is at hand. 10
The Second Coming! Hardly are those words out
When a vast image out of *Spiritus Mundi*
Troubles my sight: somewhere in sands of the desert
A shape with lion body and the head of a man,
A gaze blank and pitiless as the sun, 15
Is moving its slow thighs, while all about it
Reel shadows of the indignant desert birds.
The darkness drops again; but now I know
That twenty centuries of stony sleep
Were vexed to nightmare by a rocking cradle, 20
And what rough beast, its hour come round at last,
Slouches towards Bethlehem to be born?

William Butler Yeats (1865-1939)

THE SECOND COMING. In Christian legend the prophesied "Second Coming" may refer either to Christ or to Antichrist. Yeats believed in a cyclical theory of history in which one historical era would be replaced by an opposite kind of era every two thousand years. Here, the anarchy in the world following World War I (the poem was written in 1919) heralds the end of the Christian era. 12. *Spiritus Mundi:* the racial memory or collective unconscious mind of mankind (literally, world spirit).

THE WILD SWANS AT COOLE

The trees are in their autumn beauty,
The woodland paths are dry,
Under the October twilight the water
Mirrors a still sky;
Upon the brimming water among the stones   5
Are nine-and-fifty swans.

The nineteenth autumn has come upon me
Since I first made my count;
I saw, before I had well finished,
All suddenly mount   10
And scatter wheeling in great broken rings
Upon their clamorous wings.

I have looked upon those brilliant creatures,
And now my heart is sore,
All's changed since I, hearing at twilight,   15
The first time on this shore,
The bell-beat of their wings above my head,
Trod with a lighter tread.

Unwearied still, lover by lover,
They paddle in the cold   20
Companionable streams or climb the air;
Their hearts have not grown old;
Passion or conquest, wander where they will,
Attend upon them still.

But now they drift on the still water,   25
Mysterious, beautiful;
Among what rushes will they build,
By what lake's edge or pool
Delight men's eyes when I awake some day
To find they have flown away?   30

William Butler Yeats (1865–1939)

THE WILD SWANS AT COOLE.   Coole Park, in County Galway, Ireland, was the estate of Lady Augusta Gregory, Yeats's patroness and friend. Beginning in 1897, Yeats regularly summered there for many years.

GLOSSARY OF POETIC TERMS

The definitions in this glossary sometimes repeat and sometimes differ in language from those in the text. Where they differ, the intention is to give a fuller sense of the term's meaning by allowing the reader a double perspective on it. Page numbers refer to discussion in the text, which in most but not all cases is fuller than that in the glossary.

Accent. In this book, the same as *stress.* A syllable given more prominence in pronunciation than its neighbors is said to be accented. 166–77

Allegory. A narrative or description having a second meaning beneath the surface one. 83–85

Alliteration. The repetition at close intervals of the initial consonant sounds of accented syllables or important words (for example, *m*ap-*m*oon, *k*ill-*c*ode, *p*reach-app*r*ove). Important words and accented syllables beginning with vowels may also be said to alliterate with each other inasmuch as they all have the same lack of an initial consonant sound (for example, "*I*nebriate of *a*ir am *I*"). 154–55, 156–57, 158

Allusion. A reference, explicit or implicit, to something in previous literature or history. (The term is reserved by some writers for implicit references only, such as those in "On His Blindness," 119, and "In the Garden," 125; but the distinction between the two kinds of reference is not always clear-cut.) 115–18

Anapest. A metrical foot consisting of two unaccented syllables followed by one accented syllable (for example, ŭn-dĕr-stānd). 168, 175

Anapestic meter. A meter in which a majority of the feet are anapests. (But see *Triple meter.*) 168, 176

Apostrophe. A figure of speech in which someone absent or dead or something nonhuman is addressed as if it were alive and present and could reply. 60–62

Approximate rime (also known as *imperfect rime, near rime, slant rime,* or *oblique rime*). A term used for words in a riming pattern that have some kind of sound correspondence but are not perfect rimes. See *Rime.* Approximate rimes occur occasionally in patterns where most of the rimes are perfect (for example, arrayed-said in "Richard Cory," 39), and sometimes are used systematically in place of perfect rime (for example, "Mr. Z," 111). 155, 156–57

Assonance. The repetition at close intervals of the vowel sounds of accented syllables or important words (for example, h*a*t-r*a*n-*a*mber, v*ei*n-m*a*de). 154–55, 156–57

Aubade. A poem about dawn; a morning love song; or a poem about the parting of lovers at dawn. 49, 62, 134

Ballad. A fairly short narrative poem written in a songlike stanza form. Examples: "O what is that sound," 28; "Farewell to barn and stack and tree," 144; "Edward," 217; "La Belle Dame sans Merci," 287. Also see *Folk ballad.*

Blank verse. Unrimed iambic pentameter. 177

Cacophony. A harsh, discordant, unpleasant-sounding choice and arrangement of sounds. 189–90

Caesura. See *Grammatical pause* and *Rhetorical pause.*

Connotation. What a word suggests beyond its basic definition; a word's overtones of meaning. 32–37

Consonance. The repetition at close intervals of the final consonant sounds of accented syllables or important words (for example, boo*k*-pla*que*-thi*ck*er). 154–55, 156–57

Continuous form. That form of a poem in which the lines follow each other without formal grouping, the only breaks being dictated by units of meaning. 203–04

Couplet. Two successive lines, usually in the same meter, linked by rime. 177 (Exercise 2), 208

Dactyl. A metrical foot consisting of one accented syllable followed by two unaccented syllables (for example, mēr-rĭ-lȳ). 168

Dactylic meter. A meter in which a majority of the feet are dactyls. (But see *Triple meter.*) 168, 176

Denotation. The basic definition or dictionary meaning of a word. 32–37

Didactic poetry. Poetry having as a primary purpose to teach or preach. 225

Dimeter. A metrical line containing two feet. 168

Dipodic foot. The basic foot of *dipodic verse,* consisting (when complete) of an unaccented syllable, a lightly accented syllable, an unaccented syllable, and a heavily accented syllable, in that succession. However, dipodic verse accommodates a tremendous amount of variety, as shown by the examples in the text. 183

Dipodic verse. A meter in which there is a perceptible alternation between light and heavy stresses. See *Dipodic foot.* 183

Double rime. A rime in which the repeated vowel is in the second last syllable of the words involved (for example, politely-rightly-spritely); one form of *feminine rime.* 163 (Question 5)

Dramatic framework. The situation, whether actual or fictional, realistic or fanciful, in which an author places his or her characters in order to express the theme. 22–23

Dramatic irony. See *Irony.*

Duple meter. A meter in which a majority of the feet contain two syllables. Iambic and trochaic are both duple meters. 168

Elegy. A poem, usually formal, sustained, and meditative, expressing sorrow or lamentation over the death of someone loved or esteemed by the poet. 145, 146 (Question 2)

End rime. Rimes that occur at the ends of lines. 155

End-stopped line. A line that ends with a natural speech pause, usually marked by punctuation. 177

English (or *Shakespearean*) *sonnet.* A sonnet riming *ababcdcdefefgg*. Its content or structure ideally parallels the rime scheme, falling into three coordinate quatrains and a concluding couplet; but it is often structured, like the Italian sonnet, into octave and sestet, the principal break in thought coming at the end of the eighth line. 208–09, 209 (Exercise 3)

Euphony. A smooth, pleasant-sounding choice and arrangement of sounds. 189–90

Expected rhythm. The metrical expectation set up by the basic meter of a poem. 174

Extended figure (also known as *sustained figure*). A figure of speech (usually metaphor, simile, personification, or apostrophe) sustained or developed through a considerable number of lines or through a whole poem. 67

Feminine rime. A rime in which the repeated accented vowel is in either the second or third last syllable of the words involved (for example, ceiling-appealing; hurrying-scurrying). 155, 163 (Question 5)

Figurative language. Language employing figures of speech; language that cannot be taken literally or only literally. 56–66, 75–85, 95–103

Figure of speech. Broadly, any way of saying something other than the ordinary way; more narrowly (and for the purposes of this book) a way of saying one thing and meaning another. 56–66, 75–85, 95–103

Fixed form. Any form of poem in which the length and pattern are prescribed by previous usage or tradition, such as *sonnet, limerick, villanelle, haiku, sestina,* and so on. 206–09

Folk ballad. A narrative poem designed to be sung, composed by an anonymous author, and transmitted orally for years or generations before being written down. It has usually undergone modification through the process of oral transmission. "Edward," 217.

Foot The basic unit used in the scansion or measurement of verse. A foot usually contains one accented syllable and one or two unaccented syllables, but the *monosyllabic foot*, the *spondaic foot* (*spondee*), and the *dipodic foot* are all modifications of this principle. 167–68, 183

Form. The external pattern or shape of a poem, describable without reference to its content, as *continuous form*, *stanzaic form*, *fixed form* (and their varieties), *free verse*, and *syllabic verse*. 176, 203–10, 213. See *Structure*.

Free verse. Non-metrical verse. Poetry written in free verse is arranged in lines, may be more or less rhythmical, but has no fixed metrical pattern or expectation. 176

Grammatical pause (also known as *caesura*). A pause introduced into the reading of a line by a mark of punctuation. Grammatical pauses do not affect scansion. 174

Haiku. A three-line poem, Japanese in origin, narrowly conceived of as a fixed form in which the lines contain respectively 5, 7, and 5 syllables (in American practice this requirement is frequently dispensed with). Haiku are generally concerned with some aspect of nature and present a single image or two juxtaposed images without comment, relying on suggestion rather than on explicit statement to communicate their meaning. 213

Heard rhythm. The actual rhythm of a metrical poem as we hear it when it is read naturally. The heard rhythm mostly conforms to but sometimes departs from or modifies the *expected rhythm*. 174

Heptameter. A metrical line containing seven feet. 168

Hexameter. A metrical line containing six feet. 168

Hyperbole. See *Overstatement*.

Iamb. A metrical foot consisting of one unaccented syllable followed by one accented syllable (for example, rĕ-hēārse). 168

Iambic meter. A meter in which the majority of feet are iambs. The most common English meter. 168, 175

Iambic-anapestic meter. A meter which freely mixes iambs and anapests, and in which it might be difficult to determine which foot prevails without actually counting. 176

Imagery. The representation through language of sense experience. 46–49

Internal rime. A rime in which one or both of the rime-words occur *within* the line. 155

Irony. A situation, or a use of language, involving some kind of incongruity or discrepancy. 100. Three kinds of irony are distinguished in this book:

Verbal irony. A figure of speech in which what is meant is the opposite of what is said. 98–100

Dramatic irony. A device by which the author implies a different meaning from that intended by the speaker (or by *a* speaker) in a literary work. 101–02

Irony of situation (or *situational irony*). A situation in which there is an incongruity between actual circumstances and those that would seem appropriate or between what is anticipated and what actually comes to pass. 100, 102–03

Italian (or *Petrarchan*) *sonnet*. A sonnet consisting of an octave riming *abbaabba* and of a sestet using any arrangement of two or three additional rimes, such as *cdcdcd* or *cdecde*. 207–08, 209 (Exercise 3)

Limerick. A fixed form consisting of five lines of anapestic meter, the first two trimeter, the next two dimeter, the last line trimeter, riming *aabba;* used exclusively for humorous or nonsense verse. 206–07, 210–11

Masculine rime (also known as *single rime*). A rime in which the repeated accented vowel sound is in the final syllable of the words involved (for example, dance-pants, scald-recalled). 155, 163 (Question 5)

Metaphor. A figure of speech in which an implicit comparison is made between two things essentially unlike. It may take one of four forms: (1) that in which the literal term and the figurative term are both *named;* (2) that in which the literal term is *named* and the figurative term *implied;* (3) that in which the literal term is *implied* and the figurative term *named;* (4) that in which both the literal and the figurative terms are *implied.* 157–60, 64–65

Meter. Regularized rhythm; an arrangement of language in which the accents occur at apparently equal intervals in time. 166–77

Metonymy. A figure of speech in which some significant aspect or detail of an experience is used to represent the whole experience. In this book the single term *metonymy* is used for what are sometimes distinguished as two separate figures: *synecdoche* (the use of the part for the whole) and *metonymy* (the use of something closely related for the thing actually meant). 62–64

Metrical pause. A pause that supplies the place of an expected accented syllable. Unlike *grammatical* and *rhetorical pauses,* metrical pauses affect scansion. 183–84

Monometer. A metrical line containing one foot. 168

Monosyllabic foot. A foot consisting of a single accented syllable (for example, shīne). 168

Octameter. A metrical line containing eight feet. 168

Octave. (1) An eight-line stanza. (2) The first eight lines of a sonnet, especially one structured in the manner of an Italian sonnet. 207

Onomatopoeia. The use of words that supposedly mimic their meaning in their sound (for example, boom, click, plop). 187

Onomatopoetic language. Language employing *onomatopoeia.*

Overstatement (or *hyperbole*). A figure of speech in which exaggeration is used in the service of truth. 96–98

Oxymoron. A compact paradox, one in which two successive words apparently contradict each other. 180

Paradox. A statement or situation containing apparently contradictory or incompatible elements. 95–96

Paradoxical situation. A situation containing apparently but not actually incompatible elements. The celebration of a fifth birthday anniversary by a twenty-year-old man is paradoxical but explainable if the man was born on February 29. The Christian doctrines that Christ was born of a virgin and is both God and man are, for a Christian believer, paradoxes (that is, apparently impossible but true). 95

Paradoxical statement (or *verbal paradox*). A figure of speech in which an apparently self-contradictory statement is nevertheless found to be true. 95–96

Paraphrase. A restatement of the content of a poem designed to make its *prose meaning* as clear as possible. 25

Pentameter. A metrical line containing five feet. 168

Personification. A figure of speech in which human attributes are given to an animal, an object, or a concept. 60–62

Petrarchan sonnet. See *Italian sonnet.*

Phonetic intensive. A word whose sound, by an obscure process, to some degree suggests its meaning. As differentiated from *onomatopoetic* words, the meanings of phonetic intensives do not refer to sounds. 187–88

Prose. Non-metrical language; the opposite of *verse.* 166–67

Prose meaning. That part of a poem's *total meaning* that can be separated out and expressed through paraphrase. 126–29

Prose poem. Usually a short composition having the intentions of poetry but written in prose rather than verse. 177

Quatrain. (1) A four-line stanza. (2) A four-line division of a sonnet marked off by its rime scheme. 202

Refrain. A repeated word, phrase, line, or group of lines, normally at some fixed position in a poem written in stanzaic form. 156, 158 (Exercise), 206

Rhetorical pause (also known as *caesura*). A natural pause, unmarked by punctuation, introduced into the reading of a line by its phrasing or syntax. Rhetorical pauses do not affect scansion. 174

Rhetorical poetry. Poetry using artificially eloquent language, that is, language too high-flown for its occasion and unfaithful to the full complexity of human experience. 225

Rhythm. Any wavelike recurrence of motion or sound. 166–67

Rime (or *rhyme*). The repetition of the accented vowel sound and all succeeding sounds in important or importantly positioned words (for example, old-cold, vane-reign, court-report, order-recorder). The above definition applies to *perfect rime* and assumes that the accented vowel sounds involved are preceded by differing consonant sounds. If the preceding consonant sound is the same (for example, manse-romance, style-stile), or if there is no preceding consonant sound in either word (for example, aisle-isle, alter-altar), or if the same word is repeated in the riming position (for example, hill-hill), the words are called *identical rimes*. Both *perfect rimes* and *identical rimes* are to be distinguished from *approximate rimes*. 155, 156

Rime scheme. Any fixed pattern of rimes characterizing a whole poem or its stanzas. 206

Run-on line. A line which has no natural speech pause at its end, allowing the sense to flow uninterruptedly into the succeeding line. 177

Sarcasm. Bitter or cutting speech; speech intended by its speaker to give pain to the person addressed. 98-99

Satire. A kind of literature that ridicules human folly or vice with the purpose of bringing about reform or of keeping others from falling into similar folly or vice. 98-99

Scansion. The process of measuring verse, that is, of marking accented and unaccented syllables, dividing the lines into feet, identifying the metrical pattern, and noting significant variations from that pattern. 168

Sentimental poetry. Poetry aimed primarily at stimulating the emotions rather than at communicating experience honestly and freshly. 224-25

Sestet. (1) A six-line stanza. (2) The last six lines of a sonnet structured on the Italian model. 207

Sestina. A complex fixed form of six six-line stanzas plus an *envoi* (or *envoy*), using the same six end-words throughout but repeated in a different order in each stanza. 217 (Question 6)

Shakespearean sonnet. See *English sonnet.*

Simile. A figure of speech in which an explicit comparison is made between two things essentially unlike. The comparison is made explicit by the use of some such word or phrase as *like, as, than, similar to, resembles,* or *seems.* 57

Single rime. See *Masculine rime.*

Situational irony. See *Irony.*

Sonnet. A fixed form of fourteen lines, normally iambic pentameter, with a rime scheme conforming to or approximating one of two main types—the *Italian* or the *English.* 207-10

Spondee. A metrical foot consisting of two syllables equally or almost equally accented (for example, trūe-blūe). 168

Stanza. A group of lines whose metrical pattern (and usually its rime scheme as well) is repeated throughout a poem. 168, 204-06

Stanzaic form. The form taken by a poem when it is written in a series of units having the same number of lines and usually other characteristics in common, such as metrical pattern or rime scheme. 204-06

Stress. In this book, the same as *Accent.* But see 167 (footnote).

Structure. The internal organization of a poem's content. See *Form.*

Sustained figure. See *Extended figure.*

Syllabic verse. Verse measured by the number of syllables rather than the number of feet per line. 213 (Question 4). Also see *Haiku.*

Symbol. A figure of speech in which something (object, person, situation, or action) means more than what it is. A symbol, in other words, may be read both literally and metaphorically. 75–83, 85 (Exercise)

Synecdoche. A figure of speech in which a part is used for the whole. In this book it is subsumed under the term *Metonymy.* 62–64

Terza rima. See 209 (Exercise 2).

Tetrameter. A metrical line containing four feet. 168

Theme. The central idea of a literary work. 25

Tone. The writer's or speaker's attitude toward his subject, his audience, or himself; the emotional coloring, or emotional meaning, of a work. 138–42

Total meaning. The total experience communicated by a poem. It includes all those dimensions of experience by which a poem communicates—sensuous, emotional, imaginative, and intellectual—and it can be communicated in no other words than those of the poem itself. 126–29

Trimeter. A metrical line containing three feet. 168

Triple meter. A meter in which a majority of the feet contain three syllables. (Actually, if more than 25 percent of the feet in a poem are triple, its effect is more triple than duple, and it ought perhaps to be referred to as triple meter.) Anapestic and dactylic are both triple meters. 168

Triple rime. A rime in which the repeated accented vowel sound is in the third last syllable of the words involved (for example, gainfully-disdainfully); one form of *feminine rime.* 163 (Question 5)

Trochaic meter. A meter in which the majority of feet are trochees. 168

Trochee. A metrical foot consisting of one accented syllable followed by one unaccented syllable (for example, bār-tĕr). 168

Understatement. A figure of speech that consists of saying less than one means, or of saying what one means with less force than the occasion warrants. 96–98

Verbal irony. See *Irony.*

Verse. Metrical language; the opposite of *prose.* 166–167

Villanelle. See 209 (Exercise 1).

COPYRIGHTS AND ACKNOWLEDGMENTS *(continued from page iv)*

INDEX OF AUTHORS, TITLES, AND FIRST LINES

Authors' names appear in capitals, titles of poems in italics, and first lines of poems in roman type. Numbers in roman type indicate the page of the selection, and italic numbers indicate discussion of the poem.

6
7
H 8
I 9
J 0